)07

Urban Tourism

)9

Routledge Topics in Tourism

Series Adviser
Stephen Page, Massey University Albany, Auckland

Routledge Topics in Tourism offers a fresh, concise grounding in key themes in tourism and leisure. Each book in the series acts as a succinct and stimulating introduction to a particular topic and provides:

- comprehensive discussions of concepts
- international case studies
- key point summaries
- short questions for discussion

This series will be an excellent resource for students of tourism and leisure options at first-year undergraduate and diploma levels.

Already published:

Transport for Tourism
Stephen Page, Massey University Albany, Auckland

Forthcoming titles include:

Tourist Destination Management
Eric Laws, Christ Church College, Canterbury

People in Tourism
Tom Baum, University of Buckingham

Tourism Policy
C. Michael Hall, University of Canberra
John Jenkins, University of Central Queensland

Stephen Page

Urban Tourism

ROUTLEDGE

London and New York

First published 1995
by Routledge
11 New Fetter Lane, London EC4P 4EE

Simultaneously published in the USA and Canada
by Routledge
29 West 35th Street, New York, NY 10001

Typeset in Times by Florencetype Ltd, Stoodleigh, Devon
Printed and bound in Great Britain by
Biddles Ltd, Guildford and King's Lynn

British Library Cataloguing in Publication Data
A catalogue record for this book is available from the
British Library.

Library of Congress Cataloging in Publication Data
A catalogue record for this book has been requested

ISBN 0–415–11218–4

Contents

Plates

Figures

Tables

Preface

Urbanisation is a powerful force contributing to the development of towns and cities as places to live in, work and shop in*. Towns and cities are also places where the population concentrates in a defined area, and economic activities locate in the same area to provide the opportunity for the production and consumption of goods and services in capitalist societies. Cities can also be the focal point for diverse cultural and social activities which the population engage in, offering opportunities for entertainment, tourism and leisure activities as well as comprising meeting places, airports and conference centres which the traveller and tourist require. In other words, urban places have also developed as centres to service the needs of tourists as well as places where political power is exercised through the medium of government. Even so, the urban environment is valued by people in different ways, as their use of the city is an individualised choice related to the functions it provides. Forecasts for world urbanisation to the year 2000 indicate that more and more people will be living in urban environments, particularly the sprawling metropolises in the developed and developing world. Therefore the study of urban places will continue to occupy a prominent place in the social sciences, with anthropology, economics, geography, politics and sociology contributing to the wider pursuit of urban studies. But why should tourism researchers be interested in cities?

As long ago as 1970, P. Hall (1970: 445) predicted that 'the age of mass tourism is the biggest single factor for change in the great capitals of Europe – and in many small historic cities too – in the last 30 years of this century'. This is one immediate reason why tourism researchers might wish to study urban places, focusing on a number of questions: why should people who live in urban and non-urban environments choose to spend their free time visiting other cities as tourists and day visitors? And what are the effects for the places they visit? Now that tourism studies is gaining wider recognition as a mature area to study and research, it is appropriate for academics and practitioners to consider the wide-ranging effects of tourism as a phenomenon in different social, cultural and political environments. Why write a book on urban tourism? After all, people have been visiting cities for different reasons throughout history.

One of the continued problems facing tourism studies is the lack of integration in research, as interdisciplinary perspectives are rarely pursued to gain a holistic assessment of complex tourism issues in different environments. Nowhere is this more evident than in the case of urban tourism. The phenomenon of mass tourism is now affecting cities and generating interest from both the producers of tourism services and the consumer. The problem is that the majority of research is based on different disciplinary perspectives. Whilst the comparative neglect of urban tourism as an area of research is now being addressed, this is generating a diverse range of studies. One problem for tourism educators is that many of the studies with an interest in urban tourism are inaccessible to a general audience at undergraduate and diploma level because they are too specialised, very expensive and often written from a disciplinary basis. Although there is an ongoing interest among tourism researchers on urban tourism (e.g. Murphy 1992), such findings are rarely disseminated to a wide audience where conference proceedings result (e.g. Vetter 1985). If the complex nature of urban tourism is to be understood by students and practitioners, a book is needed which can act as a stepping stone and a foundation for further study. This is the aim of this 'Topics in Tourism' book, with the emphasis on the concepts, principles and arguments developed in the tourism and non-tourism literature by specialists.

The book does not attempt to provide a comprehensive synthesis of every possible publication which feature urban tourism in some form. The book focuses on the most notable studies and directs the reader to other studies if they want to pursue the topic in more detail. In this sense, the book should be seen as complementing the special issues of journals (e.g. *Tourism Recreation Research* 1992) and specialised monographs such as C. Law (1993) *Urban Tourism: Attracting Visitors to Large Cities* which focus on urban tourism.

Within this book, tourism is the central focus, emphasising the multi-functional nature of cities as tourist destinations and the value of a systems approach to understand the interrelated nature of tourism activity within cities. Obviously, in a book aimed at an introductory level, certain themes or issues have to be omitted due to the constraints of space. Consequently, well-documented issues such as the development process as it applies to tourism, and tourism's role in urban regeneration schemes receives a limited treatment. Wherever possible, recent innovations in the management of urban tourism problems (e.g. the role of visitor management in small historic cities) receive a prominent place as they link the theory and practice of planning and managing tourism.

One of the main limitations of the book must be its largely North American and Eurocentric approach to the literature, since there is a paucity of material generated by researchers interested in the Less Developed World, the Pacific Rim and Asia. Consequently, there is a real need for a book that raises the profile of urban areas as both the containing context and focus for specific tourist activities at an international level. If this book succeeds in stimulating the reader's interest of urban tourism outside of the existing range of specialised studies on different aspects of tourism in cities, then it will have achieved its aim of showing that cities may be complex environments to understand and analyse. Urban environments are intrinsically interesting since so much tourist activity has some contact with cities and towns in some form.

One of the principal factors which prompted me to write this concise assessment, aside from a general interest in urban tourism, is a recent involvement with a number of local authorities as a researcher and consultant in the UK and New Zealand. My frequent contact with tourism practitioners and planners, particularly as a Project Director steering a research programme to monitor the establishment and operation of Canterbury City Centre Initiative to manage tourism, crystallised my thoughts and feelings on the topic. All too often the education/industry interface remains a barrier to fruitful collaboration and research as a basis for problem-solving, with the public/private sector tourism interests viewing academics as too esoteric while academics view the private sector as too parochial or narrow in their outlook. Having joined a Steering Committee designing the future management plan for tourism in Canterbury, I recognised that these perceptions need to be addressed if a fruitful partnership is to develop. For this reason, an introductory book will help to establish a holistic view of urban tourism without losing sight of the needs of practitioners. Therefore, it is hoped that emphasis on how to conceptualise and analyse urban tourism, how to improve it through planning, managing and marketing appropriate forms of tourism, may be of value to the practitioner market by sharing examples of good practice and showing how certain constraints on achieving a successful tourism economy may be overcome. In the age of public/private sector partnerships, this book will be invaluable in understanding who is responsible for urban tourism and what organisations can do to improve the tourist's experience. I hope this will be read by both students and practitioners as a useful starting point to consider the urban tourism phenomenon in their locality.

Inevitably a number of people help to shape the book as it evolved from a simple idea to a series of interrelated chapters. Firstly, Greg Ashworth has been a constant source of help, advice and encouragement. I also wish to acknowledge the importance of his seminal study with H. Voogd on place marketing (Ashworth and Voogd 1990a). One consequence is that Chapter 6 draws extensively from their research in this area as it remains the most accessible and challenging study available. Likewise, Doug Pearce has been a great help through our regular correspondence, and his work on tourist organisations (Pearce 1992) also forms the basis for the discussion of urban organisations and their activities in Chapter 6. Chris Young has been a great source of help and a most welcome critical eye, making me rethink many of the ideas and concepts that one takes for granted in tourism research. I will sincerely miss his critical assessment of my research as I leave Canterbury and head for my new post at Massey University Albany, New Zealand – he has been a really good colleague to work with, always getting me to stop and consider other possible interpretations of material. The provision of information by friends and colleagues is also gratefully acknowledged, especially the fruitful discussions with a former research fellow on the Canterbury City Centre Initiative – Rachel Hardyman. Likewise another former research fellow – Nicola Clark on the Travel, Lifestyle and Health Project has been a source of encouragement and a good friend over the last eighteen months. I have also been fortunate enough to combine a continued interest in urban tourism with a large scale research project on Canterbury.

John Hills has provided his usual unfailing support and advice on cartography, in his usual humorous and cheerful manner. He is responsible for drawing all the maps and diagrams and for technical advice on computing. The typing services of Lisa and Chloe in the Central Secretariat, Christ Church College have also proved invaluable as well as the help received from other staff such as Ronnie Ridgeway and Maggie Watts. I am really grateful for all their help – it gave me the much needed time to focus on the manuscript rather than all the editing. They are all a real asset to the institution. I will miss them all. This is also a good place to thank both Francesca Weaver and Laura Large at Routledge. They make writing a book a less painful process, adding encouragement at each stage of preparing the manuscript, which makes working with them a real pleasure. I would also like to thank by wife Sue for her patience with the obsession that develops as a book nears completion. Lastly, I would like to thank Nick for his help and support during the first few months at Massey together with the help and advice from my new colleagues. I hope both my former and prospective students will find the book of interest.

Stephen Page
1994

Note:
* For a discussion of the concept of urban, urbanisation and its effect on people and society see Johnston *et al.* (1994).

Acknowledgements

The author would like to thank the following publishers and organisations for permission to use tables and figures: Prentice Hall for Tables 2.6 and 2.8; Greg Ashworth and Chris Cooper at the University of Surrey for Table 2.10, 6.5 and Figure 3.4; Mr G. Todd of the Economist Intelligence Unit, London for Table 3.3; Pennsylvania University Press for Table 4.3; the English Tourist Board/Employment Department for Table 4.5; Oxford University Press, Auckland for Table 5.6; Butterworth-Heinemann for Table 6.1; Pergamon Journals for permission to reproduce Figures 2.1 and 3.2 from *Annals for Tourism Research*; David Fulton Publishers for Figure 2.2 and 4.10; Wiley and Sons Ltd for Figure 3.4; Longman for Figure 4.2 and Russel King for Figure 4.10.

In addition, various organisations have granted copyright permission to quote extracts from the following material; Mansell Publishers, London to quote from C. M. Law, *Urban Tourism: Attracting Visitors to Large Cities; Pitman for permission to quote from Cooper et al., Tourism Principles and Practice*, and J. C. Holloway and R. Plant, *Marketing Tourism*; Wiley and Sons Ltd to quote from the following publications: *Progress in Tourism, Recreation and Hospitality Management*, Volume 1 (1989) and Volume 4 (1992); Greg Ashworth for permission to quote from his work on urban tourism; Longman for permission to quote from D. Pearce (1989) *Tourist Development* and A. Mathieson and G. Wall (1982) *Tourism, Economic, Physical and Social Impacts*; The *Canadian Geographer* to quote from R. Butler's (1980) article on the concept of a tourist area cycle of evolution. Permission to reproduce material from the author's article 'Urban Tourism in New Zealand: the National Museum of New Zealand Project' first published in *Tourism Management*, Vol. 14, No. 3, June 1993, by Butterworth-Heinemann, Oxford, UK, is gratefully acknowledged together with the permission from Jan van der Borg for Table 6.1.

1
Introduction

According to Law (1993: 1) 'large cities are arguably the most important type of tourist destination across the world' and yet urban areas have been neglected in most academic studies of tourism. As tourism has grown as an international phenomenon, it is viewed as a complex process associated with the culture, lifestyles and demand in different societies for holidays and travel. Major components of this process and its effect on urban places remain relatively unknown and as Law argues:

> The topic of urban tourism is only gradually being recognised . . . most textbooks on tourism make hardly any reference to it. There are only a few articles in the academic literature and some of these are calling for more study.
>
> (Law 1992: 599–600)

The expansion in discretionary leisure time and increased living standards have contributed to the demand for travel, but few researchers have considered the wide-ranging consequences for urban tourism destinations. The operation and management of this process, whereby people decide to travel to urban destinations, is poorly understood in theoretical and conceptual terms since few researchers adopt an integrated approach towards the analysis of tourism. Although researchers do identify some of the dominant origins and destinations of tourist travel, providing an indication of the patterns and flows of tourists on a global scale, much of the existing research in tourism is based on descriptions of international tourism phenomena. Pearce (1987a) cites the work of Heiberg and Hoivik (1980) which expresses the global movement of tourists from the core areas of North America, Europe and Japan to international destinations. One can also add Pacific Rim countries in South-East Asia to this expanding market for outbound travel. In other words, much of the demand originates from the urbanised and industrialised nations where high levels of disposable income facilitate tourist travel. Identifying the destinations which tourists visit is more complex, although Table 1.1 highlights the most popular tourist destinations by country. In addition to the demand for international tourism, Pearce (1987a) identifies the significance of domestic tourism, which in statistical terms, is four times greater in volume than international travel. Domestic tourism is the movement of people within their own country for the purposes of tourism, whereby they spend at least one night away from their home area.

Table 1.1 The top ten destinations for international tourism in 1991

Country	Tourist arrivals (millions)
France	55.7
USA	42.7
Spain	35.3
Italy	26.8
Hungary	21.9
Austria	19.1
UK	16.7
Mexico	16.6
Germany	15.6
Canada	15.0

Source: World Tourism Organization

A notable feature of these patterns of tourist travel is the significance of urban destinations, which serve as gateways for tourist entry to the country, as centres of accommodation and a base for excursions to rural areas as well as destinations in their own right. It is significant within the context of recent trends in tourism, since many countries such as the UK have experienced a rapid expansion in the demand for short-break domestic and international holidays to urban destinations. Therefore, urban areas are not simply places where populations concentrate together with economic activities, cultural life and the control of political power. Urban places are also assuming a greater role as centres for tourism activity.

How does one attempt to explain this phenomenon?

One approach is to consider the nature of tourism research and the extent to which its development has impeded the specialisation of research into areas such as urban tourism.

Tourism research: the search for a focus

Although a number of books now exist which examine international tourism from different perspectives such as management science (e.g. Witt *et al.* 1991) and geography (e.g. Pearce 1987a, 1989), it is apparent that major gaps exist in our understanding of the processes contributing to tourism (i.e. its growth, development, operation and management) and the way it functions in different environments, particularly urban areas. Existing knowledge of urban tourism is limited in general terms because of the way in which tourism has developed as an area of study, typically as a sub-discipline of other social science subjects in the 1970s and early 1980s. Alternatively, it could also be viewed as a branch of the tourism industry and its desire to improve the calibre and quality of its existing and future personnel. This has meant that it has lacked the direction and unity in research which one often associates with other social science subjects. For this reason, it is useful to explore the nature and purpose of research in tourism in order to examine the extent to which its diversity actually contributes to its fragmented nature, thereby constraining research on specialist areas such as urban tourism.

What is research?

Defining the purpose of research is a far from easy task, because it is undertaken for various reasons. Research, regardless of subject area, is intended at a rudimentary level to discover something new and to advance our understanding of the subject or topic under investigation. In the case of academic research, publication of research findings produces the information and material for the future development of the subject, thereby establishing new paradigms (i.e. a new focus for the subject) and a new agenda for research. Tourism does not exist as a social science discipline in its own right, and researchers usually approach the analysis of tourism with their own disciplinary perspective. These arguments are well rehearsed within the literature and were recently developed in the influential publication by Pearce and Butler (1993), *Tourism Research*. This may be one factor which has contributed towards the absence of cohesion in the analysis of tourism, a feature reinforced by the structure of tourism research (see S.L.J. Smith 1989 for a fuller discussion of this issue). One of the main practical uses of tourism research is to facilitate data collection for industry, undertaken by academics and practitioners as well as market researchers, to understand the needs and motivation of visitors together with other forms of research.

Within the context of tourism, Veal (1992) identifies three types of research in leisure and tourism:

- *Scientific research*, where specific rules, conventions and routines exist to follow particular models of thought. The use of prior logical reasoning and an understanding of scientific principles is implicit in this approach and theories and concepts may be tested to assess their validity in an abstract or applied manner;
- *Social science*, where researchers use the research methods and traditions developed within social science to examine issues which often have a human dimension. In this context, the study of people often means that the behaviour, actions, attitudes and their relationship to tourism are studied;
- *Applied research*, occurs where research is focused on the solution of a specific problem in a planning, management or policy-oriented context.

One can subdivide these categories of research into a number of approaches to research which are most commonly used:

- *Explanatory research*, where the investigation of a theme sets out to consider why something happens or occurs, which is often based on observations and social survey work as a basis to explain some phenomenon.
- *Evaluative research*, whereby the study considers the policy, management and decision-making functions or policy issues within organisations associated with the tourism process.

These different forms of research coexist within tourism and therein lies one of the major problems for the development of tourism as an area of study. With researchers adopting a disciplinary approach rather than a range of distinct tourism methodologies in the study of tourism, research remains fragmented and methodologically unsophisticated. This has meant the emphasis has tended to be on results rather than methodology, restricting the development of distinctive research methods and approaches which could be identified as the hallmark of the tourism researcher. Such criticisms have been frequently echoed by many of the leading researchers in tourism, most recently by Pearce (1993). Yet it is only recently that such criticisms have been taken seriously, as tourism searches for a purpose and direction following its massive expansion as a subject of study at vocational, degree and postgraduate study in the late 1980s (see Goodenough and Page 1993). The 1990s appear to be the decade in which the subject is reaching a state of maturity as more researchers are concerned with the search for an intellectual rigour, purpose and methodological acceptance within social science without compromising the applied and vocational nature of tourism studies.

The scattered nature of tourism literature, spread across a disparate number of sources, complicates matters. Aside from well known general textbooks, tourism material is published in a limited number of mainstream academic journals (i.e. *Annals of Tourism Research, Tourism Management* and *Journal of Travel Research*) and periodic reviews of the literature (e.g. *Progress in Tourism, Recreation and Hospitality Management*). *Ad hoc* publications, such as special issues of non-tourism journals and occasional publications and monographs, also contribute to the dispersed nature of tourism research. One useful abstracting source, which provides a contemporary review of current research in tourism – the *CAB Leisure, Recreation and Tourism Abstracts* – tends to confirm the diverse location of tourism publications. In this respect, understanding the focus and direction of current research in tourism is difficult. One consequence is that specialised research on topics, such as urban tourism, have not developed as major areas of study, despite their overwhelming significance in international and domestic patterns of tourism. Thus, *Urban Tourism* is one book in the new 'Topics in Tourism' series aimed at addressing the growing demand for more specialised yet widely accessible books for undergraduates.

Urban tourism: the existing literature

It is apparent from a preliminary assessment of the tourism literature that:

> Research on the structure of tourism in urban areas is relatively recent. . . . [and] . . . there are very few studies of urban tourism. The majority of the work is ideographic in nature and has come from Europe and the United Kingdom.
>
> (Pearce 1987a: 178)

Ashworth (1989) confirms that this neglect of urban tourism exists in his seminal study 'Urban tourism: an imbalance in attention', which remains one of the most useful and widely cited reports on the development of research and the range of studies published. For this reason, it serves as a good starting point for research on urban tourism, though its contents need not be reiterated here. Ashworth asserts that:

> A double neglect has occurred. Those interested in the study of tourism have tended to neglect the urban context in which much of it is set, while those interested in urban studies . . . have been equally neglectful of the importance of the tourist function in cities.
>
> (Ashworth 1989: 33)

A more recent review by Ashworth reaffirms the case for studying urban tourism and provides a useful rationale for its study:

> Urban tourism exists as a sufficiently distinct activity and . . . it can be studied apart from other aspects of tourism or aspects of the urban environment. Urban tourism is sufficiently important either as a particular group of tourism activities or in the role such tourism does, or might play within the broader context of cities.
>
> (Ashworth 1992a: 3)

It is evident from the recent publication of tourism textbooks (e.g. Shaw and Williams 1994) and more specialised monographs (e.g. Law 1993) that urban tourism is receiving increased attention by researchers. In fact, Shaw and Williams (1994) argue that criticisms of the neglect in attention are not as valid in the early 1990s due to the increasing academic and political attention paid to urban tourism as a spur to economic and urban environmental regeneration. However, one can question their argument in a number of respects. Firstly, urban regeneration is a highly specialised area of study which sometimes has a tourism or leisure outcome. Secondly, if the literature and research on urban tourism is now becoming established and is no longer neglected, it is surprising that Shaw and Williams (1994: 207) argue that when analysing tourists within urban areas a 'somewhat limited literature on visitor activity in urban areas' exists. Thus, while interest has focused on the significance of urban tourism as one approach to stimulate economic regeneration, it has not led to the rapid development of an urban tourism literature that is widely disseminated beyond specialist reports, journal articles and monographs. As a result, urban regeneration has formed the focus of a significant range of research that has subsequently emphasised the benefits of tourism development as a strategy for redeveloping redundant spaces in older industrial cities (Mansfeld 1992; Law 1993). One exception to this is the theoretically derived research by Mullins (1991) (which is discussed in more detail below). Law's recent (1993) synthesis of urban tourism may be a major step towards establishing urban tourism as a focus for research, but it is evident that many gaps still exist in the literature and our understanding of this complex phenomenon remains partial and incomplete.

Despite the fact that urban tourism research has developed in the 1980s and 1990s, one can identify early concerns related to the significance of tourism in cities in the recreational research by Stansfield (1964), which was symptomatic of the reluctance of researchers to examine tourism in an urban context because of the difficulty of disaggregating the tourist and non-tourist function of cities (excluding resort towns). As a result, a range of studies cited in previous reports (e.g. Ashworth 1989, 1992a; Ashworth and Tunbridge 1990; Page 1989a, b; Page and Sinclair 1989) provide evidence of work undertaken on tourism in an urban context, though much of the research is in inaccessible or dated sources. Furthermore, the existing literature does not necessarily imply that urban tourism exists as a distinct area of tourism studies. Research has often been based on case studies of particular locations which are descriptive and contribute little to the theoretical or methodological understanding of urban tourism. For this reason, one is led to consider Ashworth's contention as to whether an urban tourism exists, and if so, what is meant by the term?

Does an urban tourism exist?

According to Ashworth (1992a) tourism in urban environments has not led to the development of a distinct 'urban tourism': moreover research is focused on tourism in cities. One explanation for this strange paradox is that tourism in cities is not a distinctive attribute which is associated with the main function of the city. Many other economic activities are seen by planners, commercial interests and residents as the main rationale for the city: a place which meets both service requirements of people, commerce and industry and also fulfils a residential function. One can argue that tourism is not viewed by most urban geographers, sociologists and planners as a serious area of study since urban regeneration has been the main focus for many urban tourism studies by geographers (e.g. Hoyle and Pinder 1992). More specifically, because the demand and supply aspects of tourism in cities is entwined with other urban functions, planners, commercial interests and local governments rarely perceive tourism as a significant element within the urban economy (with the exception of resort towns). It is viewed more as an adjunct to the way in which the city operates, as an ephemeral phenomenon which is seasonal in character and transitory. Therefore, why should planners and researchers be concerned about the effects of a transitory activity, when competing demands for resources and time mean that efforts can be put to better use elsewhere? Such attitudes have meant that the collection of detailed data on the 'urban tourist', the activities they undertake in the destination and their effect on city environments, has frequently been overlooked in both applied and academic research. In essence, planners may view urban tourism as a managerial activity but as visitors have always come to an area, the need to manage and attract tourists is not always high on the agenda.

Thus, a vicious circle exists: because of the neglect of research on urban tourism, the public sector do not see the necessity of detailed research to understand the urban tourist. Therefore, researchers have access to very limited sources of data, making research difficult where large-scale funding is unavailable to generate substantive sources of primary data using social survey techniques (e.g. face-to-face interviews with tourists, residents, planners and local government officials). How can this book contribute to a better understanding of urban tourism? At this point Ashworth's (1992a) comments on the way forward for the development of urban tourism are useful, as they highlight the range of issues which need to be addressed. He argues that the development of an:

> Urban tourism requires the development of a coherent body of theories, concepts, techniques and methods of analysis which allow

comparable studies to contribute towards some common goal of understanding of either the particular role of cities within tourism or the place of tourism within the form and function of cities.

(Ashworth 1992a: 5)

For this reason, it is pertinent to consider the ways in which one might conceptualise urban tourism.

The concept of urban tourism: approaches towards its analysis

Conceptualising why tourists seek cities as places to visit is one starting point in trying to understand this phenomenon. Clearly any detailed examination of why tourists visit specific places requires an analysis of the social psychology of tourist behaviour, especially tourist motivation (P. Pearce 1982; 1993: see also Chapter 2, this volume). But at a general abstract level, one can argue that tourists are attracted to cities because of the specialised functions they offer and the range of services provided. Shaw and Williams (1994) provide a useful explanation of the significance of urban areas in tourism. They argue that such areas have a geographical concentration of facilities and attractions which are conveniently located to meet tourists' and residents' needs alike. Furthermore, they suggest that because urban areas are varied and diverse, researchers tend to examine them in three ways to understand their uniqueness and similarities. First, urban areas are heterogenous in nature, meaning that they are different and diverse when considered in terms of their size, location, function, appearance and heritage. It is this feature which makes the study of urban tourism so interesting because no two destinations are identical and yet they are characterised by a common denominator – tourism. For researchers and planners, the challenge is in understanding how to develop planning strategies which accommodate and manage specific types of tourism in their locality. Second, the sheer scale of urban areas and the different functions they simultaneously provide make them multifunctional and complex to understand. Last, urban tourist functions are 'very rarely solely produced for, or consumed by, tourists but by a whole range of users' (Shaw and Williams 1994: 201) although the work on tourism urbanisation discussed below does question this proposition in a theoretical context. In many countries, the gateway function provided by the capital or major city for incoming and outbound tourists, due to the location of transport terminals (e.g. airports) in or near the urban area, reinforces the tourist function for many urban areas. In this context, tourists cannot avoid moving through these environments when travelling.

In conceptualising the different ways one might view urban tourism, Ashworth (1992a) identifies three approaches:

1 The supply of tourism facilities in urban areas, where the categorisation and inventories of facilities by geographers has led to research on the distribution of hotels, restaurants, attractions, shopping, night-life and other tourist-related services. These approaches have also utilised the traditional approach of urban ecological models to produce regionalised descriptions of urban tourism patterns (which are discussed in the next section). More recently, the facility approach has been developed a stage further with the use of the term 'product' as a particular selected package together with many of the discrete facilities identified on tourism inventories, to highlight the diversity and variety of tourism resources available to potential visitors.

2 The demand for urban tourism, where research has largely been descriptive to establish who visits urban tourist destinations, why they visit, the patterns and behaviour of tourist activities, and the ways in which such destinations are perceived by visitors.

3 Policy perspectives on urban tourism, generated by planners and the private sector, which are not widely disseminated and restricted to those organisations who generate the studies or who have a vested interest in the tourism sector.

While these approaches are not comprehensive, they do identify the limitations of the existing literature which leads one to consider the extent to which theoretical research has been undertaken on this theme.

Theoretical perspectives on urban tourism

Within the geographical literature on tourism, a number of studies have developed models of urban tourism based on assumptions about tourist behaviour, the patterns of tourist development they observed and the extent to which this can be used to derive generalisations of urban tourist development. The principle behind the use of models, many of which can be attributed to human geography, is to develop a framework in which the complexity of the real world is simplified into a rational and logical framework. Of course, one also has to question the validity of models developed within a logical positivist tradition in social science (see Johnston 1991 for a more detailed philosophical discussion), which believed that one could rationalise human behaviour and activities into generalised models that had a wider application to the situations existing in the real world.

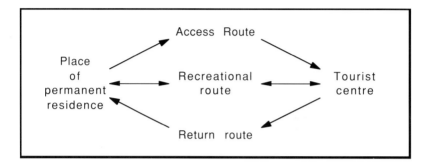

Figure 1.1 Tourist flows between two locations (after Matley 1976)

Each of the models with a direct or indirect concern for urban tourism is reviewed in detail by Pearce (1987a), where the tourist centre (urban area) is characterised as a generating and receiving area for tourism (see Matley 1976). This is illustrated in Figure 1.1 which highlights one of the dynamic elements of tourist travel – it involves a flow between the origin and destination area, which is often focused on an urban area with accommodation, attractions and infrastructure to support this activity. Other models, such as Yokeno's (1968) notion of international tourist travel, applied the concepts developed in location theory in human geography (related to the distribution of settlements and agricultural land use) to highlight how one can describe patterns of tourism. Lundgren's (1982) attempt to examine tourist places and to develop a hierarchy of tourist flows notes the mutual attraction of some tourist destinations, with flows between centrally-located tourist destinations, where a reciprocal relationship existed between the flows of tourists. However, it is Pearce's (1987a) assessment of tourist flows within an integrated framework for urban areas that draws many of these early ideographic studies into a more useful context. Even so, the recent study by Weaver (1993) is evidence of the attempt to use urban land-use models to describe the development of urban tourist zones on small Caribbean islands, using concepts from recreational geography (e.g. Getz (1993a) and the recreational or tourist business district in Chapter

3). Thus, urban areas not only perform a generating role for tourism, but also a receiving function and there is a need to consider the urban area as part of a more complex system, a feature discussed later in this chapter.

More theoretically-based models have also been developed in the context of the Less Developed World. The work of Britton (1980) analyses tourist flows using geographical concepts of core and periphery to distinguish between the demand in Western industrialised areas and the Less Developed World destinations in the Caribbean and Pacific. The significance of Britton's (1980) research is that the international transfer of tourists occurs between urban places in the generating and receiving area. In other words, tourists visiting LDCs (peripheral locations) are restricted to urban places, often focused on a resort enclave developed for the tourist market by transnational organisations with tourism interests. This is reflected in the degree of control that major tour operators in the generating country hold over the destination through contractual arrangements for accommodation, air travel and the market for tourism services. Britton argues that these patterns of control effectively present illusory benefits for LDCs which have pursued tourism as a route to economic development, often facilitated by grants and investment from the World Bank and other international aid agencies. Structural weaknesses in the economy of LDCs, which can be related to the economic system developed under colonial rule, give rise to a neocolonial pattern of control in the tourism economy where transnational corporations control the distribution of tourists and the benefits which accrue from tourist development. In some cases, profits from tourism activities are expropriated from the destination area by the transnational corporation to their headquarters in the developed world. This pattern of control is reinforced by dependent forms of development such as resort enclaves built and controlled by international tourism organisations which remove interaction with the local community and reduce the economic impact of tourism development on the local economy.

While other models exist to describe (but only rarely explain) the evolution of tourist resorts and the cycle of development they pass through (e.g. see Butler's (1980) concept of the resort cycle based on the product life cycle used in marketing science discussed in Chapter 4), there still remains a paucity of theoretically based research on urban tourism. One of the most interesting studies to fill the gap of theoretical research is by Mullins (1991).

Tourism urbanisation

Mullins argues that 'tourist cities represent a new and extraordinary form of urbanisation because they are built for consumption' (Mullins 1991: 326), compared with the rationale for industrial cities of the nineteenth and early twentieth century where industrial production, commerce and housing were the main functions. This offers a new insight into the conceptualisation of how cities develop through tourism since the consumption of goods and services in resorts and urban areas is not a permanent feature, but a transitory function not related to basic human needs, but on the quest for fun, excitement, relaxation and leisure. Stanback (1985) notes that in the USA, consumption centres (including tourist cities) have among the highest rates of urban growth highlighting the significance of this phenomenon.

If one pursues Mullins' ideas, then the growth of urban places for the purposes of tourism consumption is a logical starting point, rooted in urban sociology. The term 'consumption' is used to identify the use people make of goods and services, usually produced and sold for profit. The development of services for non-basic needs has emerged alongside the expansion of products for mass consumption. This mass consumption of goods and services is associated with the post-war growth in collective consumption, where the production of goods and services for the wider public good was the main motive as opposed to profit. In other words, a welfare function characterises the production and consumption of goods in the post-war period in Western societies (a different situation existed in command economies in the Eastern bloc). One also has to emphasise the distinction between consumption by urban dwellers and that by tourists. However, since the 1970s, many countries have seen changes in political ideology, with the rise of the *New Right* and the restructuring of services for collective consumption (for the public good) to reduce public sector expenditure. At the same time, consumption of goods and services for pleasure has expanded in many urban areas. Why should the development of these services for pleasure facilitate tourism urbanisation?

It is widely acknowledged that the post-war increase in the amount of paid holiday entitlement, free time and the rise in incomes contributed to the demand for consumer goods and services. Tourism is a notable example of this growth, initially as domestic demand and car ownership contributed to increased travel, while the introduction of package holidays assisted in the expansion in international tourism. Since the 1970s, changes in the mode of work and regime of industrial organisation led to distinct changes in the pattern of production and consumption, as shifts occurred in capital accumulation to develop new forms of productive activity in free market economies. Recent developments in leisure theory (e.g. Henry and Bramham 1990) identify how perceived structural changes in society have been accompanied by processes shaping the public provision of tourism and leisure activity. They identify shifts in regimes of capital accumulation from mass consumption and a strong commitment to public welfare (e.g. Fordism) towards new forms of consumption under conditions of post-Fordism. One clear difference under post-Fordism is the increased emphasis on the economic rationale for tourism and leisure policy as urban areas seek to develop the 'pleasure function' for profit. Roche (1992) has described these changes in post-industrial society in terms of structural changes in capitalism, thereby questioning the types of processes shaping the operation and development of tourism in many post-industrial cities. Some of the changes in public sector tourism and leisure policy underline these changes (Table 1.2). The essential difference between Fordist and post-Fordist forms of consumption is that while mass consumption still exists in parallel with the Fordist regime, under post-Fordist conditions, it is also complemented by a customised approach to consumption as goods and services are tailored more to individual's needs. This has been a development as entrepreneurs and owners of capital adapt to the new economic conditions and demands of consumers.

Whilst this remains a highly theoretical approach to tourism and leisure and requires a sound grasp of urban social theory, Mullins (1991) identifies a number of characteristics which are associated with the post-Fordist urban tourist destination. These characteristics are helpful in identifying the distinctive features of urban tourist destinations. Thus, where tourism urbanisation exists, it is:

- Geographically different, in that the observed patterns of development and land use do not coincide with those characterised in the urban ecological models of urban geography discussed earlier;
- Symbolically different, with various images and symbols used to promote the tourist function, using the natural and built environment as positive images for the consumption of pleasure, often associated with place-marketing;
- Characterised by rapid population and labour force growth;
- Distinguished by flexible forms of production, meaning that econo-

Table 1.2 Illustrations of Fordist and post-Fordist regimes of accumulation and methods of regulation

	Fordism	Post-Fordism
Local government	Large-scale bureaucratic corporate policy and management approach to social provision and accountability	Flexible forms of management and policy control: introduction of area management, decentralization: enterprise zones, urban development corporations (UDCs) and compulsory competitive tendering bring with them new management approaches and structures
Orientation of local government professionals	Bureaucratic and (liberal welfare) professionalism	Entrepreneurial and 'industrial' professionalism (e.g. accountancy)
Central–local relations	Local determination/influence on local spending and taxation levels; local management and policy for major consumption services, central responsibility for economic planning	(a) *Service provision* Central control of minimalist policy – local concern for locally flexible and appropriate means of implementation (b) *Economic development* Centrally devised policy implemented by local organs of the central state e.g. UDCs and Enterprise Zones (c) *Taxation levels* Largely decided centrally
Leisure policy emphasis	Social democratic orientation • Leisure opportunities are a right of citizenship • Leisure investment may achieve externalities (reduce anti-social behaviour and improve health)	• Provide cultural infrastructure to attract investment from new industries • Generate tourism multiplier effect • Provide infrastructure for new cultural industries (in some authorities) • Provide safety net welfare services in inner city • Minimise costs of achieving externalities
Leisure policy rationale	Largely social with some economic benefits	Largely economic with some social benefits

Source: Adapted from Henry and Bramham (1990) cited in Page (1993a)

mies are organised significantly around private sector employers and high rates of unemployment arise from the flexible work practices and insecure nature of the labour market;

- Dominated by state intervention which has a 'boosterist' tendency, whereby local government indirectly invests in the local infra-structure (physical – roads and basic services; social – schools and welfare functions; and cultural – the arts and leisure) with a view to encouraging further inward investment, often using state-funded quangos such as tourist boards and development agencies (Page 1993a; 1994a), a characteristic feature of the post-modern city;
- Associated with a mass and customised consumption of pleasure, with vast investment by developers in integrated resort complexes in coastal and inland areas (e.g. Center Parcs in Europe) and vast attraction complexes in or near urban centres of population (e.g. theme parks such as Disneyland);
- Characterised by a socially distinct resident population which has a high degree of transient people as temporary workers. These often have high levels of unemployment, with residents openly opposed to the social, cultural and environmental impact of tourism develop-ment on their locality. This often gives rise to a local conservation lobby and antagonistic views towards developers seeking to exploit the market opportunities for further tourism development in such locations. Planning restrictions are one local response favoured by conservative-minded groups while those associations favouring pro-gress and development see the positive benefits of local economic development.

Therefore, on the basis of this approach to tourism urbanisation it is possible to identify a typology of urban tourist destinations:

- Capital cities (e.g. London, Paris and New York) and cultural capi-tals (e.g. Rome);
- Metropolitan centres and walled historic cities (e.g. Canterbury and York) and small fortress cities;
- Large historic cities (e.g. Oxford, Cambridge and Venice);
- Inner city areas (Manchester);
- Revitalised waterfront areas (e.g. London Docklands and Sydney Darling Harbour);
- Industrial cities (e.g. nineteenth century Bradford);
- Seaside resorts and winter sports resorts (e.g. Lillehammer);
- Purpose-built integrated tourist resorts;

- Tourist-entertainment complexes (e.g. Disneyland and Las Vegas);
- Specialised tourist service centres (e.g. spas and pilgrimage destinations, e.g. Lourdes);
- Cultural/art cities (e.g. Florence – see Bywater 1993).

Whilst this is only a partial view, based on observations and trends within the international tourism industry, it does begin to build a profile of the complex array of destinations which tourists frequent and the value of understanding the phenomenon of urban tourism in a more systematic and detailed manner than has hitherto been the case. Nevertheless, it is only a starting point and cannot provide a framework for a more complex understanding of urban tourism. For this reason, it is necessary to consider what type of analytical approach is appropriate for the urban tourism phenomenon.

Analysing urban tourism: a systems approach

To understand the complexity and relationships which coexist within urban tourism, one needs to develop an analytical framework which is capable of synthesising the multiplicity of factors, processes and issues affecting the process of urban tourism in different contexts. The objective of developing such a framework should be to encompass the total tourist experience of urban tourism, a framework which incorporates a range of disciplinary perspectives. One methodology used by researchers to consider tourism is a systems approach, where the complexity of the real world situation can be rationalised in a simplified model to try and understand how different elements fit together. This is developed more fully in Page (1994b) in the context of tourist-transport. One of the key principles underpinning this approach is to reduce the complexity of urban tourism into a number of constructs and components which highlight the interrelated nature of different factors affecting the system. Such an approach also accommodates the multi-disciplinary nature of tourism studies, whereby the broader issues and interrelationships can by synthesised into one framework regardless of approach or discipline.

Leiper (1990) suggests that a system is a set of elements or parts that are connected to each other by at least one distinguishing principle. In this instance the urban tourism phenomenon is the distinguishing principle which forms the focus of the system. Laws (1991: 7) develops the systems idea a stage further by identifying the key features of a tourism system:

- The inputs (e.g. the supply of tourism products and tourism demand);
- The outputs (e.g. the tourist experience of urban tourism);
- External factors conditioning the system (e.g. the business environment, consumer preferences, political factors and economic issues).

The external factors exert a degree of influence on the nature of the system, and where these factors have a strong affect on the system, it can be termed an 'open' system, since the tourism inputs are not the only factors affecting it. Conversely, where external factors exert a limited influence, the system is 'closed'. To examine the links between different elements in the system, one can consider the nature of the 'flows' between the various components, where specific relationships may exist. For example, if a flow is in one direction only, then the relationship is often seen as a cause and effect (i.e. factor A affects factor B). However, if the flow is in both directions, a reciprocal relationship exists whereby the two factors are interrelated and influence each other.

A systems approach also allows one to trace the effect of different issues as well as identifying where improvements need to be made in the overall urban tourist experience. One important concept to consider at this point is the distribution channel used by researchers in marketing and operations management. This allows one to directly trace the flow of the product or service through a system from the point of production to consumption. Such an approach adopts a process-oriented approach to the analysis, operation and management of different issues. In operations management, tourism could be conceptualised as a process, and therefore the object of a systems approach would be in understanding and managing the process. In the case of urban tourism, this involves the human activities, communications between different elements in the system and the effect of tourists on the system. Therefore, urban tourism needs to be conceptualised as a service encounter and experience (see Page 1994b for a fuller discussion of the term 'service' and its significance in tourism research) which has:

- A high degree of customer involvement;
- A simultaneous supply component;

- Inconsistent demand, which varies according to seasonality;
- An intangible product which is often consumed.

Some of these elements are specifically urban in a multifunctional city (see Chapter 2), since it is the diverse urban area which can provide the intensity of resources to facilitate such an encounter.

Thus, the concept of tourist service is important because it provides a focus for the analysis of the visitor's experience of urban tourism.

The structure of the book

This books sets out to examine the international phenomenon of urban tourism and its significance as a process affecting urban areas which poses many opportunities and problems for the development, management and functioning of such destinations. Having briefly outlined some of the main features of the literature and the systems approach towards the analysis of urban tourism, it is pertinent to outline how the book is structured. It is not intended to be a comprehensive review of urban tourism: this is clearly not possible nor feasible for an introductory book. The book is designed to provide the reader with a clear understanding of the operation of urban tourism in different localities, some of the general similarities and differences in relation to the process of urban tourism and the systems developed to exploit and manage it in different tourist environments. One underlying objective is to raise awareness of the international significance of urban tourism and to develop a more integrated approach towards the study of urban tourism than has hitherto been the case. It does not adopt a theoretically determined approach, such as that advocated by Mullins (1991): it pursues a more general assessment of urban tourism, emphasising the importance of an interdisciplinary approach towards its analysis. One useful way of conceptualising the scope and extent of this book is through a systems model of the process of urban tourism and some of the interrelationships which exist. The tourist experience is the central feature (Figure 1.2) together with the interaction of different components in the system. This is probably best documented by focusing on the structure of the book which begins by examining the principal inputs – the demand and supply features of urban tourism – and then proceeds to investigate other elements and relationships within the system. The effect on the main output – the tourist experience of urban tourism – indirectly forms the focal point for other chapters to illustrate how

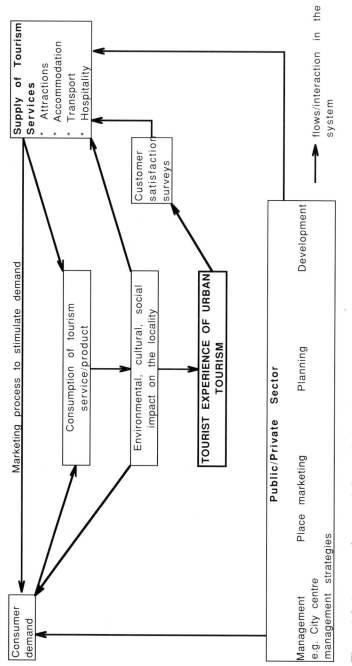

Figure 1.2 A systems framework for analysing urban tourism

improvements to this outcome can be implemented by modifying some of the principal inputs.

Chapter 2 considers the demand for urban tourism generated by visitors in terms of the locations which visitors seek and the difficulty of quantifying the scale and extent of this activity. This is followed by a discussion of how different forms of tourist motivation lead to discrete and interrelated reasons for visiting urban locations. In Chapter 3, the supply of tourism facilities is examined as a basis for an assessment of how different agencies and organisations influence and affect the provision of services and infrastructure for urban tourism. This raises the issue of the impact of urban tourist development and the need to develop approaches to understand the effect of the supply and demand in various localities. Therefore, Chapter 4 considers the methodological problems associated with examining the impact of urban tourism to illustrate the effects of urban tourism in various contexts. As a consequence of highlighting the impact of urban tourism, Chapter 5 considers the role of tourism management and planning as a natural corollary of urban tourist development. This is followed in Chapter 6 by a discussion of the trend towards place-marketing to promote towns and cities for tourism purposes. Lastly, Chapter 7 identifies some of the strategies and action needed to maintain a quality urban tourist experience in the 1990s and the role of visitor management.

Questions

1 To what extent is urban tourism a well-established area of study within tourism research?
2 What does Ashworth (1989) mean by an 'imbalance in attention' in the study of towns and cities within tourism studies?
3 How far has theoretical research in urban tourism provided explanations of why towns and cities develop as tourist destinations?
4 What is the value of a systems approach to the analysis of urban tourism?

Further reading

Ashworth, G. (1989) 'Urban tourism: an imbalance in attention', in C.P. Cooper (ed.) *Progress in Tourism, Recreation and Hospitality Management* Volume 1, Belhaven: London: 33–54.

This is a good review of the state of urban tourism research in the late 1980s and remains the most frequently cited article by most tourism researchers who examine urban tourism.

de Bres, K. (1994) 'Cow towns or cathedral precincts? Two models for contemporary urban tourism', *Area* 26 (1): 57–67

This is a critical review of urban tourism models and contains a good introduction to the literature.

Mullins, P. (1991) 'Tourism urbanisation', *International Journal of Urban and Regional Research* 15(3): 326–42.

This is a difficult, but useful theoretical analysis of tourism and urbanisation based on the authors experience in Australia.

Pearce, D. (1987) *Tourism Today: A Geographical Analysis*, Longman: London.

This has a useful chapter on this topic.

Shaw, G and Williams, A. (1994) *Critical issues in Tourism: A Geographical Perspective*, Blackwell: Oxford.

This has a good up-to-date chapter on urban tourism and should be a good starting point for those interested in a geographical approach to urban tourism.

2
The demand for urban tourism

Introduction

The demand for tourism in urban areas is poorly understood in the academic literature, and as Blank and Petkovich (1987: 165) argue 'urban tourism is almost certainly among the most misunderstood and underestimated of all tourism types. It suffers from underestimation – sometimes even unrecognition'. Accurate information on the demand for urban tourism is critical for service providers, planners and those businesses associated with the tourism industry to ensure that they meet the needs and requirements of tourists. One of the major challenges for the tourism industry is to attempt to balance the supply of services, products and infrastructure with the actual demand for such goods (see Bull 1991 for a fuller discussion of the concepts of supply and demand). Without adequate information, the day to day management of urban tourism will be difficult for planners and providers, as they will find it difficult to establish priorities for attracting, promoting and developing the market for urban tourism. This is a problem which is compounded by the heterogenous nature of urban tourism. According to Shaw and Williams:

> Within the somewhat limited literature on visitor activity in urban areas, two main perspectives can be identified. One concerns the types of users and visitor motivation, while the other, with an even smaller research base, examines visitor behaviour in the city.
>
> (Shaw and Williams 1994: 207)

This provides an important focus for this chapter, the purpose of which is to examine the nature of tourist motivation as a basis to establish why tourists choose to visit different destinations and the complex reasons associated with selecting urban areas. For this reason, a general introduction to the demand for urban tourism is followed by a discussion of tourist motivation to explain the context in which travel to urban destinations occurs. This is followed by a review of the international data sources which may be used to gauge the scale of demand for urban tourism. Following this assessment, the different types of tourists who choose to visit urban areas are discussed, and a case study is used to highlight the motivating factors shaping one particular form of urban tourism – visits to religious sites.

The demand for urban tourism

Ryan (1991) discusses the economic determinants of tourism demand which are associated with the purchase of an intangible service, usually a holiday or tourism service, which comprise an experience for the tourist (see Chapter 1). What is meant by the 'tourist experience'?

The tourist experience of urban tourism

According to Graefe and Vaske (1987), the 'tourist experience' is the culmination of a given experience which can be influenced by individual, environmental, situational and personality-related factors as well as the degree of communication with other people. It is the outcome (or output if viewed in a system framework) which researchers and the tourism industry constantly evaluate to establish if the actual experience met the tourist's expectations. In other words, the 'tourist experience' is a complex amalgam of factors which shape the tourist's feelings and attitude towards his or her visit. Yet as tourism motivation and consumer research suggests, it is almost impossible to predict tourist responses to individual situations but a series of interrelated impacts may affect the tourist's experience (Figure 2.1). For example, high usage levels of tourism resources may lead to overcrowding and this may diminish the visitor experience although the results from the recreational literature are inconclusive on this issue. In essence, when the carrying capacity (see Chapter 4) or the ability of a site to sustain a given number of visitors is exceeded, overcrowding results and that may detract from the tourist experience for some visitors. This emphasises the need to understand both the views of groups and individuals, since some people have a low tolerance threshold for an overcrowded site while others are less affected by similar conditions. However, as research has shown, increased use levels may raise the potential for conflict although 'research on all types of impact depicted in Figure 2.1 shows that the effects of increasing use levels on the recreation/tourist experience can be explained only partially, at best, as a function of use level' (Graefe and Vaske 1987: 394).

Ultimately, the individual's ability to tolerate the behaviour of other people, levels of use, the social situation and the context of the activity are all important determinants of the actual outcome. Thus, evaluating the quality of the tourist experience is a complex process which may require a careful consideration of the factors motivating a visit (i.e. how the tourist's perception of urban areas makes them predisposed to visit particular places), their actual patterns of activity and the extent to which their expectations associated with their perceptions are matched in reality.

Tourism motivation

Ryan (1991) emphasises the significance of psychological determinants of demand in explaining some of the reasons why tourists travel and their selection of particular destinations. Although there is no theory of tourist travel, a range of tourist motivators exist (P. Pearce 1982). Ryan's (1991: 25–9) analysis of tourist travel motivators (excluding business travel) identifies the following reasons commonly cited to explain why people travel to tourist destinations for holidays. These include:

- Wish fulfilment
- Shopping
- A desire to escape from a mundane environment
- The pursuit of relaxation and recuperation functions
- An opportunity for play
- The strengthening of family bonds
- Prestige, since different destinations can enable one to gain social enhancement among peers
- Social interaction
- Educational opportunities

Whilst a range of motivators can be identified, it is possible to classify

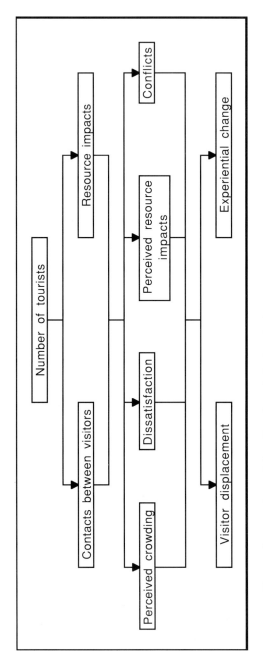

Figure 2.1 The tourist experience (after Graefe and Vaske 1987)

tourists according to the type of holiday they are seeking and the experience they desire. For example, Cohen (1972) distinguished between four types of tourist travellers:

- *The organised mass tourist*, on a package holiday who is highly organised. Their contact with the host community in a destination is minimal.
- *The individual mass tourist*, who uses similar facilities to the organised mass tourist but also desires to visit other sights not covered on organised tours in the destination.
- *The explorers*, who arrange their travel independently and who wish to experience the social and cultural lifestyle of the destination.
- *The drifter*, who does not seek any contact with other tourists or their accommodation, seeking to live with the host community (Smith 1989).

Clearly, such a classification is fraught with problems, since it does not take into account the increasing diversity of holidays undertaken and inconsistencies in tourist behaviour (P. Pearce 1982). Furthermore, the classification also fails to acknowledge the complexity of urban tourism. As Shaw and Williams (1994: 201) observe, 'urban areas of all types act as tourist destinations, attracting domestic and international visitors, including holidaymakers, as well as those on business and conference trips'. Other researchers suggest that one way of overcoming this difficulty is to consider the different destinations tourists choose to visit, and then establish a sliding scale similar to Cohen's (1972) typology, but which does not have such an absolute classification. How does this affect the identification of the tourists who visit urban areas?

Urban tourism destinations need to recognise what economic, social and psychological factors are stimulating the demand for visits, and how different types of travellers' preferences are reflected in the choice of various destinations and specific activity patterns. One important study which reviews the different approaches and models used to analyse tourist motivation, is by P. Pearce (1993). It establishes a blueprint for tourist motivation, but notes that:

Tourism demand should not be equated with tourism motivation. Tourism demand is the outcome of tourists' motivation, as well as marketing, destination features and contingency factors such as money, health and time relating to the travellers' choice behaviour . . . Tourism demand can be expressed as the sum of realistic behav-

ioural intentions to visit a specific location . . . [which is] . . . reduced
to existing travel statistics and forecasts of future traveller numbers.
Tourist motivation is then a part rather than the equivalent of tourist
demand.

(P. Pearce 1993: 113)

It is important to emphasise this author's comment that tourism
demand cannot be simply equated with tourism motivation. This
makes a convincing case for examining tourist destination choice in
the context of urban tourism if destinations are to understand
their markets. P. Pearce's (1993) blueprint for tourist motivation is
also notable because it considers both the theoretical and conceptual
issues necessary to develop an understanding of the various motives
associated with tourist behaviour (which readers should consult before
undertaking research projects on this topic, in combination with Ryan
1995 on the specific techniques which can be used to assess visitor
satisfaction).

For this reason, tour operators selling holidays to urban destinations
need to recognise the complexity of tourist motivation and the preferred
locations tourists seek to visit. More specifically, both the tourism
industry in urban areas receiving visitors and the tour operators will
need to understand the range of motives and expectations of certain
types of traveller, since the level of service they provide will need to
match the market and the requirements of travellers. This is essential if
the 'tourist experience' is to be a favourable one. Operators need to
understand not only the dimensions of demand, but the market segments and the behaviour and expectations of consumers which they will
need to accommodate in providing a high quality tourist experience (see
Ryan 1995). For this reason, attention now turns to the data sources
available to gauge patterns of demand for different destinations.

Data sources on urban tourism: a paucity of material?

The analysis of tourism, tourists and their propensity to travel and
previous travel patterns is 'a complex process . . . involving not only the
visitor and his movements but also the destination and host community'
(Latham 1989: 55). What statistical information on urban tourism is
available? How is it gathered? And who publishes it?

One immediate problem which confronts the researcher interested in
tourism is the absence of international statistics which monitor every

aspect of tourism. Although industry-specific studies exist which monitor the volume of travel, these are often confidential to organisations and one is forced to refer to tourism statistics since they are more comprehensive and consistent, providing an insight into:

- Tourist arrivals in different regions of the world and for specific countries;
- The volume of tourist trips;
- Types of tourism (e.g. holidaymaking, visiting friends and relatives and business travel);
- The number of nights spent in different countries by tourists;
- Tourist expenditure on services.

Latham's (1989) excellent study on tourism statistics is essential reading, since it provides a useful insight into the complex process of assessing the general patterns of demand for tourism. Recent studies by Jefferson and Lickorish (1991) and Veal (1992) document the procedures associated with the generation of tourism statistics, which often use social survey techniques, such as questionnaire-based interviews with tourists at departure and arrival points. These surveys often form the basis for calculations by tourism organisations who estimate the volume of tourism for specific countries, regions and individual localities.

Unlike other forms of social survey work, tourists are a transient and mobile population. This poses many problems in relation to which social survey method and sampling technique one should use to generate reliable and accurate statistical information, to ensure that it is representative of the real world. Due to the cost involved in undertaking social surveys, it is impossible and impractical for organisations to interview all tourists travelling on a specific mode of transport. (The exception here is the self-completion customer satisfaction questionnaires which tour operators such as Thomson Holidays in the UK use – see Page 1994b for a specimen copy of the Thomson questionnaire.) A sampling framework is normally used to select a range of respondents who are representative of the population being examined. Whilst there are a number of good sources which deal with this technical issue (see S.L.J. Smith 1989; Veal 1992), it is clear that no one survey technique and sampling framework is going to provide all the information necessary to enable managers and planners to make decisions related to planning and service provision. It is possible to discern three common types of tourism surveys:

- Pre-travel studies of tourists' intended travel habits and likely use of tourist-transport;
- Studies of tourists in transit, or at their destination, to provide information on their actual behaviour and plans for the remainder of their holiday or journey;
- Post-travel studies of tourists once they have returned to their place of residence.

Clearly there are advantages and disadvantages with each approach. For example, pre-travel studies may indicate the potential destinations which tourists would like to visit on their next holiday, but it is difficult to assess the extent to which holiday intentions are converted to actual travel. In contrast, surveys of tourists in transit or at a destination can only provide a snapshot of their experiences to date rather than a broader evaluation of their holiday experience. Yet retrospective post-travel studies incur the problem of actually locating and eliciting responses from tourists which accurately record a previous event or experience. Each approach has a valuable role and individual operators and tourism organisations use the approach appropriate to their information needs.

International data sources

The most comprehensive and widely used sources of tourism statistics that directly and indirectly examine international tourist travel are produced by the World Tourism Organization (WTO) and the Organization for Economic Cooperation and Development (OECD) (see Pearce 1987a for a more detailed discussion of these sources). National governments also compile statistics on international tourism for their own country (in-bound travel) and the destinations chosen by outbound travellers. WTO publishes a number of annual publications which include the Yearbook of Tourism Statistics (published since 1947 as *International Travel Statistics*, then as *World Travel Statistics*, and now as *World Travel and Tourism Statistics*). This has a summary of tourism statistics for almost 150 countries and areas with key data on tourist-transport and includes statistical information in the following order:

1 A world summary of international tourism statistics;
2 Tourist arrivals;
3 Accommodation capacity by regions;

4 Trends in world international tourism arrivals, receipts and exports;
5 Arrivals of cruise passengers;
6 Domestic tourism;
7 Tourism payments (including international tourism receipts by countries calculated in US$ millions, excluding international fare receipts);
8 Tourist transport (tourist arrivals from abroad by mode of transport);
9 Tourism motivations (arrivals from abroad and purpose of visit);
10 Tourism accommodation;
11 Country studies which examine the detailed breakdown of tourism statistics collected for each area, including tourism seasonality.

In addition to WTO, OECD produces *Tourism Policy and International Tourism in OECD Member Countries*. Although the data collected are restricted to twenty-five countries, it deals with other issues such as government policy and barriers to international tourism.

How do these studies relate to urban tourism?

International data on urban tourism

Tourism statistics collated by OECD and WTO are largely based on the information which governments supply to them in relation to the criteria set out by each organisation. Despite the existence of WTO and OECD data sources, which document different aspects of domestic tourism, neither organisation collects data which directly assesses urban tourism. No international sources exist to identify patterns, trends and the associated impact of urban tourism. This is supported by Shaw and Williams (1994: 212) who argue that 'unfortunately it is difficult to document the scale and importance of urban tourism in a comparative context, since few statistics exist'. Even so, they do refer to Ashworth and Tunbridge (1990), compiling Table 2.1 to identify the scale and volume of tourism in selected European cities. The result is that researchers have to revert to individual locations and tourism organisations (e.g. national and regional tourism organisations – see Pearce 1992 for a discussion of these organisations), city governments and commercial bodies who have a vested interest in assembling market intelligence on urban tourism (see Touche Ross 1991). For this reason, it is pertinent to consider the types of data available in WTO and OECD publications which may be used as an indirect measure of the scale and volume of urban tourism.

Table 2.1 International visitor nights in major
European cities

City	Number of visitor nights (millions)
London	20
Paris	16
Rome	5.6
Madrid	5.5
Athens	4.7
Vienna	4.6
Munich	2.6
Amsterdam	2.5
Brussels	2.4
Copenhagen	2.1

Source: Shaw and Williams (1994: 213) based on Ashworth
and Tunbridge 1990

One important indicator recorded by WTO and OECD is the amount
and use made of tourist accommodation by domestic and international
tourists in relation to the occupancy and volume of usage. But what
relevance does this have to establishing estimates of urban tourism?
Within the tourism literature, accommodation is normally regarded as a
'supply-side' variable (Bull 1991), but its use can be regarded as indica-
tive of the aggregate demand generated by tourists. Therefore, if one
makes the assumption that serviced tourist accommodation (e.g. hotels
and guest houses) has a tendency to locate in urban areas (Ashworth
1989), it is clear that tourists will stay in locations where accommodation
is available. In fact the tourist accommodation is the main source used
by Shaw and Williams (1994) to illustrate the scale of tourism in major
European cities. Of course, there are many situations where hotels
locate outside urban areas (e.g. country house hotels and similar establishments in rural areas) but the combination of serviced accommodation in tourist cities, seaside resorts and specialised resorts makes an
overwhelming case for arguing that accommodation tends to locate
close to urban areas (the locational characteristics of hotels is dealt with
in more detail in the next chapter).

Accommodation provides the base for tourists staying in one location
for a holiday or travelling on a package or itinerary to visit other urban
places on a predefined circuit (Pearce 1987b), although the weakness of
using serviced accommodation as an approximation of demand is that it
may not capture those tourists staying with friends and relatives and

camping. Therefore, whilst not being able to identify the precise patterns of urban tourism for individual countries from WTO and OECD
data, it is possible to look at the patterns of arrivals to individual
countries (i.e. arrivals at frontiers and gateways) and to compare those
statistics with tourist use of accommodation. Admittedly, a proportion
of tourist use of accommodation will be non-urban in some cases but a
significant proportion will be urban and this is a useful starting point for
the assessment of the scale of urban tourism. This provides researchers
with initial estimates of the likely scale of urban tourism and is a starting
point for more detailed investigation of the situation in individual
countries and their urban tourist destinations, if appropriate data exist.
To illustrate the type of information which exists, a range of data
collated by OECD is considered as it is more manageable for comparative purposes although it only covers a limited range of countries. The
worldwide coverage by WTO, which deals with the data on a country by
country basis, is more complex and one would have to be selective in
identifying the potential demand for urban tourism.

OECD tourism data: the international scale of urban tourism demand

As with all forms of tourism data, there are difficulties in the degree of
comparability in the categories of data collated by different countries.
As Table 2.2 shows, there are significant variations in the types of
accommodation recorded by OECD countries and this limits the extent
to which precise comparisons can be made. However, the motives for
overseas tourist visits (Table 2.3) highlights the diversity in tourism
markets and their demand for different types of accommodation in 1989
and 1990. This is an important starting point for establishing the extent
of demand for accommodation (although more detailed assessments for
individual countries are provided in the Economist Intelligence Unit's
comprehensive *International Tourism Reports* and *Travel and Tourism
Analyst* and Horwath International's (1990) international survey of
tourism accommodation).

In terms of demand, Table 2.4 provides an indication of the nights
spent by foreign and domestic tourists in all forms of accommodation
while Table 2.5 focuses on hotels and similar establishments. It is
apparent from Table 2.5 that the use of hotel accommodation by foreign
tourists is comparatively high for Spain, Austria, France, Greece,
Germany and Switzerland (and the former Yugoslavia). In contrast, the

Table 2.2 Types of accommodation covered by OECD statistics

Countries	Hotels and similar establishments						Supplementary means of accommodation						
	Hotels[1]	Motels[2]	Boarding houses[3]	Inns[4]	Others[5]	Youth hostels[6]	Camping and caravan sites[7]	Holiday villages	Mountain huts and shelters	Rented rooms flats and houses	Sanatoria, health est'ments	Recreation homes for children[8]	Others[9]
Australia	X	X	X		X	X	X			X			X
Austria	X					X	X	X	X	X	X	X	X
Belgium	X				X		X		X	X	X	X	X
Canada	X	X					X						X
Denmark[10]	X		X		X	X	X						X
Finland	X		X		X		X			X			
France	X		X		X	X	X	X					X
Germany	X		X	X	X	X	X	X			X		
Greece	X	X	X	X	X		X						
Ireland	X		X				X			X			
Italy	X				X	X	X						X
Netherlands	X		X		X	X	X						
Norway[10]						X	X					X	
Portugal	X	X	X	X	X		X						
Spain	X						X						
Sweden	X	X	X			X	X	X		X			X
Switzerland	X	X		X		X	X				X		
Turkey	X	X	X	X	X		X	X	X		X		
Yugoslavia	X	X	X	X	X	X	X	X	X	X	X		X

Source: OECD (1992) *Tourism Policy and International Tourism*

Table 2.2 cont.

Notes

1 Includes: Germany: hotels serving breakfast only; Belgium: motels, boarding houses and inns; Finland: motels; France: motels; Ireland: motels; Portugal: studio-hotels; Spain: *Paradores* and boarding houses (*Fondas*) and *Casa de Heuspedes*); Sweden: motels; Switzerland: boarding houses; Turkey: thermal hotels.

2 Includes: Greece: bungalows.

3 Includes: Finland: inns; Ireland: inns; Sweden: resort hotels.

4 Includes: Portugal: private and state-owned inns.

5 Includes: Australia: hotels and motels with facilities in most rooms and not necessarily providing meals and alcoholic drinks; Belgium: non-licensed establishments; Finland: lodging houses and part of youth hostels; Greece: bungalow-hotels, studio-hotels and recreation homes for children; Netherlands: youth hostels in Amsterdam; Portugal: holiday flats and villages; Spain: Fondas; Sweden: boarding houses, inns and resort hotels; Turkey: special licensed hotels and studio-hotels.

6 Includes: Germany: mountain huts and shelters.

7 Includes: Australia: cabins and flats; Finland: holiday village cottages.

8 Includes: Portugal: youth hostels.

9 Includes: Australia: rented farms, house-boats, rented camper-vans, boats, cabin cruisers, camping outside commercial grounds; Austria: mountain huts and shelters; Belgium: youth hostels, holiday villages and social tourism establishments; Canada: homes of friends or relatives, private cottages, commercial cottages and others, (universities, hostels); Germany: recreation and holiday homes, institutions providing educational services; Greece: holiday centres; Italy: recreation homes for children, mountain huts and shelters, holiday homes and religious establishments; Spain: secondary residences, private apartments, chalets and bungalows; Switzerland: dormitories in recreation homes for children, tourist camps, mountain huts and shelters, holiday villages; Yugoslavia: children and student homes, sleeping cars, cabins and ships, mountain huts and shelters.

10 Total available without breakdown for 'hotels and similar establishments'.

Table 2.3 Foreign tourism by purpose of visit

	1989						1990					
	Business journeys (%)[1]	Private journeys (%)[2]				Total volume in thousands	Business journeys (%)	Private journeys (%)				Total volume in thousands
		Holidays	VFR[2]	Others	Total			Holidays	VFR	Others	Total	
Greece[3]	9.1	81.1	4.0	5.8	90.9	8081.9	9.1	82.8	3.9	4.1	90.9	8873.3
Ireland[4]	17.2	38.8	37.3	6.6	82.8	2733.0	16.5	43.3	34.5	5.7	83.5	3068.0
Portugal[5]	2.4	92.2	0.8	4.6	97.6	7115.9	2.4	92.0	0.9	4.7	97.6	8019.9
Spain[6]	7.0	84.0	3.0	6.0	93.0	35350.0	7.9	83.2	4.0	4.9	92.1	34666.0
Turkey[7]	10.4	78.1	2.3	9.2	89.6	4459.2	8.0	79.4	3.2	9.4	92.0	5389.3
United Kingdom[8]		56.1	26.9	16.9	100.0	12976.0		58.3	25.4	16.4	100.0	12589.0
Canada[9]	17.7	54.2	24.1	3.9	82.3	15111.2						
Australia[10]	12.3	53.2	22.1	12.4	87.7	2080.3	11.9	55.7	20.6	11.8	88.1	2214.8
New Zealand[11]	11.7	49.9	24.4	14.0	88.3	901.1	11.3	50.2	24.1	14.5	88.7	976.0
Japan[12]	29.2	52.9		18.0	70.8	2835.1	27.7	58.1		14.2	72.3	3235.9
Yugoslavia[13]	2.6	81.5		15.9	97.4	8.6						

Source: OECD (1992) *Tourism Policy and International Tourism*

Notes

1 Includes: business, congresses, seminars, on missions, etc.
2 VFR: visits to friends and relatives
3 Greece: number of tourists includes journeys combining visiting relatives and holiday or business holiday.
4 Ireland: number of visits on overseas routes.
5 Portugal: number of tourists 'Other' includes visits for cultural purposes and journeys for educational reasons.
6 Spain: number of tourists 'Other' includes journeys for educational reasons.
7 Turkey: 'Others' includes journeys combining shopping and transit and journeys for study, health, religious and sports purposes.
8 United Kingdom: number of visits, 'Other' includes visits for religion, sports, health and visits of more than one purpose where none predominates.
9 Canada: number of tourists.
10 Australia: short-term visitors (less than one year), 'Others' includes journeys for educational reasons.
11 New Zealand: number of tourists, 'Others' includes journeys for educational reasons.
12 Japan: number of visits, 'Others' includes journeys for educational reasons.
13 Yugoslavia: number of tourists, 'Others' includes visits to friends and relatives, tours (cruises) and visits for sports, health and religion purposes. Estimate on basis of sample survey of foreign tourists in accommodation establishments.

Table 2.4 Nights spent by foreign and domestic tourists in all types of accommodation[1] (thousands)

	Nights spent by foreign tourists			Nights spent by domestic tourists			Total nights			Proportion spent by foreign tourists (%)	
	1989	1990	% change	1989	1990	% change	1989	1990	% change	1989	1990
Austria	94968.5	94788.3	−0.2	28815.6	28841.2	0.1	123784.2	123629.5	−0.1	76.7	76.7
Belgium[2]	12168.3	12886.2	5.9	23798.8	23953.1	0.6	35967.1	36839.3	2.4	33.8	35.0
Denmark	8574.4	9338.0	8.9	12677.5	13333.6	5.2	21251.9	22671.7	6.7	40.3	41.2
Finland	2846.0	2829.8	−0.6	10130.3	10261.1	1.3	12976.4	13090.9	0.9	21.9	21.6
Germany[3]	38028.2	39146.5	2.9	222833.6	234579.0	5.3	260861.8	273725.5	4.9	14.6	14.3
Greece	34157.7	36298.6	6.3	11985.8	11831.9	−1.3	46143.5	48130.5	4.3	74.0	75.4
Netherlands	14171.9	16387.0	15.6	36787.1	39270.3	6.8	50959.0	55657.3	9.2	27.8	29.4
Norway	5538.6	5840.4	5.4	11122.7	11578.7	4.1	16661.3	17419.1	4.5	33.2	33.5
Portugal	18229.8	19349.4	6.1	12588.6	13206.5	4.9	30818.3	32555.9	5.6	59.2	59.4
Sweden	7584.0	6574.7	−13.3	28634.9	27111.9	−5.3	36218.9	33686.6	−7.0	20.9	19.5
Switzerland	35952.3	36875.6	2.6	39817.6	38934.8	−2.2	75769.9	75810.4	0.1	47.4	48.6
Turkey[4]	11864.7	13270.6	11.8	5565.6	6878.4	23.6	17430.3	20149.0	15.6	68.1	65.9
Canada					253673.0						
Australia	30210.0	36358.2	20.4	122901.0	120811.0	−1.7	153111.0	157169.2	2.7	19.7	23.1
Yugoslavia	49175.9	43370.5	−11.8	51112.9	45002.7	−12.0	100288.8	88373.1	−11.9	49.0	49.1

Source: OECD (1992) *Tourism Policy and International Tourism*

Notes
1 For the 'Types of accommodation covered by the statistics' see Table 2.2.
2 Belgium: preliminary data for 1990.
3 The data relate to the territory of the Federal Republic of Germany prior to 3 October 1990; after the unification tourists from the former German Democratic Republic are regarded as domestic tourists.
4 Turkey: figures based on a monthly sample survey carried out among establishments licensed by the Ministry of Tourism.

Table 2.5 Nights spent by foreign and domestic tourists in hotels and similar establishments[1] (thousands)

	Nights spent by foreign tourists			Nights spent by domestic tourists			Total nights			Proportion spent by foreign tourists (%)	
	1989	1990	% change	1989	1990	% change	1989	1990	% change	1989	1990
Austria	61428.4	61893.6	0.8	14875.6	15152.1	1.9	76304.0	77045.7	1.0	80.5	80.3
Belgium[2]	6574.8	6873.5	4.5	2610.7	2706.9	3.7	9185.5	9580.4	4.3	71.6	71.7
Denmark	4887.1	5429.4	11.1	4949.8	5205.2	5.2	9836.9	10634.6	8.1	49.7	51.1
Finland	2517.3	2468.1	−2.0	8054.1	8208.9	1.9	10571.4	10677.0	1.0	23.8	23.1
France[3]	51704.8	55934.2	8.2	87685.1	89869.3	2.5	139389.8	145803.5	4.6	37.1	38.4
Germany[4]	28388.7	29766.2	4.9	118591.1	125620.7	5.9	146979.9	155387.0	5.7	19.3	19.2
Greece	32938.5	35012.1	6.3	11396.2	11346.4	−0.4	44334.7	46358.5	4.6	74.3	75.5
Netherlands	7178.5	8104.0	12.9	5941.1	6380.7	7.4	13119.6	14484.7	10.4	54.7	55.9
Norway	3431.4	3536.6	3.1	8192.9	8484.9	3.6	11624.3	12021.5	3.4	29.5	29.4
Portugal	15467.5	16710.3	8.0	6585.5	7103.2	7.9	22053.0	23813.5	8.0	70.1	70.2
Spain	78301.4			53123.1			131424.5			59.6	
Sweden	3366.9	3193.0	−5.2	13607.9	13033.0	−4.2	16974.8	16226.0	−4.4	19.8	19.7
Switzerland	20489.4	21040.7	2.7	13659.9	13586.9	−0.5	34149.3	34627.6	1.4	60.0	60.8
Turkey[5]	9673.3	10255.1	6.0	4975.2	6091.0	22.4	14648.5	16346.1	11.6	66.0	62.7
Canada[6]					51514.0						
Australia	11400.0			40614.0	43370.0	6.8	52014.0			21.9	
Yugoslavia	27931.0	27020.4	−3.3	20705.5	19267.6	−6.9	48636.5	46288.0	−4.8	57.4	58.4

Source: OECD (1992) *Tourism Policy and International Tourism*

Notes
1 For the 'Types of accommodation covered by the statistics' see Table 2.2.
2 Belgium: preliminary data for 1990.
3 France: data covering all France except three regions (Pays de la Loire, Champagne-Ardennes and Corse).
4 The data relate to the territory of the Federal Republic of Germany prior to 3 October 1990; after reunification, tourists from the former German Democratic Republic are regarded as domestic tourists.
5 Turkey: does not include thermal hotels.
6 Canada: includes nights spent by Canadians in the United States with final destinations in Canada.

use of hotels and similar accommodation by domestic tourists is also comparatively high in Greece, Germany, Spain and Australia. The number of nights spent then drops to a much lower threshold to include the remaining countries with less than 15 million nights spent in such accommodation by domestic tourists. Such figures have to be treated cautiously as they do not enumerate the number of tourists but the total nights spent in accommodation. The average number of nights spent by each tourist varies by country although OECD only collates detailed statistics on the average length of stay by country for international visitors. For example, international tourists visiting Australia stayed an average of 32 days in 1990, whereas for Portugal this was only 7.4 days. For this reason, the number of tourist nights spent only provides an indication of the magnitude and scale of tourist movements to those urban areas where hotels are located (as well as non-urban areas). It is clear from these statistics that the volume of nights spent is variable between domestic and international tourists, depending on the structure of the tourism industry and markets each country serves. Nevertheless, for most OECD countries, urban destinations feature prominently as the containing context for all or part of the tourist's visit where serviced accommodation is used. In addition to these statistics, there are those categories of tourists who visit friends and relatives as well as the day trip and leisure market. For this reason, it is pertinent to consider how to identify the market for urban tourism.

The identification of urban tourists: market segmentation

Market segmentation is the process developed within marketing to identify whether:

> People with similar needs, wants and characteristics are grouped together so that an organisation can use greater precision in serving and communicating with its chosen customers. Market segmentation, then, is a two-step process of . . . deciding how to group all potential tourists (the market segments) and . . . selecting specific groups from among these (target markets) to pursue.
>
> (Mill and Morrison 1992: 423)

In other words, market segmentation assumes that various tourist segments exist with different needs, and those tourists in different segments have common characteristics which enables the tourism industry to develop a product or service which is likely to appeal to these groups.

As Middleton (1988), Holloway and Plant (1988) and Kotler and Armstrong (1991) have shown, the process of market segmentation is part of the strategic planning process in tourism marketing in relation to identifying the type of market one is dealing with (see Chapter 6 for a more detailed discussion of marketing).

Within the literature on tourism marketing, various approaches can be used to segment the market (S.L.J. Smith 1989) and these use a number of bases to identify the market. Prior to segmenting the tourist market for products or services, one needs to consider whether a potential market exists. Once this assumption is agreed, the marketer usually seeks to:

- Measure the value and volume of the market;
- Assess the geographical distribution of the tourist market in different locations or regions, and how it will be reached through marketing and promotion, as well as its likely effectiveness;
- Establish whether the market segments are large enough to support a marketing campaign, or if the segments can be combined with other markets to establish a critical threshold for a financially viable campaign;
- Examine if the market is durable, and to establish whether the attributes of the destination or product are sufficiently distinctive to stand the test of time and the efforts of competitors;
- Consider the competitive advantage of the service provider or destination in its target market.

There are different research methods employed by consultancy companies and marketing and advertising agencies as well as tourism operators to implement the process of market segmentation. Two of the most commonly used techniques are:

Forward segmentation

This is where the marketer predetermines the basis for segmentation using existing research data, reports and studies of tourist behaviour. A particular base is used (e.g. geographic origin of visitors or purpose of visit) to establish the likely market. In the case of urban tourism, a short break brochure targeted at North American visitors to Venice may emphasise the cultural and historic appeal of the destination as a particular characteristic in identifying this market segment.

Factor and clustering techniques

These are techniques which apply sophisticated statistical techniques on existing sources of tourism data from visitor surveys and tourist intention surveys (i.e. where and why they intend to visit a particular location on their next holiday). For example, the survey information is coded to establish a number of variables and input into a powerful statistical package such as SPSS-PC (see Ryan 1995 for a fuller discussion of the technique and methodology). The statistical technique is selected to cluster the variables around a series of common themes. The usual outcome is the identification of common groupings of tourists according to their behaviour, preferences and activities. A good illustration of this can be found in Clark, Clift and Page (1993) in the context of British package holidaymakers and health problems they experienced in Malta. Mill and Morrison (1992) suggest that there are a range of approaches one can use in market segmentation which include:

Demographic or socio-economic segmentation

This occurs where statistical data such as the census are used together with other statistical information to identify the scale and volume of potential tourists likely to visit an urban area. Key factors such as age and income are important as these are important determinants of the demand. For example, the amount of paid holidays and an individual or family's income have an important bearing on demand. Holloway and Plant (1988) highlight the value of social class in identifying the spending potential of tourists. In the UK, the Institute of Practitioners in Advertising use the following socio-economic grouping:

A   Higher managerial, administrative or professional;
B   Middle managerial, administrative or professional;
C1 Supervisory, clerical or managerial;
C2 Skilled manual workers;
D   Semi and unskilled manual workers;
E   Pensioners, the unemployed, casual or lowest grade workers.

After: Holloway and Plant (1988)

There are a number of variants on this classification, but they tend to have one common purpose in relation to tourism: to group people according to their income potential and propensity to spend discretionary time and income on travel (see below for a discussion of discretionary time). For example, in the UK those people in categories A and B account for 40 per cent of the market for short breaks and visits to heritage and cultural attractions (Holloway and Plant 1988). Although one cannot predict the destinations and urban locations of potential tourists from such classifications, they do help to segment the market for urban tourism when the group behaviour and activities of such people are examined. However, an important facilitating feature (and constraining factor when there is an absence of it) is leisure time and annual holiday entitlement.

The availability of time for travel is a significant factor which conditions the potential for tourist trips. Researchers normally express the amount of time available for tourist trips as *discretionary time* – that time remaining after one has fulfilled daily obligations such as working, sleeping, shopping, housework and childcare. In the context of urban tourism, both the daily and weekly amount of time available for leisure trips to urban areas and the annual holiday entitlement of different groups helps to shape the potential demand for urban tourist trips. As most tourism analysts note, the amount of leisure time and annual holiday entitlement in westernised countries has risen since 1945 and this has helped fuel a growth in these forms of activities. Although there is often a tendency by tourism researchers to distinguish between leisure time for weekend recreational or day trips and annual holiday entitlement used for short breaks (a holiday of up to 3 days) and long holidays, it is the individual or family's predisposition towards using leisure or holiday time for specific activities which affects the outcome – visits to urban areas.

The growth of consumer spending associated with tourism and leisure expenditure now competes with other forms of discretionary spending in advanced industrial societies. It is important to note that urban areas in Europe have benefited from the growth in short break holidays in the 1980s and 1990s, as such spending by people in groups A, B and C1 is reflected in second and third holidays. Yet criticisms of using socio-economic data as predictors of tourist segmentation has meant that there has been a trend towards including the concept of life cycle into the segmentation process. This is a combination of a household's marital status, age, children and ages which is incorporated with the socio-economic data. It assists the marketer in identifying those groups who have the most disposable income for tourism and leisure spending, typically when they reach middle age, have no children at home and have paid off a mortgage.

Product-related segmentation

This occurs where the tourist market is identified in relation to the product available and the demand for it. One difficulty with this approach is that other aspects of consumer behaviour are often introduced from other forms of segmentation such as psychographic approaches.

Psychographic segmentation

This is often introduced to complement more simplistic approaches based on socio-economic or geographic data. It involves the complex process of using socio-economic and life cycle data to predict a range of consumer behaviours or purchasing patterns associated with each stage (see Table 2.6). This is further developed by examining the psychological profile of consumers to establish their traits or characteristics in relation to different market segments. The VALS (Value and Lifestyles) research conducted by the Stanford Research Institute in North America used socio-economic data, the aspirations, self-images, values and consumption patterns of Americans to establish nine lifestyles which people could move through. This has been followed by other forms of lifestyle segmentation in consumer behaviour research to reduce the complex reality of the market for products and services into a series of identifiable groupings.

Geographic segmentation

This is commonly used to assess the catchment, and accessibility of the destination to each market and their propensity to travel. Such approaches are frequently used by organisations such as the London Tourist Board to establish which markets to target for promotional campaigns overseas. Table 2.7 provides a geographic segmentation for urban tourists for the Wellington City region in New Zealand in 1990.

Purpose of trip

This term is used to segment markets to distinguish between a number of simple categories of tourists such as day trippers, business travellers and visiting friends and relatives.

Behavioural segmentation

Behavioural segmentation is a relatively recent approach to defining markets. It has been used in recent years by airlines to highlight frequent flyers and the particular marketing potential for cultivating a group of customers to maintain brand loyalty for a product by offering service enhancements where frequent use is made of the service.

Channel of distribution segmentation

This is used where other organisations (e.g. intermediaries) can assist in marketing the product to a distinct group of clients. Here the marketer needs to establish who comprises the target market and what type of distribution channel to use. The most commonly used outlets for the marketing of short city breaks are travel agencies who receive a commission on the sale of products and services. These points are summarised in Table 2.8 which identifies the variables one needs to consider in any form of market segmentation.

Having outlined the principles and methods used to identify segments, attention now turns to the development of a typology of urban tourists.

Towards a typology of urban tourists

Any assessment of 'who visits' and 'why they visit' urban areas requires one to develop a typology of urban tourists. According to Blank and Petkovich (1987), there are a number of important points to consider when attempting to assess why visitors seek urban tourist destinations, a number of which were examined in Chapter 1. These are:

- Cities are places of high population density, with the result that there is a high propensity to visit friends and relatives;
- Urban areas are often the focal point of tourist-transport interchanges and termini;
- The concentration of commercial, financial, industrial and producer services in urban areas acts as a focus for different people to visit cities for employment-related purposes such as conferences, exhibitions, business travel, etc;
- Cities provide a wide range of cultural, artistic and recreational experiences.

Table 2.6 A traditional family life cycle

Stage in life cycle	Buying or behaviour pattern
1 Bachelor stage: young,single people not living at home	Few financial burdens; fashion opinion leaders; recreation oriented; buy basic kitchen equipment, basic furniture, cars, equipment for the mating game, holidays.
2 Newly married couples: young, no children	Better off financially than they will be in near future; highest purchase rate and highest average purchase of durables; buy cars, refrigerators, cookers, sensible and durable furniture, holidays.
3 Full nest I: youngest child under six	Home purchasing at peak; liquid assets low; dissatisfied with financial position and amount of money saved; interested in new products; buy washers, dryers, TV, baby food, chest rubs and cough medicines, vitamins, dolls prams, sleds, skates.
4 Full nest II: youngest child six or over	Financial position better; some wives work; less influenced by advertising; buy larger-sized packages, multiple-unit deals; buy many foods, cleaning materials, bicycles, music lessons, pianos.
5 Full nest III: older couples with dependent children	Financial position still better; more wives work; some children get jobs; hard to influence with advertising; high average purchase of durables; buy new, more tasteful furniture, auto travel, non-necessary appliances, boats, dental services, magazines.
6 Empty nest I: older couples, no children living with them, head in labour force	Home ownership at peak; most satisfied with financial position and money saved; interested in travel, recreation, self-education; make gifts and contributions; not interested in new products; buy holidays, luxuries, home improvements.
7 Empty nest II: older married couples, no children living at home, head retired	Drastic cut in income; keep home; buy medical-care products that improve health, sleep and digestion.
8 Solitary survivor, in labour force	Income still good, but likely to sell home.
9 Solitary survivor, retired	Same medical and product needs as other retired group; drastic cut in income; special need for attention, affection and security.

Source: William D. Wells and George Gubar, 'Life cycle concept in marketing research', *Journal of Marketing Research*, November 1986, pp.355–363, in J. Paul Peter and Jerry C. Olson, *Consumer Behavior: Marketing Strategy Perspectives* (Homewood, Illinois, Richard D. Irwin), p.459. Cited in Mill and Morrison (1992: 82).

Table 2.7 Geographic segmentation of the market for urban tourism in Wellington, New Zealand (1990)

TOTAL NUMBER OF VISITORS:		1,363,000
Domestic tourists		1,099,000
Region of origin	*(%)*	
Auckland	18	
Wellington Region	13	
Manawatu	8	
Wanganui	10	
Hawkes Bay	8	
Bay of Plenty	6	
Rest of North Island	18	
Canterbury	8	
Rest of South Island	10	
Purpose of visit	*(%)*	
Holiday	18	
Visiting friends and relatives	38	
Business	29	
Hobbies/other	9	
Sports	6	
Overseas tourists		264,000
Region of origin	*(%)*	
Australia	33.4	
USA	14.5	
UK	13.1	
Canada	4.9	
West Germany	5.3	
Japan	2.5	
Other	26.3	
Purpose of visit	*(%)*	
Holiday	53	
Visiting friends and relatives	21	
Business	16	
Other	9	

Source: Wellington Regional Council (1991: 16) *Wellington Region Tourism Strategy*

Yet Blank and Petkovich (1980) also argue that while visitors may have a major purpose for visiting urban areas (e.g. for business), they may undertake other activities related to the attractions and facilities in urban destinations. In other words, it is not simply the case that tourists visit such areas for a single purpose. Visits may be motivated by a range of factors. However, for the purposes of developing an initial typology of tourist visits, one has to examine the principal force motivating such a visit.

Table 2.8 Recreation and tourism market segmentation bases

Socio-economic and demographic variables
Age
Education
Sex
Income
Family size
Family life cycle
Social class
Home ownership
Second home ownership
Race or ethnic group
Occupation

Product-related variables
Recreation activity
Equipment type
Volume usage
Brand loyalty
Benefit expectations
Length of stay
Transportation mode
Experience preferences
Participation patterns

Psychographic variables
Personality traits
Life-style
Attitudes, interests, options
Motivations

Geographic variables
Region
Market area
Urban, surburban, rural
City size
Population density

Source: Mill and Morrison (1992: 426)

There have been various attempts to construct typologies of tourists visiting urban areas. For example, research in North America by Blank and Petkovich (1980) identifies the motivating factors associated with visits to urban areas in terms of:

- Visiting friends and relatives
- Business/convention
- Outdoor recreation
- Entertainment and sightseeing
- Personal reasons
- Shopping
- Other factors.

Their research noted that the significance of each factor varied by destination and its attraction. Yet this does not deal with the more complex methodological problems of distinguishing between urban tourists. As Jansen-Verbeke (1986: 88) notes, visitors can be distinguished according to 'their place of residence and . . . motives for visiting'. Much of the data relating to visitor demand and motivation for visiting urban areas are based on questionnaire-based research focused on individual locations. It forms part of a wider spectrum of urban tourism research and a range of studies in North America (Blank and Petkovich 1987), the Netherlands (e.g. Jansen-Verbeke 1986; Ashworth and Tunbridge 1990), and the UK (initiated by local authority and tourist-boards) have highlighted a range of commonly cited motives:

- Visiting friends and relatives
- Business travellers
- Conference and exhibition visitors
- Educational tourists
- Cultural and heritage tourists
- Religious travellers (e.g. pilgrims)
- Hallmark event visitors
- Leisure shoppers
- Day visitors.

But, as Jansen-Verbeke (1986) rightly acknowledges, urban tourists are only one set of visitors using the city because day visitors and residents also have distinct uses for the city. A notable study by Burtenshaw *et al.* (1991) confirms this finding and identifies functional areas within the tourist city which expresses the relationship between the supply and demand for urban services (Figure 2.2). In other words, different visitors to cities have a wide range of motivating factors shaping their visit which emphasises the significance of motivation research to understand the different groups of users. Burtenshaw *et al.* (1991) identify both the demand from users including:

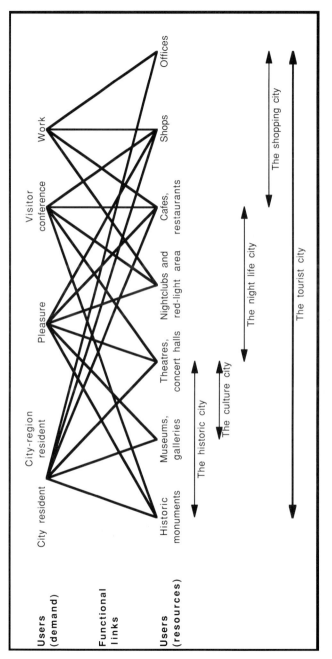

Figure 2.2 Functional areas in the tourist city (after Burtenshaw *et al.* 1991, reproduced with permission from David Fulton Publishers)

- City residents
- City-region residents
- Visitors seeking pleasure from their visit
- Conference visitors
- People working within the city,

and the resources which the users use including:

- Historic monuments
- Museums and galleries
- Theatres and concert halls
- Night clubs and the red-light area
- Cafes and restaurants
- Shops and,
- Offices in which the workers undertake their employment.

As a result, urban tourists are but one set of users in the multifunctional city which comprises the 'historic city', the 'culture city', the night-life city', the 'shopping city' and the 'tourist city'. The latter embraces all of the other functional cities and their resources.

What is clear from existing studies, is that the multifunctional nature of tourist cities complicates any attempt to develop a complex typology or taxonomy of users. As emphasised above, devising a simple classification of users based on a single motive for visiting is straightforward until the functional areas in cities noted by Jansen-Verbeke (1986), Ashworth (1989) and Burtenshaw *et al.* (1991) are acknowledged. In other words, simple labels such as 'tourist', 'day-tripper', 'excursionist' or 'business traveller' are descriptive and assume that the use of services and facilities is for one specific purpose. Although the market segmentation approaches discussed above can also be descriptive and:

> May appear superficially similar in their division of actual or latent users into categories. . . . these are based upon the actual nature of the use itself rather than any general characteristics of groups of users.
>
> (Ashworth and Tunbridge 1990: 119)

Therefore, a segmentation approach is a useful starting point in developing a classification of urban tourists in the multifunctional tourist city. Ashworth and Tunbridge (1990) develop the approach in terms of the consumer market and motives of visitors using concepts such as the 'purchasing intent' of visitors, the attitudes, opinions and interests of users of specific urban tourism products and the frequency of use. Clearly the most important issue is the distinction between use/non-use of specific tourism resources within tourist cities and it is useful to introduce their initial division of users of urban tourist areas in terms of:

- Intentional users (those motivated by the character of the city);
- Incidental users (those who see the character of the city as irrelevant to their use).

By imposing a geographical component to their analysis, Ashworth and Tunbridge (1990) also recognise the importance of residents and day visitors in the urban system, thereby identifying four specific types of user in the context of the tourist-historic city:

1 Intentional users from outside the city region, who may be holidaymakers staying in the city or outside it using the city for excursions – *Tourists* and in the case of these resources quite specifically, *Heritage tourists*.
2 Intentional users from inside the city-region, making use of the city's recreational and entertainment facilities or merely enjoying its historic character while engaging in other activities – *Recreating residents*.
3 Incidental users from outside the city-region, which would include most business and congress visitors and those on family visits – *Non-recreating visitors*.
4 Incidental users from inside the city-region, the most numerous group, being ordinary residents going about their ordinary affairs – *Non-recreating residents*.

Ashworth and Tunbridge (1990: 120–1).

This typology can be refined for other urban destinations since it recognises the significance of attitudes and the use made of the city and its services rather than the geographical origin of users as a fundamental starting point in the segmentation. Yet as Ashworth and Tunbridge (1990) observe, the difficulty in operationalising such an approach is the tendency for tourists to classify themselves according to the principal reason for visiting the destination, while in reality, any destination will have a range of users akin to the classification above. Nevertheless, Ashworth and de Haan's (1986) study of users in the tourist-historic city of Norwich, based on the self-allocation of the most important reasons for visiting Norwich supports their multimotivation argument on the diverse uses made of the city by visitors. Even so, among holidaymakers

Table 2.9 Main reasons for visiting Norwich (percentages)

	Holiday-makers	Day visitors	Business visitors	Shoppers
Castle/cathedral	18.9	19.5	2.2	0.0
Other historic site	2.5	9.5	11.1	9.1
General sightseeing	26.9	23.3	4.4	18.2
Shopping	2.5	10.0	4.4	54.5
Family/friends	22.3	10.0	2.2	4.5
Sport	0.8	1.7	0.0	0.0
Business/congress	0.4	1.4	55.6	0.0
Other	25.6	24.6	20.0	13.6

Source: Ashworth and de Haan (1986)

Sample size = 907 visitors

only 50 per cent were intentional users of the historic city (Table 2.9) while variations existed in the day visitor, business traveller and shoppers' use of the historic city. The multimotivation and multifunctional hypothesis developed by urban tourism researchers emphasises the different purposes and complexity of tourist behaviour in such locations. It is a major development within the urban tourism research to encourage a more complex approach towards the demand and motivation for such visits.

The purpose of the next section is to examine one group of tourism and leisure users in more detail to establish what motivates such visitors, since as Pearce (1989: 87) argues, 'if typologies are to be formulated, it must also embrace a range of examples from various countries'. One case study is used to examine the demand for visits to religious sites in urban areas focusing on one site in Europe – Lourdes.

Urban tourism and pilgrimages

Urban tourism and religious visits: an overview

The concept of religious tourism, defined by the Roman Catholic Church in Europe as a system that includes a range of holy places, from large cathedrals to small rural chapels and the service facilities associated with them, attracts both devout and secular visitors. It therefore plays a major role in the development of urban tourist destinations serving a variety of needs. Jackowski and Smith (1992) highlight the significance of this form of tourism, which is often oriented towards urban sites or pilgrimages which pass through them. They argue that:

Visitors at the pilgrimage centres remain at the site city for at least two days. Their stays generate substantial economic opportunities for local entrepreneurs, providing lodging, meals, and multiple other services, as well as the manufacture and sale of devotional and secular crafts.

(Jackowski and Smith 1992: 105)

which highlights the significance of this form of tourism which often has an urban bias in Europe.

This is supported by Nolan and Nolan who argue that:

Sacred places and ceremonial events are among the most ancient of travel destinations. These shrines, temples, churches, landscape features and religious festivals . . . are among the most complex of attractions because of their appeal to a spectrum of visitors . . . Regardless of their motivations, all visitors to these attractions require some level of services, ranging from providing for the most basic of human needs, to full secular development that rivals the most secular resort.

(Nolan and Nolan 1992: 68–9)

There is a growing literature on religious tourism and its spatial distribution and development among different faiths, and Rinschede (1990) suggests that while it is one of the oldest forms of tourism it has been neglected in research. For example, Rinschede (1990) cites the case of Mecca where the growth of pilgrims to an urban destination has risen from 50,000 per annum in the 1930s to over 1 million in the mid-1980s. This has been facilitated by developments in tourist-transportation and similar impacts on the scale and volume of pilgrimages is discussed in a special issue of *Annals of Tourism Research* (1992).

One of the immediate consequences of the greater accessibility of pilgrimage sites is the potential for conflict which mass tourism poses for sensitive and special religious sites. While pilgrimages fulfil an important emotional and religious need, the effect of secular visitors on traditional religious festivals has now posed a serious challenge to their rationale. The authenticity of religious festivals, which have become secularised and commercialised in popular tourist areas, has meant that they disappear in the tourist season to reappear at a later date. For this reason, the examples of urban tourism development associated with pilgrimages is considered in relation to Lourdes in France, because of its international significance as a pilgrimage shrine. However, before considering Lourdes it is useful to consider the different forms of pilgrimage in Europe as a context in which to understand the religious tourism system and the relationship with urban areas.

A large proportion of religious tourism in Europe is based on urban destinations and Nolan and Nolan (1992) provide a comprehensive typology of Christian pilgrimage which includes:

- Pilgrimage shrines (which fulfil the needs of religiously motivated journeys beyond the immediate locality, although they are not necessarily sites of wider tourist interest);
- Religious tourist attractions (sites of religious significance as well as artistic or historic significance);
- Festivals in religious associations (in towns and villages).

A very good insight into the religious tourism system in one country can be found in Jackowski and Smith's (1992) analysis of Polish pilgrim tourists.

The market for religious forms of tourism can be segmented according to the religious motives and intrinsic needs of the visitors, although it is apparent that they operate as a distinct religious tourism system in Europe. As Jackowski and Smith (1992: 93) note it is important to distinguish between two types:

- *The pilgrims*, who have a religious motivation and spend their time in meditation and prayer, while also performing religious rites and stop at identifiable sanctuaries en route. Jackowski and Smith argue that:

  most of these pilgrims are poorly informed (or disinterested) about the historic or cultural (i.e. non-religious) significance of the cities and villages through which they travel. Their primary purpose is the 'special pilgrimage' to a worship centre where miraculous healing of the ill or salvation and entry to paradise may be attained . . .

- *Religious tourists*, where the motivation for the journey is largely knowledge-based as the tourist seeks information on the route, the people and the centre they visit. They may participate in some of the religious rites.

Complex interactions exist within the variety of religious attractions because popular religious shrines often act as secular tourist attractions (e.g. Westminster Abbey and Canterbury Cathedral in the UK) where

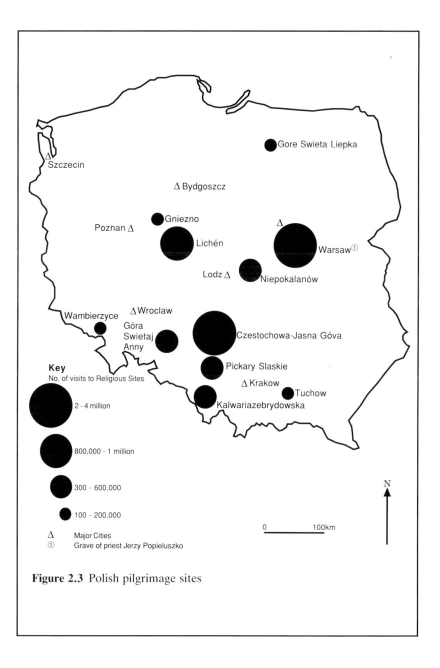

Figure 2.3 Polish pilgrimage sites

pilgrims are often outnumbered by tourists. In fact Jackowski and Smith (1992) note that Poland now has several shrines that are now exclusively visited by religious tourists, as opposed to pilgrims (e.g. Gore Swieta Liepka, Gore Swiete Anny and Wambierzyce). Figure 2.3 indicates the geographical distribution of the scale and volume of visits to these pilgrimage sites with more than 100,000 visitors per annum. The expansion of pilgrimages was given a significant impetus after the pontification of John Paul II in 1978 and three personal pilgrimages in the 1980s. In present-day Poland, some 500 Roman Catholic pilgrimage centres exist and a number rank on the same scale as Lourdes in France. In some cases, distinctive urban forms have developed to serve the needs of pilgrims and more recently, religious tourists. For example, 6–7 million people currently participate in pilgrimages in Poland each year, equivalent to 15 per cent of the population. In addition, over 100,000 overseas visitors from more than 100 countries visit Poland for religious purposes. Having outlined some of the principal features and characteristics of religious tourism and pilgrimages, attention now turns to the case of Lourdes.

Case study 1

Pilgrimage tourism in Lourdes

The historical development of Lourdes can be dated back to 1858 and the series of visions witnessed by Bernadette Soubirous (St Bernadette) and the miraculous healing powers of a spring which developed during one of the visions of Our Lady, the Mother of Christ . The development of the railway after 1866 and the centre's expansion as a French national pilgrimage was closely followed by the international pilgrimages organised from North America, Eastern and Western Europe. As Rinschede (1986) notes, Lourdes population rose from 4,155 in 1844 to 18,000 by 1980 as it developed as one of the world's most famous Roman Catholic shrines. For example, in 1987 over 4 million visitors travelled to Lourdes during its pilgrimage season (April–October). The result of this stimulus to development is that Lourdes contains over 30,000 beds in hotels and guest houses, with a further 50,000 in military and youth camps and a further 10,000 in private

Case study 1 (*continued*)

quarters (e.g. religious houses, hospitals and camp sites). This is the largest concentration of accommodation in France, outside Paris. The majority of hotels are located adjacent to the 'domain' (centre of the shrine). Whilst many visitors arrive by car, Lourdes fulfils a variety of tourist functions as a centre of pilgrimage and as part of a wide religious itinerary which consists of visits to other French centres or international sites of religious significance. As Nolan and Nolan (1992) suggest, large shrines such as Lourdes which have high levels of visitation tend to offer a variety of activities for tourists and pilgrims alike. Furthermore, a high degree of commercialism now affects sacred sites but the site can accommodate multiple uses to ensure that the devotional activities are not disturbed. As Eade (1992) argues, an intensely hierarchical and institutional character of voluntary work exists at Lourdes under the auspices of the Hospitality which has partly dis-tinguished pilgrims and helpers from more general tourists. In other words, pilgrims and visitors are:

> Sharply differentiated from each other in ways that reflect both differences within the wider society [of Lourdes] and divisions peculiar to the shrine.
>
> (Eade 1992: 29)

However, outside the sacred area of Lourdes (the domain), a highly commercialised tourist centre exists, with distinct class differences existing in the perception of middle class helpers who find the souvenir shops distasteful, and working class pilgrims who provide the bulk of customers. What Eade (1992) observes is that many pilgrims behave like tourists, particularly the pilgrims who purchase the trivia and commercialised memorabilia of the shrine. In contrast, it is argued that many tourists who visit the shrine each year are touched by its qualities, especially its spiritualism. Thus, distinguishing between pilgrims and tourists outside the 'domain' is difficult, in contrast to the highly structured environment of the shrine. Whilst it is possible to segment the market for visitors to Lourdes according to nationality, language, motives for visiting, the individual's meaning and behaviour outside the domain makes

Case study 1 (*continued*)

---

any formal classification difficult from a sociological perspective, in view of the meaning associated with the visitors' experience of Lourdes. Pilgrims and tourists may participate in activities and events organised by entrepreneurs in the town, but it is the attitudes, behaviour and meaning derived from the visit which makes any simplistic classification difficult. In this context, Ashworth and Tunbridge's (1990) arguments on the use, views and motivation of visitors to urban areas holds true as the simple demand characteristics of visitors to specialised tourist destinations like Lourdes are complex to understand. Even the simple distinction between tourist and pilgrim is complicated by the visitors' experience of Lourdes as it is the individual and group meaning of the visit which is important, rather than the tourist market they are allocated to.

Conclusion

This chapter has indicated that understanding the demand for urban tourism is not a simple mechanistic exercise related to statistical analysis of tourist visits to destinations. The absence of urban tourism statistics at an international and national level in most countries means that most research has emphasised the significance of individual case studies rather than the scale and volume of urban tourism at an international and national scale. Although some useful preliminary approximations of tourism demand can be gauged from the use of accommodation, this approach is not without its problems. Furthermore, it is not appropriate to simply equate demand with aggregate statistics when the motivation and use made of tourist facilities offers many insights into tourist and non-tourist interaction in the urban environment. In fact, the arguments put forward by Ashworth and Tunbridge (1990) criticise simplistic attempts to reduce urban tourists to static classifications which do not incorporate:

- The multifunctional nature of the tourist city;
- The existence of different groups of users within any tourist city;
- The different use made of tourist resources by visitors;
- The multimotivational nature of visits by urban tourists.

The example of Lourdes and the brief discussion of the distinction between tourist and pilgrim highlights the importance of considering these key points in any analysis of urban tourism. This suggests that the effective analysis of urban tourists requires one to consider the behaviour and activity patterns of tourists which is partly conditioned by their motivation and the availability of tourist facilities within different cities. For this reason, the next chapter considers the supply of urban tourism services and facilities and use made by different types of visitors.

Questions

1 What sources of data are commonly used as an approximation of urban tourism demand?
2 What techniques are used to segment urban tourism markets?
3 What are the problems associated with the use of typologies of urban tourists?
4 What studies can you identify which focus on the 'tourist-historic' city?

Further reading

Bywater, M. (1993) 'The market for cultural tourism in Europe', *Travel and Tourism Analyst* 6: 30–46.

This is a good comprehensive article that focuses on the market segments for a specific form of tourism that has an urban bias.

Bywater, M. (1994) 'Religious travel in Europe', *Travel and Tourism Analyst* 2: 39–52.

This is a useful overview of religious sites as tourism attractions in Europe, particularly the role of towns and cities as the location of sites and shrines.

Eade, J. (1992) 'Pilgrimage and tourism at Lourdes', *Annals of Tourism Research* 19(1): 18–32.

This is one of the most detailed articles published on tourism at Lourdes.

Ryan, C. (1995) *Researching Tourist Satisfaction: Issues, Concepts, Problems*, London: Routledge.

This is by far the best book available on tourism research and methodology.

3
The supply of urban tourism: services, infrastructure and activities

Introduction

In the last chapter, the issue of tourist motivation was considered in relation to some of the approaches used to identify the market for urban tourism. Yet the fundamental question – why do people visit urban areas – is not easily reduced to simple classifications of motives among visitors. The diverse range of activities users engage in within individual cities complicates the use of typologies of visitors since 'people may visit cities for business including conferences and exhibitions, and also to see friends and relatives' (Law 1993: 68). At a general level, Law (1993) also argues that an urban area's reputation and attractions may be significant in influencing the tourist's visit. This means that visitors may often have a preconceived notion or perception of the 'tourist experience' or service encounter they expect. In other words, tourists and other visitors are not passive agents within the tourism system that exists in urban areas (see Figure 1.2), as they have views or expectations of the services, facilities and products they may consume. Shaw and Williams (1994: 16) acknowledge that the production and consumption of tourism are important approaches to the analysis of tourism since:

- *Production*, is the method by which a complex of businesses and industries are involved in the supply of tourism services and products, and how they are delivered to consumers; and
- *Consumption*, is how, where, why and when the tourist actually consumes tourism services and products.

Law (1993) expands upon these simple notions arguing that

> In many respects tourism is the geography of consumption outside the home area; it is about how and why people travel to consume . . . on the production side it is concerned to understand where tourism activities develop and on what scale. It is concerned with the process or processes whereby some cities are able to create tourism resources and a tourism industry.
>
> (Law 1993: 14)

While production and consumption have been the focus of the more theoretically derived explanations of urban tourism (e.g. Mullins 1991), such approaches raise conceptual issues related to how one should view production and consumption in the context of urban tourism. The purpose of this chapter is to address how one can examine the relationship between production and consumption in terms of the supply of products, services and facilities as a means of understanding why tourists visit urban areas. Both the tourists consumption (often expressed as the demand – dealt with in Chapter 2) and the products and services produced for their visit (the supply) form important inputs in the overall system of urban tourism (Figure 1.2). To provide a logical framework for the chapter, the concept of the urban area as a 'leisure product' (Jansen-Verbeke 1986) is introduced. This is followed by a discussion of how to analyse the supply and distribution of urban tourism, then the elements of Jansen-Verbeke's (1986) notion of a leisure product is examined. The role of the public and private sector as agents affecting the supply of urban tourism is then discussed and a number of other approaches to the analysis of urban tourism supply issues are considered in relation to the concept of the tourism business district and the role of tourism attractions in research on tourism supply issues. Attention finally turns to the various elements of Jansen Verbeke's (1986) leisure product, with reference to *tourist facilities* and the *conditional elements*.

Approaches toward the analysis of urban tourism: supply-side variables

One of the most poorly researched areas in tourism remains the supply-side of the industry (Sinclair and Stabler 1991). However, in the context of urban tourism, a well-established approach developed by Jansen-Verbeke (1986) is to view the urban area as a leisure product (Figure 3.1) which comprises *primary elements* including:

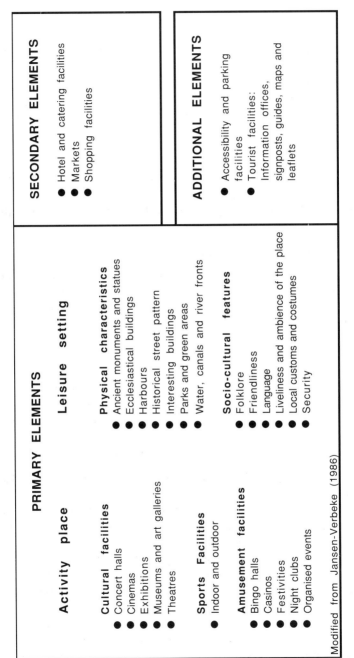

PRIMARY ELEMENTS

Activity place

Leisure setting

Cultural facilities
- Concert halls
- Cinemas
- Exhibitions
- Museums and art galleries
- Theatres

Sports Facilities
- Indoor and outdoor

Amusement facilities
- Bingo halls
- Casinos
- Festivities
- Night clubs
- Organised events

Physical characteristics
- Ancient monuments and statues
- Ecclesiastical buildings
- Harbours
- Historical street pattern
- Interesting buildings
- Parks and green areas
- Water, canals and river fronts

Socio-cultural features
- Folklore
- Friendliness
- Language
- Liveliness and ambience of the place
- Local customs and costumes
- Security

SECONDARY ELEMENTS
- Hotel and catering facilities
- Markets
- Shopping facilities

ADDITIONAL ELEMENTS
- Accessibility and parking facilities
- Tourist facilities: Information offices, signposts, guides, maps and leaflets

Modified from Jansen-Verbeke (1986)

Figure 3.1 The elements of tourism (based on Jansen-Verbeke 1986)

- A variety of facilities that can be grouped into:
- *An activity place*, thereby defining the overall supply features within the city, particularly the main tourist attractions;
- *A leisure setting*, which includes both the physical elements in the built environment and the socio/cultural characteristics which give a city a distinct image and 'sense of place' (see Walmesley and Jenkins 1992 for a discussion of this concept) for visitors;

and *secondary elements* which consist of:

- The supporting facilities and services which tourists consume during their visit (e.g. hotel and catering outlets and shopping facilities) which shape the visitor's experience of the services available in the city;

as well as *additional elements* which consist of:

- The tourism infrastructure which conditions the visit, such as the availability of car parking, tourist-transport provision and accessibility and tourist-specific services (e.g. visitor information centres and tourist signposting).

Shaw and Williams (1994: 202) rightly argue that

> While such an approach allows a systematic consideration of the supply side of urban tourism, it is not without its difficulties. For example, in many cities, the so-called secondary elements of shops and restaurants may well be the main attractions for certain groups of visitors.
>
> (Shaw and Williams 1994: 202)

Nevertheless, the supply-side variables within the context of the urban tourism system need to be analysed to understand the interrelationships between the supply and demand for urban tourism and the interaction between the consumers and the products. In this respect, it is also useful to identify what aspect of the leisure product urban tourists consume; some may consume only one product (e.g. a visit to an art gallery) while others may consume what Jansen-Verbeke (1988) terms a 'bundle of products' (i.e. several products during their visit or stay such as a visit to a theatre, museum and a meal in a restaurant).

Jansen-Verbeke (1986) examines this concept within the inner city tourism system to identify the nature of tourists visiting the inner city and the organisations responsible for the promotion of the inner city as an area for tourists to visit. The role of organisations promoting urban areas for tourism is discussed in more detail in Chapter 6, but to explain Jansen-Verbeke's (1986) analysis it is useful to consider the relationship which she believes exists between the product, tourist and promoter. Promoters affect the relationship in two ways:

1 They build an image of the inner city and its tourists' resources to attract potential tourists;
2 The promotion of the inner city also leads to direct product improvements.

Consequently, the model Jansen-Verbeke (1986) constructs (Figure 3.1) illustrates how different elements of the inner city tourism system are interrelated and the significance of the inner city as a leisure product.

The role of the public and private sector in urban tourism

Pearce observes that the:

> Provision of services and facilities characteristically involves a wide range of agents of development. Some of these will be involved indirectly and primarily with meeting the needs of tourists, a role that has fallen predominantly to the private sector in most countries [the Eastern bloc is the exception]. Other agents will facilitate, control or limit development . . . through the provision of basic infrastructure, planning or regulation. Such activities have commonly been the responsibility of the public sector with the government at various levels being charged with looking after the public's interest and providing goods and services whose cost cannot be attributed directly to groups or individuals.
>
> (Pearce 1989: 32)

This illustrates the essential distinction between the role of the private and public sector in the provision of services and facilities for tourists.

The private sector

The private sector's involvement in tourism is most likely to be motivated by profit, as tourism entrepreneurs (Shaw and Williams 1994) invest in business opportunities. This gives rise to a complex array of large organisations and operators involved in tourism (e.g. multinational chain hotels – Forte and Holiday Inns) and an array of smaller

businesses and operators, often employing less than 10 people or working on a self-employed basis. If left unchecked, this sector is likely to
give rise to conflicts in the operation of tourism where the state takes a
laissez-faire role in tourism planning and management.

The public sector

In contrast to the private sector, the public sector involves government
at a variety of geographical scales and may become involved in tourism
for various reasons. These include:

Economic reasons

- To improve the balance of payments in a country;
- To aid regional (or local) economic development;
- To diversify the economy;
- To increase income levels;
- To increase state revenue from taxes;
- To generate new employment opportunities.

(Based on Pearce 1989)

Social and cultural reasons

- To achieve social objectives related to 'social tourism' to ensure the
  well-being and health of the individual is protected, as illustrated by
  the former Soviet Union's network of spas and holiday centres for
  workers;
- To promote a greater cultural awareness of an area and its people.

Environmental reasons

- To undertake the stewardship of the environment and tourism resources to ensure that the agents of development do not destroy the
  future basis for sustainable tourism development.

Political reasons

- To further political objectives as illustrated by the Franco government in Spain in the 1960s where it promoted the development of

tourism to broaden the political acceptance of the regime among visitors;

- In the context of the Less Developed World, Jenkins and Henry (1982) argue that the state should have a role in controlling the development process associated with tourism;
- In socialist countries (e.g. Albania and Cuba), the state has maintained a dominant role in tourism to ensure that forms of development are consistent with its political ideology.

In many cases, the state's involvement is to ensure a policy of intervention so that political objectives associated with employment generation and planning are achieved, although this varies from one country to another and from city to city according to the political persuasion of the organisation involved. The public sector's role is also evident from national government funding of tourism promotion among national tourism organisations. In addition, public sector regional and local organisations (e.g. tourist boards) advise on planning, promotion and development, although the trend among developed countries in recent years has been to encourage the private sector to play a greater role in funding these activities. Pearce rightly acknowledges, however, that:

> The public sector then is by no means a single entity with clear cut responsibilities and well-defined policies for tourist development. Rather, the public sector becomes involved in tourism for a wide range of reasons in a variety of ways at different levels and through many agencies and institutions . . . [and] . . . there is often a lack of co-ordination, unnecessary competition, duplication of effort in some areas and neglect in others.
>
> (Pearce 1989: 44)

Analysing the supply and distribution of urban tourism services and facilities

According to Ashworth (1989) one of the most frequently used approaches towards the supply of urban tourism is the descriptive research by geographers based on inventories and lists of the facilities and where they are located. In view of the wide range of literature that discusses the distribution of specific facilities or services, it is more useful to consider these approaches and concepts as they derive generalisations of patterns of urban tourism activity. For this reason, two aspects are considered:

1 the tourism business district;
2 tourism attraction research.

The tourism business district

Within the literature on the supply of urban tourism, Ashworth (1989) reviews the 'facility approach' which offers researchers the opportunity to map the location of specific facilities, undertaking inventories of facilities on a city-wide basis. The difficulty in such approaches is that the users of urban services and facilities are not just tourists, as Chapter 2 emphasised. Therefore, any inventory will only be a partial view of the full range of facilities and potential services tourists could use. One useful approach is to identify the areas in which the majority of tourist activities occur and to use it as the focus for the analysis of the supply of tourism services in the multifunctional city. This avoids the individual assessments of the location and use of specific aspects of tourism services such as accommodation (Page and Sinclair 1989), entertainment facilities such as restaurants (S.L.J. Smith 1989) and night-life entertainment facilities (Ashworth *et al.* 1988) and other attractions. This approach embraces the *ecological approaches* developed in human geography to identify regions within cities as a basis to identify the processes shaping the patterns.

The ecological approach toward the analysis of urban tourism dates back to Gilbert's (1949) assessment of the development of resorts, which was further refined by Barrett (1958). The outcome is a resort model where accommodation, entertainment and commercial zones exist and the central location of tourism facilities are dominant elements. The significance of such research is that it identifies some of the features and relationships which were subsequently developed in urban geography and applied to tourism and recreation. The most notable study is Stansfield and Rickert's (1970) development of the 'recreational business district' (RBD). This study rightly identifies the multifunctional land use of the central areas of cities in relation to the central area for business ('central business district' – CBD). Meyer-Arendt (1990) also expands this notion in the context of the Gulf of Mexico coastal resorts while Pearce (1989) offers a useful critique of these studies. The essential ideas in the RBD have subsequently been extended to urban tourism to try and understand the location and distribution of the range of visitor-oriented urban functions in cities. What is meant by the 'tourism business district' (TBD)?

Burtenshaw *et al.*'s (1991) seminal study of tourism and recreation in European cities deals with the concept of the 'central tourist district' (CTD) where tourism activities in cities are concentrated in certain areas. This has been termed the TBD by Getz (1993a) who argues that it is the:

> Concentration of visitor-oriented attractions and services located in conjunction with urban central businesses (CBD) functions. In older cities, especially in Europe, the TBD and CBD often coincide with heritage areas. Owing to their high visibility and economic importance, TBDs can be subjected to intense planning by municipal authorities . . . The form and evolution of TBDs reveals much about the nature of urban tourism and its impacts, while the analysis of the planning systems influencing TBDs can contribute to concepts and methods for better planning of tourism in urban areas.
>
> (Getz 1993a: 583–4)

Therefore, TBDs are a useful framework in which to understand the components of urban tourism and how they fit together. Figure 3.2, based on the analysis by Getz (1993a) of the TBD, is a schematic model in which the functions rather than geographical patterns of activities are considered. This model illustrates the difficulty of separating visitor-oriented services from the CBD and use of services and facilities by residents and workers. Yet as Jansen-Verbeke and Ashworth (1990) argue, while tourism and recreational activities are integrated within the physical, social and economic context of the city, no analytical framework exists to determine the functional or behavioural interactions in these activities. They argue that more research is needed to assess the extent to which the clustering of tourism and recreational activities can occur in cities without leading to incompatible and conflicting uses from such facilities. While the TBD may offer a distinctive blend of activities and attractions for tourist and non-tourist alike, it is important to recognise these issues where tourism clusters in areas such as the TBD. Even so, the use of street entertainment and special events and festivals (Getz 1991) may also add to the ambience and sense of place for the city worker and visitor. By having a concentration of tourism and non-tourism resources and services in one accessible area within a city, it is possible to encourage visitors to stay there, making it a place tourists will want to visit. However, the attractions in urban areas are an important component in the appeal to potential visitors.

Tourism attractions

Attractions are an integral feature of urban tourism, which offer visitors passive and more active activities to occupy their time during a visit. They also comprise a key component of Jansen-Verbeke's (1986) 'primary element' (Figure 3.1). Recent studies have adapted descriptive analyses of specific types of attractions (e.g. Law 1993) rather than exploring their relationship with urban tourists. Lew (1987: 554) acknowledges that 'although the importance of tourist attractions is readily recognized, tourism researchers and theorists have yet to fully come to terms with the nature of attractions as phenomena both in the environment and the mind'. As a result, Lew's (1987) study and Leiper's (1990) synthesis and conceptual framework of 'tourist attraction systems' remain among the most theoretically-informed literature published to date. Lew (1987) identifies three perspectives used to understand the nature of tourist attractions. These are:

- *The ideographic perspective*, where the general characteristics of a place, site, climate, culture and customs are used to develop typologies of tourism attractions, involving inventories or general descriptions. For example, the use of Standard Industrial Classification codes (SICs) are one approach used to group attractions (see S.L.J. Smith 1989). These approaches are the ones most commonly used to examine tourist attractions in the general tourism literature;
- *The organisational perspective*, in contrast, tends to emphasise the geographical, capacity and temporal aspects (the time dimension) of attractions rather than the 'managerial notions of organisation' (Leiper 1990: 175). This approach examines scales ranging from the individual attraction, to larger areas and their attractions;
- *The cognitive perspective*, is based on 'studies of tourist perceptions and experiences of attractions' (Lew 1987: 560). P. Pearce (1982: 98) recognises that any tourist place (or attraction) is one capable of fostering the feeling of being a tourist. Therefore, the cognitive perspective is interested in understanding the tourists' feelings and views of the place or attraction.

The significance of Lew's (1987) framework is that it acknowledges the importance of attractions as a research focus, although Leiper (1990)

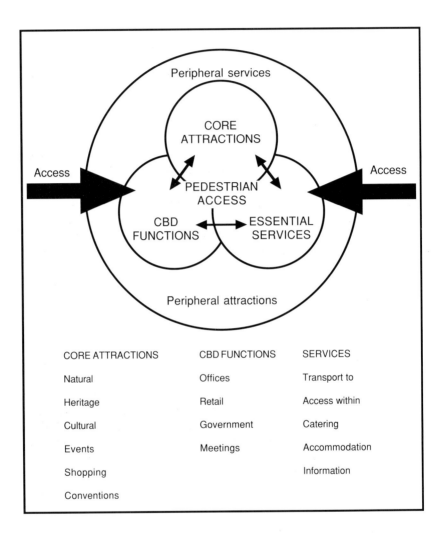

Figure 3.2 The tourism business district (after Getz 1993a)

questions the definition of attractions used by many researchers. He
pursues the ideas developed by MacCannel (1976: 41), that an attraction
incorporates 'an empirical relationship between a tourist, a sight and a
marker, a piece of information about a sight'. A 'marker' is an item of
information about any phenemenon which could be used to highlight
the tourists awareness of the potential existence of a tourist attraction.
This implies that an attraction has a number of components, while
conventional definitions only consider the sight (Leiper 1990: 177). In
this respect, 'the tourist attraction is a system comprising three elements: a tourist, a sight and a marker' (Leiper 1990: 178). Although
sightseeing is a common tourist activity, the idea of a sight really refers
to the nucleus or central component of the attraction (Gunn 1972). In
this context a situation could include a sight where sightseeing occurs,
but it may also be an object, person or event. Based on this argument,
Leiper (1990: 178) introduces the following definition of a tourist attraction as 'a system comprising three elements: a tourist or human element,
a nucleus or central element, and a marker or informative element.
A tourist attraction comes into existence when the three elements are
interconnected'. On the basis of this alternative approach to attractions,
Leiper (1990) identifies the type of information which is likely to give
meaning to the tourist experience of urban destinations in relation to
their attractions.

These ideas are developed more fully in Leiper's model of a tourist
attraction system (Figure 3.3), breaking the established view that tourists are not simply 'attracted' or 'pulled' to areas on the basis of their
attractions. Instead, visitors are motivated to experience a nucleus and
its markers in a situation where the marker reacts positively with their
needs and wants. Figure 3.3 identifies the linkages within the model and
how tourist motivation is influenced by the information available and
the individual's perception of their needs. Thus, it is only once the
following become connected together that an attraction system
develops:

- A person with tourist needs;
- A nucleus (a feature or attribute of a place that tourists seek to visit);
- A marker (information about the nucleus).

This theoretical framework has a great deal of value in relation to
understanding the supply of urban tourism resources for visitors. Firstly,
it views an attraction system as a subsystem of the larger tourism system
in an urban area. Secondly, it acknowledges the integral role for the

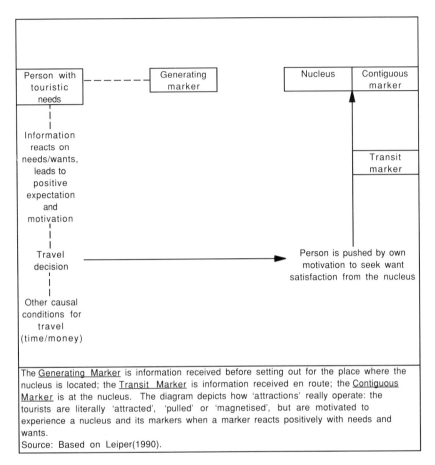

Figure 3.3 A model of a tourism attraction system (after Leiper 1990)

tourist as consumers – without the tourist (or day tripper) the system would not exist. Thirdly, the systems approach offers a convenient social science framework in which to understand how urban destinations attract visitors, with different markers and nuclei to attract specific groups of visitors. For these reasons, it is useful to consider a case study of how one organisation – Dover District Council – pursued an interventionist strategy towards tourism by investing in one major attraction as part of an attempt to establish a new 'attraction system' to promote economic development in the town.

Case study 2

Developing a tourism attraction system in Dover

In the 1980s the revenue-generating role of tourism gained greater importance, and consequently public and private sector interest in tourism increased significantly, particularly where its potential for regenerating urban areas has been recognised (see Law 1992 on the role of tourism and urban regeneration). The strategy adopted by the coastal town of Dover (Kent) (see Figure 3.5 later in this chapter for the location of Dover) in response to the threat to its prosperity posed by the Channel Tunnel, provides a recent example of attraction-based development inspired by tourism. The decision to build the Channel Tunnel and the ensuing *Kent Impact Study* raised the question of Dover's future as one of Britain's major tourist gateways. Initial estimates by the Kent Impact Study suggested that the Channel Tunnel could lead to a loss of up to 6,000 jobs once the fixed link was completed. Although recent experience casts new light on the likely impact of job losses associated with the Channel Tunnel, the fixed link will affect Dover's tourism industry since it has tended to be perceived as a *transit town*, attracting passing trade rather than serving as a destination in its own right (Sinclair and Page 1993).

In 1987 Dover District Council's *Tourism and Operational Marketing Strategy* highlighted the threat posed by the Channel Tunnel, noting that 'it is essential that the town of Dover be transformed from what is principally a transit ferry port to an international tourist destination of distinction'. It argued that this could be achieved by restoring business confidence in the town's future, which was being undermined by growing uncertainty associated with its dependence on the ferry industry as an employer and the impact of the Channel Tunnel. Dover District Council responded to this immediate problem by commissioning *The Dover Tourism Initiative* (Peat Marwick *et al.* 1994) which provided a detailed analysis of tourism in Dover. An earlier report by Eurotunnel, the Channel Tunnel operator, took a gloomy view of Dover's future, arguing that Dover and Folkestone have no major tourist draws of their own. However, the Dover Tourism

Case study 2 (*continued*)

Initiative recommended that the negative impact of the Channel Tunnel could be counteracted by upgrading existing facilities and infrastructure and providing new tourist attractions. It suggested that action was needed to improve the environment of the town, the number and quality of hotels, restaurants and shops, and the presentation of existing historic sites to capitalise on the heritage theme. It also argued that there was a need for a new and major visitor attraction to act as a catalyst to further development. It was suggested that up to 1,500 new tourism-related jobs might be created if these recommendations were implemented, although it was acknowledged that Dover would need to take an aggressive stance on marketing. The optimum forecasts for visitor arrivals for Dover in the 1990s were 300,000 staying and 600,000 day visitors per annum, generating £30 million for the town. However, it was acknowledged that the town's image as a transit town could work against any attempt to attract domestic and overseas visitors using the ferry or the Channel Tunnel – a problem which needed urgent attention.

The White Cliffs Experience

Dover District Council responded to the Dover Tourism Initiative by promoting the historic and heritage assets of its 'White Cliffs County' – comprising the towns of Dover, Deal and Sandwich. An effort was made to develop an integrated 'Dover experience' and this called for a new and major visitor attraction. The Dover Tourism Initiative acknowledged that the private sector had shown little interest in investing in tourism projects in the town (although interest had been shown in Dover Castle). It was clear that tourism development would require a public sector lead – which would then, it was hoped, encourage investment from the private sector. A feasibility study for a major tourism attraction called the White Cliffs Experience was commissioned by Dover District Council. On the basis of this, it proceeded with plans for a £14 million heritage centre funded almost entirely by the local authority (partly through land and building sales).

Case study 2 (*continued*)

Tourism-based regeneration

The underlying principle of finding suitable investment to attract business to the town is commendable, but the Dover project also raises a number of important considerations for other towns contemplating a similar strategy. The decision to use tourism to boost business confidence in Dover is understandable: according to the South East Economic Development Strategy, in 1987 tourism contributed approximately £18,000 million to the British economy and provided employment for 1.4 million people. Overseas visitors contribute a significant amount to tourist spending in the UK. In 1988, 15.9 million visits were made by overseas tourists, accounting for 44% of all tourist spending. It is hardly surprising that Dover District Council should wish to take advantage of such opportunities, particularly as the town is likely to suffer some loss of trade and employment as a result of the competition posed to the ferry companies by the Channel Tunnel.

In support of its decision to concentrate investment in tourism, the Council pointed to Portsmouth's success in developing a naval heritage theme, in which tourism products associated with the Tudor warship – the *Mary Rose* – and Portsmouth's naval history are used to generate visitor interest and tourism investment in the town. However, such a strategy is not without its critics. The first criticism that can be made is that the tourist trade is notoriously fickle; the tourism industry's domestic and overseas markets are easily affected by factors beyond its control, such as those influencing disposable income. Second, many of the jobs provided by tourism are characterised by low pay and low skill (Hudson and Townsend 1992). Often the industry relies upon casual employment and varied shift patterns, and it tends to offer limited protection for its workers. Furthermore, tourism is an industry which tends to place its employees in servile relationships with the public. It could be argued that a local authority using public funds should consider the quality of the employment it promotes. Third, there are inherent risks in using a major tourism attraction as a leader for investment in towns such as Dover, especially when the

Case study 2 (*continued*)

venue is oriented towards the domestic tourism market rather than the more lucrative incoming overseas visitors. Domestic tourism levels in Britain have been relatively static in recent years, and some of Dover's potential market may be tempted to take advantage of leisure opportunities in mainland Europe once the travel time has been reduced by the fixed link. This raises the problem of whether the White Cliffs Experience has the 'right ingredients' to attract visitor interest.

Delivery and Presentation

Under the guidance of the project designer John Sutherland (of the highly successful Jorvik Viking Centre in York), the White Cliffs Experience attempts to bring the story of Dover to life and attract visitors by exploiting Dover's cultural heritage. Dover is in fact following a significant national and international trend which has seen a major growth in heritage-based tourism attractions. Dover's strategy is to integrate Roman archaeological remains with the story of Dover's development as a frontier town, to interest visitors of a wide age range. What makes heritage attractions such as Jorvik so appealing, and does the White Cliffs Experience manage to capture those essential elements? The visitor experience at Jorvik follows a unified theme, focusing on the Viking settlement in York; but one wonders whether the story of Dover has the same intrinsic fascination. The focus on the educational market and the national curriculum has obvious appeal and fascination for school parties (see Cooper and Latham 1988 on educational visits and tourism), which comprise 20% of the visitors to Jorvik. The White Cliffs Experience reflects its ability to capture the schools market, having exceeded its initial visitor forecasts in the first few years of operation, reflecting initial visitor interest with a new attraction. Unfortunately the impact of local management in schools in the 1990s may actually militate against any growth in this market: budgets may be reduced for 'luxury items' such as educational visits.

Case study 2 (*continued*)

A further aspect that probably adds to the success of Jorvik is the provision of a relaxed, comfortable, undemanding visitor experience. Visitors are conveyed effortlessly back in time, through the replica Viking settlement and on into the archeological site, in small electric cars. This appears to add to the visitor's enjoyment and gives welcome relief and comfort for the elderly and weary tourist. It is a dimension likely to contribute to the overall success of a heritage project, and a feature absent from Dover's new heritage attraction. There is another factor which may be important in the continued success of Dover's scheme: the improvements to the road and rail networks associated with the Channel Tunnel. Dover has already experienced the effects of a road opened in 1977, which takes potential visitors on a direct route from the ferry terminal to the A2 dual-carriageway, so encouraging tourists to bypass the town. The Channel Tunnel–M20 link through Dover may have a similar effect on the town once it opens, thereby encouraging tourists to bypass the town and avoid stopping off as visitors.

What lessons does the Dover experience provide for our understanding of tourism attraction systems?

- Tourist attractions cannot be isolated from the urban tourism system in a town when seeking to use tourism as a method of stimulating economic development;
- The tourists are an integral part of the system – where the focus is on a new tourist attraction to boost the local economy via tourist spending and induced economic development;
- The concept of a marker is critical to the strategy of attraction development since the promotion of the attraction is central to its future commercial success;
- Recognising that 'tourism attraction systems are highly differentiated . . . [is fundamental to the marker and message conveyed to visitors as] . . . Behaviourally, there are many types of tourists, and individually tourists might relate to virtually any feature or characteristic of places as nucleus informative elements, markers, are likewise found in very diverse media and may perform many functions in the system' (Leiper 1990: 91);

- Organisations seeking to attract additional visitors to a town need to ensure the markers for tourists are based on consistent information. This is one of the real advantages of Dover's White Cliffs Country image as most visitors associate Dover with the White Cliffs; though promoting the town as a place to visit rather than as a transit destination requires innovative marketing and the identification of markers at each stage in the tourism attraction system to enable the District Council to achieve its ultimate economic regeneration objectives;
- The case study identifies a relationship between tourism and economic development which is considered in more detail in Chapter 4.

Having examined the significance of different approaches towards the analysis of tourism supply in urban areas, attention turns to the significance of different components of Jansen-Verbeke's leisure product and urban tourism destinations.

Tourist facilities

Among the 'secondary elements' of the leisure product in urban areas, three components emerge as central to servicing tourist needs. These are:

- Accommodation
- Catering
- Shopping
- Conditional elements.

Accommodation

Tourist accommodation performs an important function in cities: it provides the opportunity for visitors to stay for a length of time to enjoy the locality and its attractions, while their spending can contribute to the local economy. Accommodation forms a base for the tourists exploration of the urban (and non-urban) environment. The tendency for establishments to locate in urban areas is illustrated in Figure 3.4, which is based on the typical patterns of urban hotel location in West European cities (Ashworth 1989; also see the seminal paper by Arbel and Pizam 1977 on urban hotel location). Figure 3.4 highlights the importance of infrastructure and accessibility when hotels are built to serve specific markets (i.e. the exhibition and conference market will need hotels adjacent to a major conference and exhibition centre as Law 1988 emphasised). This point is also illustrated in the case of Kent (see Figure 3.5) where the majority of new hotel developments are being constructed adjacent to the major transit routes in the County to attract business travellers once the Channel Tunnel is fully operational (Page *et al.* 1990). As Figure 3.5 suggests even in a rural county, such as Kent, the majority of existing and projected hotel projects are located in towns (see Sinclair and Page 1993 for a more detailed discussion in the context of the 'Euroregion').

The accommodation sector within cities can be divided into serviced and non-serviced sectors (Figure 3.6). Each sector has developed in response to the needs of different markets, and a wide variety of organisational structures have emerged among private sector operators to develop this area of economic activity. As Pearce (1989) notes, many large chains and corporations now dominate the accommodation sector, using vertical and horizontal forms of integration to develop a greater degree of control over their business activities (see McVey 1986 for a more detailed discussion). Integration usually consists of:

- Horizontal integration, whereby hotel chains or franchising arrangements allows the accommodation sector to expand or acquire the business from other operators;
- Vertical integration, where one organisation seeks to diversify into other areas of activity. For example, in the 1970s and 1980s, it was commonplace for state owned airlines to have a chain of airport or city-centre hotels for its customers (e.g. Aer Lingus in Ireland had the Copthorne Hotel chain until their recent sale to realise the company's assets).

(A useful set of studies which focus on the issue of tourist accommodation can be found in Goodall 1989.) In terms of understanding the supply and demand for this type of facility, it is useful to focus on one specific country – Japan, as this will reinforce the arguments put forward in chapter two on the value of data to assess the demand and supply for urban tourism.

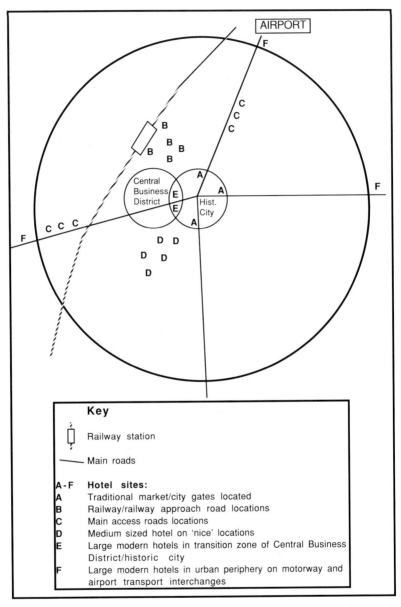

Figure 3.4 Model of urban hotel location in West European cities (after Ashworth 1989)

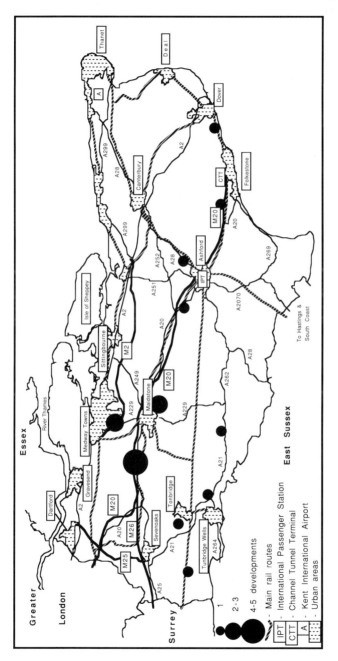

Figure 3.5 The distribution of hotel development projects in Kent in 1990

Sector	Serviced sector		Non-serviced sector (self-catering)	
Market segment	Destination	Routes	Destination	Routes
Business and other non-leisure	City/town hotels (Monday–Friday) Resort hotels for conferences, exhibitions Educational establishments	Motels Inns Airport hotels	Apartments	Not applicable
Leisure and holiday	Resort hotels Guest house/pensions Farm houses City/town hotels (Friday-Sunday) Some educational establishments	Motels Bed and breakfast Inns	Apart hotels Condominia Holiday villages Holiday centres/camps Caravan/chalet parks Gîtes Cottages Villas Apartments/flats Some motels	Touring pitches for caravans, tents, recreation vehicles YHA Some hotels

Figure 3.6 Types of tourism accommodation (after Middleton 1988, reproduced with permission from Butterworth-Heinemann)

Case study 3

Urban tourism accommodation in Japan

Japan has attracted a great deal of attention from researchers and analysts in relation to its outbound tourism market, which is renowned for its high spending visitors (Morris 1990). Its location in the Pacific Rim, which is one of the world's fastest growing regions for tourism activity (Morris 1990), has benefited both inbound and outbound travel. Yet the emphasis in the existing literature has been on outbound travel despite the recent development of inbound markets (Hall 1994). As this author argues (1994: 19), 'Japan is not only the dominant economic power of the Pacific but in tourism terms it is the largest inbound market for many of the countries of the region'. Shirawska's rather dated (1982) study still has an important bearing on patterns of inbound tourism to Japan, where a 1979 visitor survey noted the tendency of visitors to arrive and depart from the same gateways. Tokyo and Osaka dominate these patterns and a significant number of visitors did not venture beyond major gateways such as Tokyo (see Figure 3.7 for the location of these gateways). When visitors do travel around the country, there is a tendency for them to follow established tourist circuits such as the 'Golden Route' based on travel through central Japan to the Fuji-Hakone National Park and the old imperial cities of Kamakura, Kyoto and Nara. The significance of these travel patterns is the emphasis on urban tourism centres as accommodation bases and as places to visit outside of Tokyo and other large cities. This creates a demand for tourism accommodation in urban locations to serve the well-established visitor market in international and 'domestic travel [which] has grown substantially in Japan over the past decade' (Hall 1994: 21). In 1990, 363 million person-nights were spent in Japan by domestic tourists, the majority for pleasure and leisure travel (see Hall 1994 for more detail). What sources of data are available to assess the demand and supply of tourism accommodation in Japan?

Much of the data upon which tourism analysts base their studies of tourism are generated by the Ministry of Justice (MOJ), Ministry of Transport (MOT) and the Japanese National Tourist

Case study 3 (*continued*)

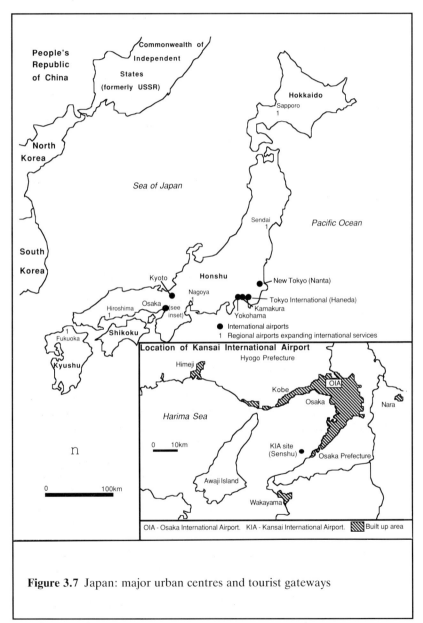

Figure 3.7 Japan: major urban centres and tourist gateways

Case study 3 (*continued*)

Organization (JNTO) (Pearce 1987a; Page 1994b). In terms of accommodation, the real difficulty is the limited basis of the official data because only 3% of the total accommodation stock is registered with the MOT, although this is likely to change in the near future (the Japanese government intends to expand the amount of accommodation registered by revising the 1949 International Tourist Hotel Law). The following data exist for 1991:

- For government-registered hotels, based on the western-style model with similar facilities, there are 636 hotels containing 119,114 rooms (although the total stock for this sector is 5,837 hotels with 422,211 rooms);
- For government-registered Japanese style hotels (Ryokans), there are 1,649 hotels and 97,117 rooms (although the total stock in this sector is 74,889 Ryokans and 1,015,959 rooms).

However, to assess the use of this accommodation, it is useful to examine the demand among international visitors as a source of urban tourism demand.

Inbound Tourism Demand in Japan

Table 3.1 outlines the pattern of arrivals for Japan and it is clear that the Asian market is by far the most important source area for inbound travel. For example, the Asian market has risen from 1,257,400 arrivals (1988) to 2,195,000 (1991), a growth of 74.5%. This has been fuelled by the decision of the South Korean government to ease restrictions on overseas travel. Both Taiwan and Hong Kong are also major markets contributing to Japanese inbound tourism. The total share of international Asian arrivals increased from 53.4% (1988) to 62.1% (1991), while the share of European and North American arrivals decreased (Table 3.2). Yet such data contain a number of problems as JNTO includes some business travellers and VFR traffic in their 'tourist' category, which may overestimate the actual number of inbound tourists at the expense of other categories. Thus, in 1991, the inbound

Case study 3 (*continued*)

market comprised: business travellers (26.1%); tourists (59.5%); others (12%) and shore excursionists (2.4%). Although Taiwan is the largest source market for inbound tourism (26.9%), closely followed by South Korea (24%), the South Korean business travel market outnumbers the Taiwanese market by a ratio of 5:1. In order to boost inbound tourism, the Japanese government has developed a number of initiatives. For example, in 1985 the MOT designated 15 prefectures as areas in which NRW Sites of Discovery were located. These sites covered 153 towns, cities and villages

Table 3.1 Inbound tourist arrivals in Japan 1965–91

Year	Number (000s)	% growth rate
1965	367	3.9
1966	433	18.1
1967	477	10.1
1968	519	8.9
1969	609	17.3
1970	854	40.2
1971	661	−22.7
1972	724	9.5
1973	785	8.4
1974	764	−2.6
1975	812	6.2
1976	915	12.7
1977	1028	12.4
1978	1039	1.0
1979	1113	7.1
1980	1317	18.3
1981	1583	20.2
1982	1793	13.3
1983	1968	9.8
1984	2110	7.2
1985	2327	10.3
1986	2062	−11.4
1987	2155	4.5
1988	2355	9.3
1989	2835	20.4
1990	3236	14.1
1991	3532	9.2
1989–91		24.6

Source: C.M. Hall (1994) and Economist Intelligence Unit (1992) Japan Country Report, *International Tourism Report* 2

Table 3.2 Major inbound markets to Japan by region and nationality 1988–91 (thousands)

Region	1988			1989			1990			1991		
	Number	% Change	% Share	Number	% Change	% Share	Number	% Change	% Share	Number	% Change	% Share
Asia & Middle East	1,257	19.9	53.4	1,637	30.2	57.8	1,919	17.2	59.3	2,195	14.4	62.1
Europe	401	5.2	17.0	455	13.6	16.1	516	13.4	16.0	521	0.9	14.7
Africa		5.3	0.4	12	13.1	0.4	12	2.1	0.4	15	0.9	14.7
North America	590	−5.3	25.0	605	2.6	21.3	633	4.7	19.6	619	−2.2	17.5
South America	32	17.5	1.4	49	52.7	1.7	78	59.8	2.4	108	37.6	3.0
Oceania	62	0.3	2.6	74	19.3	2.6	75	0.9	2.3	75	0.3	2.1
Nationality												
USA	516	−6.2	21.9	532	3.0	18.8	555	4.4	17.1	543	−2.1	15.4
Taiwan	411	7.2	17.5	528	28.4	18.6	608	15.1	18.8	658	8.3	18.6
South Korea	341	57.7	14.5	610	78.7	21.5	740	21.4	22.9	862	16.4	24.4
UK[A]	155	4.2	6.6	177	14.7	6.3	214	21.0	6.6	219	2.3	6.2
China	109	56.0	4.6	97	−10.2	3.4	106	8.8	3.3	130	23.1	3.7
UK (Hong Kong)[B]	66	NA	3.0	84	26.5	3.0	112	34.0	3.5	116	3.6	3.3

Source: Hall (1994) and Economist Intelligence Unit (1992) Japan Country Report, *International Tourism Report 4*, 1992

Notes
[A] Includes Hong Kong holders of British passports
[B] Hong Kong holders of British passports
Numbers of visitors have been rounded to the nearest thousand so percentages may not be exact.

Case study 3 (*continued*)

which were likely to appeal to international visitors. Whilst this has stimulated the development of urban tourism, the more recent government-initiated 'Five Million Programme' aims to raise inbound arrivals to 5 million by 1995. However, the programme is much more low profile than the highly publicised 'Ten Million Programme' for outbound travellers. The 'Five Million Programme' is largely focused on niche markets such as the incentive and convention market.

The business travel market also affects the age and sex profile of international visitors, since the typical profile of visitors is male and aged 30–50, although such demand is less seasonal than the 'tourist' category with its predisposition towards travel in July–October. However, the nature of demand does show a particular bias towards urban destinations as more detailed accommodation data suggest. For example, the Japanese Hotel Association, with its 400 member hotels, provides a partial but detailed insight into the concentration of visitors in the Tokyo and Yokohama region and occupancy rates (see Table 3.3). Whilst this data source suggests that only 15% of foreign bednights are spent at members' hotels, the dominance of Tokyo with 50% of the overseas staying market highlights the urban concentration in terms of supply and demand. To attract the lucrative overseas business travel market, many luxury hotels in Tokyo have invested in product development. At least 80% of luxury accommodation use in Tokyo is by business travellers, rising to over 90% in some cases. Not surprisingly, the needs of corporate clients has led to major refurbishment programmes and the investment in specialised facilities such as business centres and meeting rooms to satisfy the demand in this market.

Even so, the Japanese hotel market is notable for its limited degree of foreign penetration due to the high entry costs for overseas companies. As a result, domestic leisure and transportation companies have a major stake in Japan's hotels at home and abroad (Murakami and Go 1990). Yet this has not slowed down the rate of development. To the contrary, plans are in place for a major expansion in the luxury hotel market with 50 hotels and a

Table 3.3 Average occupancy rates and share of foreign bednights as a percentage of total bednights of Japan Hotel Association hotels, 1988–91

	Tokyo/Yokohama		Osaka/Kyoto/Kobe		Local cities		Resorts		Average	
	Occupancy rate	Share of foreign bednights	Occupancy rate	Share of foreign bednights	Occupancy rate	Share of foreign bednights	Occupancy rate	Share of foreign bednights	Occupancy rate	Share of foreign bednights
1988	79.0	29.0	72.2	15.7	70.7	7.9	58.2	2.0	71.3	14.3
1989	83.0	32.1	75.0	17.1	74.5	8.6	60.9	2.3	74.8	15.7
1990	84.9	33.3	81.9	16.2	76.0	8.4	64.7	3.1	77.6	15.0
1991	82.4	32.7	76.6	16.2	75.8	8.7	64.6	3.8	75.9	15.1

Source: Economist Intelligence Unit (1992), Japan Country Report, *International Tourism Report* 4, 1992 and Japan Hotel Association. Reproduced with permission from the Economist Intelligence Unit, London.

Case study 3 (*continued*)

capacity of 16,000 rooms, due for completion by 1997. The development of these new hotels is limited in the Tokyo region due to the scarcity of land and high development costs, with other large cities benefiting from the investment programme. For example, the new Kansai International Airport (see Page 1994c) has stimulated development of eight schemes to benefit from the expected growth in tourism associated with the new airport (see Figure 3.7). However, this focus on the luxury market may pose certain problems for inbound tourists using budget hotels on packages or as independent travellers. One consequence may be the increase in price for budget accommodation following a similar pattern to that in London (Page and Sinclair 1989). This is likely to be particularly acute in the Tokyo region. One market that has seen a major growth in its use of urban accommodation is the meetings and convention market.

The Meetings and Convention Market and Urban Tourism

The number of meetings and conventions in Japan has risen from 371 in 1981 to 1244 in 1991, making Japan the world's eleventh most popular venue for meetings and conventions. This rapid growth has been stimulated by the decision of the MOT to identify twenty-five Japanese cities as International Convention Cities in 1988, though this subsequently rose to thirty-three in 1992. The international marketing of these cities is handled by a specialist agency attached to the JNTO – the Japan Convention Bureau which targets and markets venues overseas in liaison with the travel trade in Japan. The regional development of convention cities has weakened Tokoyo's standing as a venue and led to the development of accommodation and tourist facilities in other cities. In 1991 Kyoto became Japan's leading convention venue, having hosted 209 events compared to only 181 in Tokyo. However, Tokyo is responding to the aggressive and competitive market for meetings and conventions among the domestic and overseas market by investing in new facilities. Yet this also applies to many other Japanese cities as the recent expansion of Nagoya as a regional meetings and convention centre suggests. In 1990,

Case study 3 (*continued*)

---

the city opened its own convention centre benefiting from the expansion of its regional airport to facilitate international travel. A similar situation exists in the Kansai region of Japan, where the cities of Kyoto, Kobe and Osaka now have a 37% share of this market, having developed accommodation and infrastructure to serve this expanding area of tourism activity within its urban area (see Fujita and Child 1993 for further details of Japanese urban development). It is clear that this is both a highly competitive activity for cities in Japan seeking to optimise their potential as urban tourism destinations and a further niche within the growing market for urban tourism in Japan. As a result, the following points summarise the situation in Japan:

- Japan is an expanding market for inbound (and outbound) travel largely based on the Asian market;
- Business travel in Japan is a major component of urban tourism and it is reflected in the supply and demand for accommodation in its major cities;
- While Tokyo has traditionally dominated patterns of urban tourism among international visitors, the developments in accommodation outside the region and the expansion of the Convention and Meetings market has challenged this position;
- Potential shortages in supply may affect the budget end of the market, although high yielding market segments such as business travel have been the main focus of investment strategies.

Catering facilities

Ashworth and Tunbridge (1990) note that catering facilities are among the most frequently used tourism services after accommodation. For example, of the £15 billion of overseas and domestic tourist spending in the UK in 1990, nearly £2 billion is estimated to be on eating and drinking (Marketpower 1991). What is meant by catering facilities? Bull and Church (1994) suggest that one way of grouping this sector is to use the Standard Industrial Classification which comprises:

- Restaurants
- Eating places
- Public houses
- Bars, clubs, canteens and messes
- Hotels and other forms of tourist accommodation.

Using the products which this sector produces, they further subdivide the groups into:

- The provision of accommodation
- Food for immediate consumption.

Whilst there is considerable overlap between the two sectors, there are organisational links between each sector as integration within larger hospitality organisations (e.g. the Forte Group) with their subsidiaries offering various products. In the context of urban tourism, one of the immediate difficulties is in identifying specific outlets for tourist use, as many such facilities are also used by residents. Therefore, tourist spending at such facilities also has to be viewed against total consumer spending in this sector. In 1989, Marketpower (1991) found that total consumer spending in the UK on alcoholic drinks and meals outside the home totalled £15 billion. Extracting tourism and leisure spending from this amount can only be an estimate. Tourist use of catering facilities varies according to the specific service on offer, being located throughout cities, often in association with other facilities (S.L.J. Smith 1983). Many catering establishments in cities reflect local community needs and tourism complements the existing pattern of use. Nevertheless, Ashworth and Tunbridge do acknowledge that

> Restaurants and establishments combining food and drink with other entertainments, whether night-clubs, discos, casinos and the like, have two important locational characteristics that render them useful in this context: they have a distinct tendency to cluster together into particular streets or districts, what might be termed the 'latin-quarter effect', and they tend to be associated spatially with other tourism elements including hotels, which probably themselves offer public restaurant facilities.
>
> (Ashworth and Tunbridge 1990: 65)

Furthermore, a recent British Tourist Authority report (1993) recognises that while the quality of food and service in Britain has improved in recent years, food can be a persuasive ingredient in Britain's overall tourist appeal, particularly in urban areas. Nevertheless, the report supports the reform of Britain's Sunday trading laws and licensing hours, as well as the investment in upgrading the language skills of tourism and hospitality workers, in pursuit of improvements to customer service. As the report suggests, food may have improved, but tourist perceptions still lag behind the reality of provision in many urban areas; illustrating the significance of this element is the 'tourist experience' of urban areas. Catering facilities also have a predisposition to cluster within areas where shopping is also a dominant activity.

Tourist shopping

The English Historic Towns Forum's (1992) study on retailing and tourism highlights many of the relationships between:

> Tourism and retail activity [which] are inextricably linked to historic towns with three-quarters of tourists combining shopping with visiting attractions . . . The expenditure is not only on refreshments and souvenirs, as might be expected, but also on clothing and footwear, stationery and books.
>
> (English Towns Forum 1992: 3)

The study also emphasises the overall significance of the environmental quality in towns which is vital to the success of urban tourism and retailing. In fact the report argues that:

> For towns wishing to maintain or increase leisure visitor levels, the study reveals a number of guide lines. For example, cleanliness, attractive shop fronts and provision of street entertainment are all important to tourists.
>
> (English Historic Towns Forum 1992: 3)

Unfortunately, identifying tourist-shopping as a concept in the context of urban tourism is difficult, since it is also an activity undertaken by other users such as residents (Kent 1983). The most relevant research undertaken in this field, by Jansen-Verbeke (1990, 1991), considers the motives of tourists and their activities in a range of Dutch towns. She makes a number of interesting observations on this concept. However, the range of motives associated with tourism and leisure shopping are complex: people visit areas because of their appeal and shopping may be a spontaneous as well as a planned activity. Even so, the quality and range of retail facilities may be a useful determinant of the likely demand for tourism and leisure shopping: the longer the visitor is enticed to stay in a destination – the greater the likely spending in retail outlets.

One important factor which affects the ability of cities to attract tourism and leisure shoppers is the retail mix – namely the variety of goods, shops and presence of specific retailers. For example, the English Historic Towns Forum (1992) notes that over 80% of visitors consider the retailing mix and general environment of the town the most important attraction of the destination. Although the priorities of different tourist market segments vary slightly, catering, accessibility (e.g. availability of car parking, location of car parks and public transport), tourist attractions and the availability of visitor information, shape the decision to engage in tourism and leisure shopping. The constant search for the unique shopping experience, especially in conjunction with day trips in border areas and neighbouring countries (e.g. the UK cross-channel tax-free shopping trips from Dover to Calais) are well-established forms of tourism and leisure shopping.

The global standardisation of consumer products has meant that the search for the unique shopping experience continues to remain important. The growth of the North American shopping malls and tourist specific projects (see Getz 1993b for more detail) and the development in the UK of out-of-town complexes (e.g. the Metro Centre in Gateshead and Lakeside at Thurrock, adjacent to the M25) have extended this trend. For example, in the case of Edmonton Mall (Canada) Jansen-Verbeke (1991) estimates that 10% of the total floor space is used for leisure facilities with its 800 shops and parking for 27,000 cars. Such developments have been a great concern for many cities as out of town shopping has reduced the potential in-town urban tourism in view of the competition they pose for established destinations. The difficulty with most existing studies of leisure shopping, is that they fail to disentangle the relationships between the actual activity tourists undertake and their perception of the environment. For this reason, Jansen-Verbeke (1991) distinguishes between intentional shopping and intentional leisure shopping in a preliminary attempt to explain how and why tourists engage in this activity; she also suggests that several criteria need to be considered to distinguish between intentional shopping and intentional leisure and tourism in relation to the following.

Behaviour pattern of visitors

- Trip length – short, possibly longer;
- Length of stay – limited or rather unplanned;
- Time of stay – a few hours during the day, an evening, a full day;
- Kinds of activity – window shopping, intentional buying, drinking, eating, various leisure activities, cultural activities, sightseeing;
- Expenditure – goods, possibly some souvenirs, drinks, meals, entrance fees to leisure facilities.

Functional characteristics of the environment

- Wide range of retail shops, department stores, catering, leisure and other facilities, tourist attractions, spatial clustering of facilities;
- Parking space and easy access;
- Street retailing, pedestrian priority in open spaces.

Quality of the environment

- Image of the place, leisure setting, display of goods on the street, street musicians and artists;
- Accessibility during leisure time, including weekends and evenings;
- Aesthetic value, image of maintenance and safety;
- Architectural design of buildings, streets, shops, windows, sign boards, lighting;
- Social effective value, liveliness of the open space;
- Animation, entertainment, amusement and surprise.

Hospitableness of the environment

- Social, visual, physical;
- Orientation, information, symbolism, identification.

Source: Jansen-Verbeke (1991: 9–10)

For many cities, finding the right mix between shops, leisure facilities and tourist attractions to appeal to a wide range of visitors and residents involves a process of development and promotion to attract investment in town centres. However, critics have argued that the out-of-town shopping malls and complexes are only a passing trend which do not pose a long-term challenge to tourism and leisure spending in town centres. So why is tourism and leisure shopping attracting so much attention among planners and researchers?

One immediate reason is the potential for using shopping as a marketing tool by the tourism industry in towns and cities. The English Historic Towns Forum (1992) emphasises this relationship, as 75% of visitors to the cities surveyed combine tourism and shopping. But what changes are occurring and how is tourism and leisure shopping changing in the 1990s?

Only certain shopping centres have the essential ingredients to be promoted as tourism and day trip destinations. The image and manner in which these places are promoted is assuming growing significance (see Chapter 6 for a fuller discussion of place-marketing). Historic cities in Europe have many of the key ingredients in terms of the environment, facilities, tourism attractions and the ability to appeal to distinct visitor audiences. Many successful cities in Western Europe have used tourism and leisure shopping to establish their popularity as destinations as a gradual process of evolution. In particular, improvements to town centres by city authorities have acted as catalysts to this process by:

- Establishing pedestrian precincts;
- Managing parking problems and implementing park and ride schemes to improve access and convenience;
- Marketing the destination based around an identifiable theme, often using the historical and cultural attractions of a city;
- Investing in new and attractive indoor shopping galleries, improving facades, the layout and design of the built environment and making the environment more attractive. For example, Dover's Tourism Initiative (Case Study 2) included a number of key environmental improvements. The English Historic Towns Forum (1992: 12) identifies the following factors which tourism and leisure shoppers deemed important:

  - The cleanliness of the town
  - Pedestrian areas/pavements which are well maintained
  - Natural features such as rivers and parks
  - The architecture and facades/shopfronts
  - Street furniture (seating and floral displays)
  - Town centre activities (e.g. outdoor markets and live entertainment).

One illustration of the effect of specific factors which tourists may view as important is evident from the Tidy Britain Group's qualitative study of the cleanliness of capital cities in Europe and the conditions at major tourist sites. The survey examines litter levels and environmental problems, awarding points for cleanliness. While the results of such surveys may be highly variable, due to the sampling methodology used, London featured as the overall winner in relation to the criteria used. Although Berne's 'the Bear Pit' emerges as the most clean tourist site among those locations surveyed (while Athens Syntagma Square came bottom of the league), the environment around other facilities visited and used by tourists (e.g. shopping streets, railway stations and parliament buildings) provide additional insights into the environmental quality of those areas which tourists also visit. Although it is difficult to place a great deal of store by *ad hoc* and random surveys such as the Tidy Britain Group, it does illustrate the point that cleanliness, litter and the perceived quality of the local environment may influence tourist views, particularly those seeking to visit shopping streets in major capital cities such as Oxford Street (London), Puerto del Sol (Madrid), Rue de Neuve (Brussels), Kalverstraat (Amsterdam), Bahnhof Platz (Berne), Ermou (Athens), Boulevard Haussmann (Paris), Kurfustendamm (Berlin) and Via del Corso (Rome). The impressions which shoppers form of the environmental quality of urban areas may also influence other potential visitors as word of mouth communication is a powerful force in personal recommendation of shopping areas.

Changes which alter the character of the town, where it becomes more tourist orientated, are sometimes characterised by the development of speciality and gift/souvenir shops and catering facilities in certain areas. However, as Owen (1990) argues, many traditional urban shopping areas are in need of major refurbishment and tourism may provide the necessary stimulus for regeneration. Recent developments such as theme shopping (Jones Lang Wootton 1989) and festival marketplaces (Sawicki 1989) are specialised examples of how this regeneration has proceeded in the UK and North America.

The 1990s, therefore, would seem to be set for tourism and leisure shopping development to further segment markets by seeking new niches and products. Jansen-Verbeke (1991) describes the 'total experience' as the future way forward for this activity – retailers will need to attract tourism and leisure spending using newly built, simulated or refurbished retailing environments with a variety of shopping experiences. Keown's (1989) experience is that the opportunity to undertake a diverse range of retail activities in a locality increases the tourists propensity to spend. However, the growing saturation of retailing provision in many industrialised countries may pose problems for further growth in tourism and leisure shopping due to the intense competition for such spending. Urban tourism destinations are likely to have to compete more aggressively for such spending in the 1990s.

The conditional elements

The last features which Jansen-Verbeke (1986) views as central to the city's 'leisure product' are the conditional elements, such as transport, physical infrastructure and the provision of signposting. To illustrate the significance of these elements in the context of tourist activities, a case study of London Docklands follows. The case study describes how the expectations of developers to create a new focus for tourism and leisure shopping failed to materialise due to the inadequate infrastructure provision and the reluctance of tourists to divert from established patterns of visitor activity.

Case study 4

Developing tourism in London Docklands: infrastructure contraints

The London Docklands development covers an area of 20 km², with 180 ha of redundant docks and 88.5 km of redundant waterfront which stretches from the Tower of London in the West to Becton in the East (Figure 3.8). The decline and subsequent redevelopment of London Docklands has been extensively documented (Page 1994a) and it has followed a similar pattern to other waterfront schemes (Hoyle and Pinder 1992). London Docklands represents one of the world's largest waterfront revitalisation programmes, stimulated and directed by a central government funded quango – the London Docklands Development Corporation (LDDC), with Canary Wharf as its focal point (Plate 3.1). It has caused a great deal of controversy in relation to its accountability and impact on the local planning process. LDDC proceeded to redevelop the land, improve the region's infrastructure and pursue

Case study 4 (*continued*)

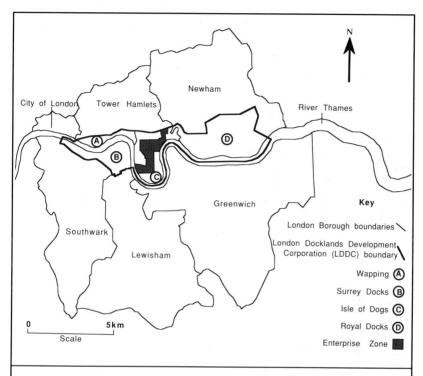

Figure 3.8 The location of London Docklands

a policy of image promotion (Plate 3.2). By 1990, LDDC claimed that some £8,057 million of investment by the private sector had been committed to redevelopment compared to government funding of £803 million, providing a private to public leverage ratio of 10:1 for investment in the area.

Central to the redevelopment was the development of the Dockland's Light Railway (DLR) at a cost of £77 million in the 1980s, prior to the planned extension of the Jubilee Underground Line to the area in the late 1990s (Figure 3.9). Transport is a critical factor in relation to regenerating new centres for tourism and leisure shopping (e.g. Tobacco Dock) as the discussion will show and for this reason it is useful to consider the significance of transport for tourism in Docklands.

Plate 3.1 Canary Wharf (reproduced by kind permission from LDDC)

Venue Directory 1994

London Docklands

Plate 3.2 Recent marketing and publicity literature to promote London Docklands (reproduced by kind permission from LDDC)

Case study 4 (*continued*)

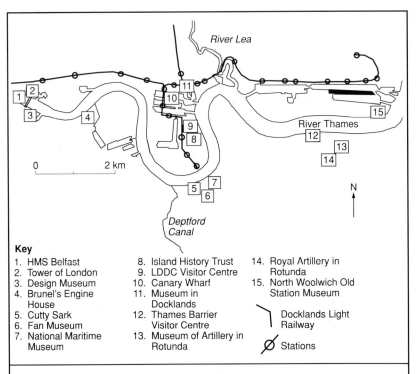

Figure 3.9 Tourist-transport infrastructure in London Docklands

Transport for tourism in London Docklands

The relationship between transport and tourism is reviewed in Page (1994b), being vital to the mobility of visitors to travel at their destination. Church (1990) argues that the LDDC's transport policy reflects the ideological goals of central government, which emphasises: limiting public transport expenditure; allowing the market to set priorities and resolve problems; limiting state intervention; promoting private ownership of transport; meeting the demands of road users; promoting wealth creation and the enterprise culture. The absence of strategic transport planning by the LDDC has also meant that the region's transport network has failed to meet accessibility targets emphasised in the LDDC's

Case study 4 (*continued*)

brief from central government. Its preference for investment in environmentally-damaging road projects (e.g. the 12km Docklands Highway) exemplifies the LDDC ideology on transportation and a certain degree of synergy with central government transport objectives. What does this mean for tourism in the region?

In the context of London Docklands, awareness of the potential relationship between tourism and urban regeneration was reflected in the LDDC's commissioning of the *Tourist Development in Docklands* report (Llewelyn-Davies 1987). Prior to 1987, tourism was not a key priority for the LDDC as capital investment in outdoor recreation projects consumed the majority of leisure budgets. Yet the tourism potential of Docklands had been recognised in the mid 1980s by Horwath and Horwath (1986: 149) who argue that it is necessary to raise 'the ambience and image of part or parts of Dockland to establish Docklands as a prime tourist destination in its own right which tourists would seek as a desirable location for their London stay'. Furthermore, London Tourist Board (1987) estimate that between 1986 and 1996, up to half of London's new tourism developments could be located in Docklands, highlighting its potential role as a new tourism destination. To understand how tourism could be used to stimulate economic development in Docklands, it is pertinent to examine the LDDC's tourism development strategy embodied in the Llewelyn-Davies (1987) report and the effect of demand-led planning on the region's tourism potential.

Tourism Planning and Development in Docklands

The LDDC *Tourism Strategy for Docklands* identified the main direction which tourism accommodation and attraction development should follow in Docklands, examining the underlying principles of tourism development in Docklands which sought to maximise the geographical distribution of visitors using three concepts to guide tourist development.

- First, a riverside corridor bordering Dockland was to be the main focus for visitors. Within this corridor a series of 'visitor

Case study 4 (*continued*)

destinations' were to be to developed at major docks (Figure 3.10). Each 'destination' should be capable of attracting at least 2 million visitors per annum spread throughout the year. Public transport (DLR) and river boat access was essential to ensure that these focal points were accessible, offering a wide range of attractions including shops, restaurants, nightlife and hotels. LDDC identified five areas which were suitable as 'visitor destinations': Tower Bridge, Wapping, West India Dock, Greenwich (which is outside of the LDDC boundary, although it has been incorporated in view of its significance in a London-wide context) and Royal Victoria Dock.

• Second, a series of 'visitor places' were to be developed near the main corridor of Docklands which comprised single attractions or groups of small attractions capable of attracting up to 1 million visitors per annum, although their visitor markets were likely to be seasonal. Like the 'visitor destinations', they were aimed at visitor leisure activities.

• Last, a number of small scale, isolated and less well known 'visitor features' were to be promoted. These were to be at least 1 km from the main tourist attractions and capable of attracting up to 100,000 visitors per annum. Therefore, as Figure 3.10 suggests, tourist development in Docklands emphasises the principle of concentrated activity at accessible waterside locations.

To complement the planned development of tourism, in 1990 the LDDC introduced an 'Arts Action Plan for Docklands' which would be an essential part of the quality of life of Docklands providing a creative use of leisure time and enhancing the built environment for workers although the underlying rationale of LDDC's approach to tourism and urban redevelopment is to stimulate 'the supply side of the economy by rolling back the frontiers of the state – decreasing the degree of regulation and intervention by government' (Page and Sinclair 1989: 135). In Docklands, the result has been that private investment has gravitated towards existing areas of tourism development which reveal

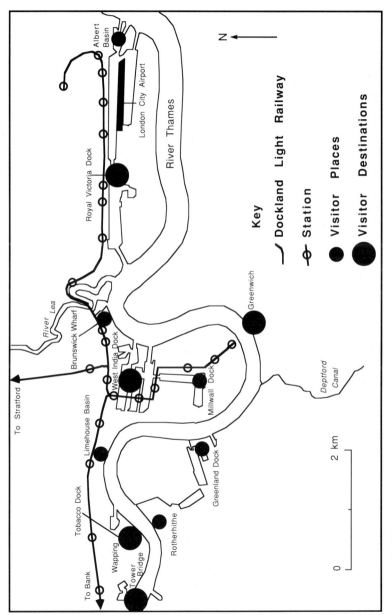

Figure 3.10 Visitor destinations and visitor places in London Docklands

Plate 3.3 Recent marketing and publicity literature to promote London Docklands (reproduced by kind permission from LDDC).

Case study 4 (*continued*)

market potential. In cases where private sector investment in tourism has been pump-primed by LDDC grants (e.g. Tobacco Dock), the LDDC's prioritisation of investment in infrastructure has failed to make destinations accessible.

The case in point is Tobacco Dock. This project cost £50 million and is situated in a restored Grade 1 listed building providing specialist shops and tourist attractions. It was hoped that such developments would resemble the highly successful Covent Garden scheme in central London. Tobacco Dock was expected to create 800 new job vacancies, of which 75% may be filled by local labour in an area of high unemployment. However, due to the recession, the development of tourism at Tobacco Dock has been limited; many shops have closed down, the visitors have not materialised since it is inaccessible and not on tourist itineraries (Plate 3.4). Thus, its potential as a speciality shopping centre for tourism and leisure visitors has, therefore, not been realised. One important consideration is the effect of the recent recession on new projects such as Tobacco Dock (see Figure 3.11 for a recent assessment of business failures in Docklands). Even where urban programme grants have been directed towards tourism projects in Docklands, these have not enjoyed the high rates of employment of Liverpool Docks (Department of the Environment 1990). As the Department of the Environment acknowledges:

> Tourism projects appear to have greater impacts when they are grouped with other tourism projects in a relatively small geographical area. This clustered approach gives a higher profile, enables links to be developed between projects, facilities joint marketing.
>
> (Department of the Environment 1990: 69)

In Docklands, the spirit of the free market economy has meant that co-operative ventures and partnership schemes have been limited, particularly since few destinations within the region have sufficient attractions to enjoy benefits of clustered development. While the effects of market-led planning and its impact on the landscape of Docklands has placed the region on the tourist map

Plate 3.4 Docklands Light Railway (reproduced by kind permission from LDDC).

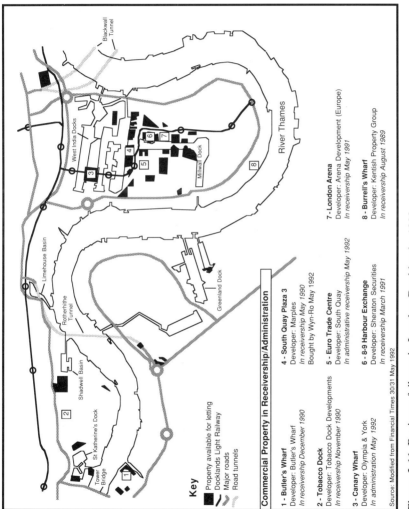

Key

■ Property available for letting
  Docklands Light Railway
  Major roads
  Road tunnels

Commercial Property in Receivership/Administration

1 - Butler's Wharf
Developer: Butler's Wharf
In receivership December 1990

2 - Tobacco Dock
Developer: Tobacco Dock Developments
In receivership November 1990

3 - Canary Wharf
Developer: Olympia & York
In administration May 1992

4 - South Quay Plaza 3
Developer: Marples
In receivership May 1990
Bought by Wyn-Ro May 1992

5 - Euro Trade Centre
Developer: South Quay
In administrative receivership May 1992

6 - 8-9 Harbour Exchange
Developer: Sheraton Securities
In receivership March 1991

7 - London Arena
Developer: Arena Development (Europe)
In receivership May 1991

8 - Burrell's Wharf
Developer: Kentish Property Group
In receivership August 1989

Source: Modified from Financial Times 30/31 May 1992

Figure 3.11 Business failures in London Docklands, 1992

Case study 4 (*continued*)

of London, the emphasis on encouraging private sector investment
to realise development opportunities in tourism and leisure facilities has been notoriously difficult in a climate of commercial
uncertainty. Without adequate investment in public transport
infrastructure in Docklands, tourism is unlikely to reach its full
potential, remaining a day trip destination, with visitors concentrated at those locations which are easily accessible.

Conclusion

This chapter has examined a range of issues and concepts associated
with the analysis of tourism supply issues. The 'leisure product' concept
developed by Jansen-Verbeke (1986) provides a convenient and mean-
ingful framework in which to explore the supply of different components in urban tourism destinations that influence visitors and provide
opportunities for activities. Yet even this framework is not without its
problems. Some researchers question the approaches one might adopt
towards the analysis of different aspects of urban tourism supply. The
public and private sectors each have distinct roles to perform, although
as the case studies show, there is growing evidence of public–private
sector partnerships to expand and improve the provision of services and
facilities for tourists, day visitors and residents alike.

This chapter argues that it is not simply the case that tourists visit
urban areas due to the attractions and facilities available. The supply of
services and essential tourism infrastructure is part of the tourism
system that researchers can construct to analyse the functional links and
activities tourists undertake in specific destinations. While this chapter
discusses the different elements of tourism supply, in reality the elements coexist and interact to produce an identifiable 'bundle' of services
and facilities. Therefore, it is impossible to isolate any one element of
the supply as the main determinant of tourism in a specific location.
Although some elements may appear dominant (e.g. attractions),
without a well-developed infrastructure and network of services and
facilities for tourists, tourism may fail to develop to its full potential
as the case of Tobacco Dock implies. Yet where tourism develops as a

successful enterprise, supported by the private and public sector, a variety of impacts occur in given locations which affect the tourists experience of the destination and environment. For this reason, the next chapter examines the impact of tourism in urban areas.

Questions

1 How would you develop a framework to analyse the supply of tourism services in urban areas ?
2 What is the value of the tourism business district as a framework for analysing the location and interrelationships between tourism and non-tourism services in the central area of cities?
3 How would you go about developing a tourism attraction system for a local authority client?
4 To what extent has London Docklands emerged as a distinctive tourism destination in London?

Further reading

Fujita, K. and Child, R. (eds) (1993) *Japanese Cities in the World Economy*, Philadelphia: Temple University Press.

This is a useful up-to-date assessment of urbanisation in Japan which provides a context in which to understand how certain cities in Japan have developed and maintained their position as industrial and commercial centres and how this has influenced the market for conference tourism.

Goodall, B. (ed.) (1989) Tourism Accommodation: Special Issue, *Built Environment* 15(2).

This set of papers is a good introduction to tourist use of accommodation in towns and cities.

Jansen-Verbeke, M (1994) 'The synergy between shopping and tourism: the Japanese experience' in W. Theobald (ed.) *Global Tourism: The Next Decade*, Oxford: Butterworth-Heinemann: 347–62.

This is a good up-to-date assessment of the relationship between shopping and tourism.

Jones Lang Wootton (1989) *Retail, Leisure and Tourism*, London: English Tourist Board.

This is a good report which considers the relationship between retailing and tourism and highlights the area of leisure shopping.

4
Analysing the impact of urban tourism: economic, socio-cultural and environmental perspectives

Introduction

The development, expansion and operation of tourism in urban areas has both beneficial and negative effects for the city and its population: in simple terms – tourism leads to impacts in urban areas. Yet this concern for the impact of tourism is not confined to urban areas: it is part of a growing concern for the impact and long-term sustainability of tourism across the world. But the combination of the expansion of tourism and world population growth based in mega-cities (O'Connor 1993) means that, by the twenty-first century, a greater emphasis will be placed on urban areas as places to work, live and visit. By understanding the impact of modern tourism, it is possible to understand how tourism actually coexists with other economic activities in urban areas and its real contribution to the life, economy and environment of the city. As Pearce (1989) argues, research on the impact of tourism has led to varying degrees of emphasis on economic, cultural, social and environmental impacts induced by tourism.

One of the main criticisms of many studies of the impact of tourism is that they do not pay adequate attention to the various types of tourism which induce the impacts. All too often the studies are unable to identify and understand the processes creating the impacts. While detailed literature exists on the impact of tourism, there are no comprehensive studies which assess the diverse range of impacts of tourism in urban areas, mainly because of the methodological problems. The purpose of this chapter is to examine the range of impacts which are associated with urban tourism and the different approaches used to analyse the scope and nature of specific impacts. The chapter commences with a discussion of methodological problems in assessing the impact of tourism and the constraints in developing a comprehensive approach towards impact analysis. This is followed by a detailed discussion of specific impacts which are illustrated by a range of representative case studies and the implications for the planning and management of urban tourism.

Methodological problems associated with analysing the impact of urban tourism

In any attempt to assess the impact of urban tourism, the immediate problem facing researchers and planners is the establishment of an appropriate baseline on which to measure the existing and future changes induced by tourism. This is a problem that affects all aspects of impact assessment, although it is frequently cited in 'environmental assessment' (EA). Numerous studies of EA acknowledge the practical problems of establishing baseline studies and in disaggregating the impact of tourism from other economic activities in urban areas (Vetter 1985), and their different contribution to environmental impacts. Mathieson and Wall highlight the precise nature of the problem since:

> In many tourist destinations public use has existed for long periods of time so that it is now almost impossible to reconstruct the environment minus the effects induced by tourism. However, failure to establish baseline data will mean that it will be impossible to fully assess the magnitude of changes brought by tourism.
>
> (Mathieson and Wall 1982: 5)

Even when it is possible to establish a baseline of data for a specific urban destination the problem, which Pearce (1989) identifies, is the extent to which pre-existing processes and changes in the physical and built environment of specific urban destinations is induced by tourism. While it is widely acknowledged that tourism is a major agent affecting the natural and built environment at a general level, isolating the precise causes or processes leading to specific impacts is difficult: is tourism the principle agent of change or is it part of a wider process of economic development in a particular destination? Mathieson and Wall (1982: 5) highlight the common problem that 'tourism may also be a highly visible scapegoat for problems which existed prior to the advent of modern tourism. It certainly is easier to blame tourism than it is to address the conditions of society and the environment'. This is compounded by the reality of impact assessment – that the complex interactions of tourism, urban areas and the built and physical environment make it virtually impossible to model or measure with any degree of precision. Even if it is possible to precisely gauge these impacts, they may not manifest themselves in a tangible form that is easily measured or gauged by survey methods. Impacts may be large scale and tangible (e.g. where a destination is saturated by visitors) and/or small scale and intangible: but how does this affect the interaction between the resident and visitor? And when should one measure these impacts?

The real difficulty is in attributing cause and effect in relation to urban tourism which is not necessarily continuous in time (due to seasonality) and space (as tourism activity tends to concentrate in certain locations within cities in relation to the supply of services and facilities – see Chapter 3). Once researchers have decided on a direction to pursue in the analysis of tourism impacts in urban areas, the precise indicators chosen to represent the complex interaction of tourism and the urban destination require the establishment of a methodological framework in which to guide the impact assessment. It is not surprising, therefore, to find many general texts in tourism studies reducing the impact of tourism to costs and benefits for specific destinations, rather than entering into the complex relationships that exist for specific forms of tourism such as urban tourism.

Law's (1993) research monograph on urban tourism reaffirms this tendency to avoid methodological discussion of assessing the impact of tourism in large cities. For example, he states (1993: 156) that 'the first task of any impact study is decide who is to be counted as a visitor or tourist' as a basis for calculating visitor numbers for a destination. As Chapter 2 has shown, various indicators such as accommodation can also be used to gauge demand as a baseline for estimating the magnitude of the likely impact of tourism. Where visitor surveys are undertaken, Law (1993) criticises their value as they are often undertaken at visitor attractions, to establish the nature and scale of visitors to urban destinations. Their reliability and ability to yield a representative sample or picture of what is actually happening at destinations is also questioned. It needs to be recognised that where towns and cities have visitor management projects in place, the derivation of baseline information on visitors from surveys is only one part of a more systematic attempt to recognise the impact of urban tourism from the visitor, resident and planning perspective. Nevertheless, Law (1993) does acknowledge that where visitor information is collected, it needs to be related to other forms of statistical information.

Pearce (1989) presents an interesting framework for impact assessment, pointing to the stimulus from EA in North America to consider impacts, especially in relation to proposed developments. It is in this context that the work by Potter (1978) is of interest, since it provides a general methodology for impact assessment. As Figure 4.1 shows, the assessment of the impact incorporates environmental, social and economic issues, all of which can be applied to tourism. As Pearce (1989: 185) argues, the real value is in its ability to assess both the existing and proposed developments. Potter's (1978) methodology comprises a number of steps, beginning with the context of the development and proceeding through to making a decision on a particular development. Pearce (1989) moves a stage further, arguing that impact studies should also consider the wider context of development rather than just the destination (i.e. the urban area). In this respect, both the origin of visitors, the processes and linkages between origin and destination area and factors influencing the outcome – the impact – need to be considered. Pearce (1989) argues that a systems model may help to provide a more holistic framework for understanding the impact of tourism. This approach is embodied in Figure 4.2 and extends the discussion of the value of a systems approach to tourism. In fact, Figure 4.2 can be applied to urban tourism so that the relationship between the supply and demand for tourism are set in a wider geographical context, as impacts occur from tourists while in transit and also at the destination (see Page 1994b). Pearce (1989) acknowledges that the integration of both Potter (1978) and Thurot's (1980) work reinforces the significance of the contextual factors and the type of tourist development involved as well as the range of mitigation measures necessary to reduce the range of impacts associated with tourism. Attention now turns to different aspects of tourism's impact in urban areas.

The economic impact of urban tourism

Tourism is increasingly being viewed by many national and local governments as a mechanism to aid the regeneration of the ailing economies of industrial cities (Law 1993). But why is tourism being incorporated into the economic development strategies of different towns?

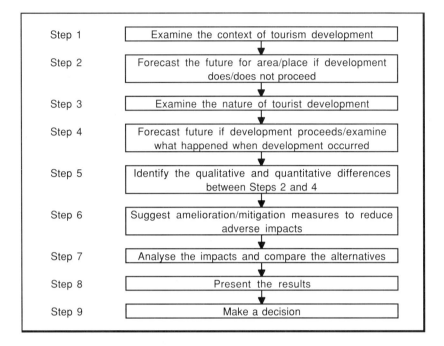

Figure 4.1 A framework for assessing the impact of tourism development

There is a prevailing perception among national and local governments that economic benefits accrue to tourism destinations, which then creates employment opportunities and stimulates the development process in resorts and localities. For the local population, it is often argued by proponents of tourism development, that investment in tourist and recreational facilities provides a positive contribution to the local economy. Such assumptions are not without their problems since tourists are not noted for their high levels of customer loyalty to tourism destinations and a number of features support this argument:

- Tourism is a fickle industry, being highly seasonal and this has implications for investment and the type of employment created. Tourism employment is often characterised as being low skill, poorly paid, low status and lacking long-term stability;
- The demand for tourism can easily be influenced by external factors (e.g. political unrest, unusual climatic and environmental conditions) which are beyond the control of destination areas;

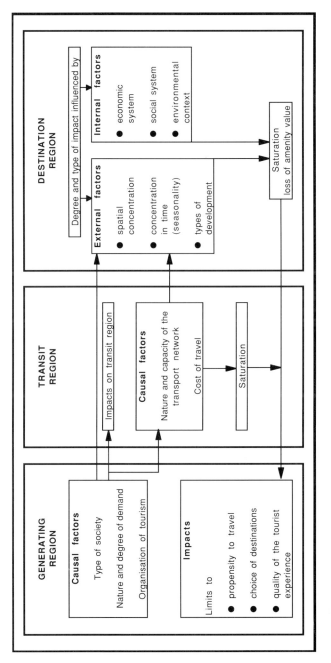

Figure 4.2 Interrelationships and causal factors and impacts associated with generating, transit and destination regions (after Pearce 1989, reproduced courtesy of Longman)

- The motivation for tourist travel to urban destinations is complex and variable and constantly changing in the competitive market in the 1990s;
- In economic terms, tourism is price and income elastic (see Bull 1991), which means that it is easily influenced by small changes to the price of the product and the disposable income of consumers;
- Many cities are becoming alike, a feature Harvey (1989) has described as 'serial reproduction'. This means that once an idea for urban economic development is successful in one location, the concept diffuses to other places. The example of waterfront revitalisation is a case in point; many projects are similar in structure and character across the world. For many cities seeking to harness tourism, the competition for visitors will intensify in the 1990s as more locations compete for the same market.

Despite these underlying concerns, the growth of structural unemployment has led governments to promote the development of urban tourism, since it may hold many employment opportunities for cities, particularly in those redundant areas which have lost their economic rationale. As a service sector activity, tourism may offer new opportunities for cities seeking to reposition their economies to the reality of the service economy and information age of the 1990s. However, it must be stressed that making an attempt to gauge the likely long-term benefits of tourism development in cities is complicated by the difficulty of measuring the diffuse nature of tourism as an economic activity.

In fact Pearce (1989: 192) argues that 'the objective and detailed evaluation of the economic impact of tourism can be a long and complicated task'. One immediate problem is that there is little agreement within the literature on what constitutes the tourism industry. As Chapter 3 indicates, the sectors which are usually included under the heading of the tourism industry are:

- Accommodation
- Transport
- Attractions
- The travel organisers sector
- Destination organisation sector

while hospitality and ancillary services may also have a role to play. Therefore, one has to agree a working definition of what to include in the category urban tourism industry.

Even once a working definition has been agreed, isolating the flow of income in the local urban tourism economy is notoriously difficult. This is because it is difficult to attribute the proportion of tourist expenditure on goods and services in relation to the total pattern of expenditure by all users of the urban area (e.g. residents, workers and visitors). In practice, one is trying to identify the different forms of tourist expenditure and how it then affects the local economy. However, there are common factors which influence the scale of the impact in urban areas including:

- The nature of the urban area and its 'leisure product', particularly its facilities, physical characteristics and 'secondary elements';
- The volume and scale of tourist expenditure in the particular city;
- The state of the economic development and economy in the individual city;
- The size and nature of the local economy (i.e. is it dependent on services, manufacturing or is it a mixed economy?);
- The extent to which tourist expenditure circulates around the local economy;
- The degree to which the local economy has addressed the problem of seasonality and extended the city's appeal to an all-year-round destination.

On the basis of these factors, it is possible to assess whether the economic impact will be beneficial to the city or if it will have a detrimental effect on its economy. In this respect, it is possible to identify some of the commonly cited economic benefits of tourism for urban areas:

- The generation of income for the local economy
- The creation of new employment opportunities for the city
- Improvements to the structure and balance of economic activities within the locality
- Encouraging entrepreneurial activity.

In contrast, there are also a range of costs commonly associated with urban tourism and these include:

- The potential for economic overdependence on one particular form of activity;
- Inflationary costs in the local economy as new consumers enter the area and potential increases in land prices as the tourism development cycle commences;

- A growing dependence on imported rather than locally produced goods, services and labour as the development of facilities and infrastructure proceeds;
- Seasonality in the consumption and production of tourism services leading to limited returns on investment;
- Leakages of tourism expenditure from the local economy;
- Additional costs for city authorities (e.g. it is estimated that these costs in Canterbury exceed £2 million a year).

Techniques and methodologies used to analyse the economic impact of urban tourism

Cooper *et al.* (1993: 115) argue that 'the measurement of the economic impact of tourism is far more complicated than simply calculating the level of tourist expenditure'. It is important to distinguish between the economic impact derived from tourist expenditure and that due to the development of tourism (e.g. the construction of facilities). Whilst a diverse literature now exists on the economics of tourism (see Bull 1991; Sinclair 1991), there is an absence of specific studies which review and illustrate the economic impact of tourism for specific genre of tourist cities. Murphy (1985) points to the necessity of understanding the tourism economy of localities and the concept of economic cycles, since tourism experiences the following:

Short-term economic cycles

These commonly occur within a one-year time span and reflect the seasonality in demand which destinations and their economies have to accommodate.

Medium-term economic cycles

These are where changes in the circumstances of the tourism market may lead a destination to readjust to conditions occurring over a couple of years. For example, changes in the exchange rate and costs of producing tourism services make specific urban destinations expensive for overseas visitors.

Long-term economic cycles

This is where long-term business cycles become important and the destination is viewed in relation to the product life cycle concept used in marketing and subsequently applied to resort development (Butler 1980). What is suggested is that the long-term economic viability of a destination may follow the growth curve of a new product where it is produced and seeks to establish an identity. If the product is a success with consumers, it gains growing acceptance leading to increased sales and peak production. However, as the number of suppliers increase, the demand for the product, patronage and sales decline and a state of low sales emerges and the product may be replaced or re-launched in a new form to stimulate sales. This principle has also been applied to resort areas to explain their evolution. It is also useful to understand the stage of development of specific urban tourism economies since it will condition the scale, volume and extent of tourist expenditure. Butler's (1980) concept of the resort cycle is extensively documented and reviewed in the tourism literature thus:

> Visitors will come to an area in small numbers initially, restricted by a lack of access, facilities, and local knowledge. As facilities are provided and awareness grows, visitor numbers will increase. With marketing, information dissemination, and further facility provision, the area's popularity will grow rapidly. Eventually, however, the rate of increase in visitor numbers will decline as levels of carrying capacity are reached. . . . As the attractiveness of the area declines relative to other areas, because of overuse and the impacts of visitors, the actual number of visitors may also eventually decline.
>
> (Butler 1980: 6)

Butler's (1980) model is divided into six stages:

1 The 'exploration stage' (e.g. only small numbers of tourists visit the destination);
2 The 'involvement stage' (e.g. the local community provides limited facilities for tourism);
3 The 'development stage' (e.g. rapid tourism growth occurs which corresponds with the same process in the product life cycle);
4 The 'consolidation stage' (e.g. a slower rate of growth, visitor numbers continue to expand and marketing activity is undertaken to maintain market share and to extend the season);
5 The 'stagnation stage' (e.g. peak numbers are reached and economic,

environmental and social problems occur due to pressure on the locality by visitors);

6 'Future options' (e.g. how should the area respond to the future once stagnation has set in? Can a long-term decline be prevented by marketing the unique appeal of the city to visitors? Can a process of rejuvenation be implemented through development of new resources, as in the case of Dover in conjunction with innovative marketing, to promote the city?).

Although such models have limitations in terms of their application to the real world, they do assist in establishing the state of economic development for specific urban tourist destinations. Yet how does one then proceed to establish the economic impacts accruing from tourism within the city's economy? Law (1993) provides a good synthesis of the ways of assessing the economic impact of tourism in large cities. He argues that expenditure information gleaned from visitor surveys together with other published data can be used to establish the following.

Direct expenditure

This is expenditure by tourists on goods and services consumed (e.g. hotels, restaurants and tourist transport services), although this is not a definitive account of expenditure due to leakage of tourist spending to areas and corporations outside the local economy.

Indirect expenditure

Expenditure by visitors which is often estimated by identifying how many tourism enterprises use the income derived from tourists' spending. This spending is then used by enterprises to pay for services, taxes and employees which then recirculates in the urban economy. In other words, tourist expenditure stimulates an economic process which passes through a series of stages (or rounds). Specific forms of economic analysis, such as input–output analysis may be used to identify the types of transactions which occur between tourism businesses to assess how indirect expenditure influences the tourism economy. Input–output analysis may illustrate how the output from each sector of the urban economy contributes to other economic activities or consumption (see

Bull 1991). In this context, it may help to identify the role of tourism in these interactions within the local economy.

The Induced Impact

This is arrived at by calculating the impact of expenditure from those employed in tourism and the effect of the spending in the local economy. On the basis of the direct, indirect and induced impacts, one can produce an estimate of the total impact of tourist spending on the urban economy. These different impacts are indicated in Figure 4.3 where the tourism economy is viewed as an open system which varies according to the degree of penetration by outside interests and quantity of goods imported.

Figure 4.3 is useful as it highlights the interrelationships which exist with the tourism economy of urban areas and the flow of income within the economic system. It also introduces the concept of 'leakage', which occurs due to the taxation of income derived from tourist spending, and loss of expenditure to other areas and economies. Clearly, 'visitor expenditures represent only the first stage of economic impact on a destination community, for like other generators of basic income, tourism's contribution can multiply as the extra income passes throughout an economy' (Murphy 1985: 90).

Tourism multiplier analysis

There is a vast literature which reviews the concept of multiplier analysis (e.g. Archer 1987; Fletcher and Archer 1991), which Mathieson and Wall (1982: 64) define as 'the number, by which initial tourist expenditure must be multiplied in order to obtain the total cumulative income effect for a specified period'. The multiplier concept is 'based on the recognition that the various sectors which make up the economy are interdependent. . . . Therefore, any autonomous change in the level of final demand will not only affect the industry which produces that final good or service, but also that industry's suppliers and the suppliers' suppliers' (Fletcher and Archer 1991: 28). The multiplier is expressed as a ratio which measures those changes, the final demand resulting from the effect of changes in variables such as economic output, income, employment, government revenue and foreign exchange flows (if appropriate). The multiplier ratio (see Cooper *et al.* 1993 for more detail on the formulae used to calculate different types of multipliers), measures

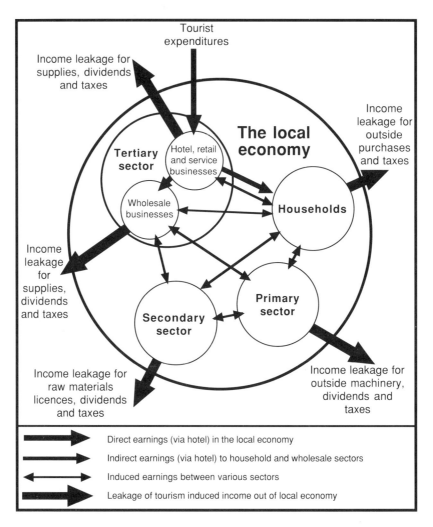

Figure 4.3 The economic impact of tourist spending in an urban area (after Murphy 1985)

the changes to the final demand resulting from the aforementioned changes and expresses the estimate of the total change in output (the output multiplier). A similar value can also be derived to estimate the total change in income (the income multiplier) to illustrate the effect of changes in demand on tourism income. These concepts help to establish

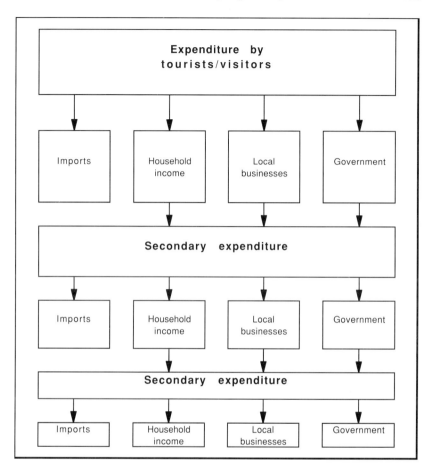

Figure 4.4 How the multiplier process operates (modified from Cooper *et al.* 1993)

the estimated changes in the direct, indirect and induced effects on the tourism economy, resulting from changes in demand.

Figure 4.4 illustrates how the multiplier concept operates from the point at which tourist expenditure is spent in the urban area on goods and services. Leakages occur where imported goods are supplied to meet tourist needs (e.g. food and beverages). Where they are not provided locally, money leaks outside the economy and is not retained within the area. The tourist expenditure which remains after the imports

Table 4.1 Tourism income multipliers for selected urban destinations

Metropolitan Victoria	0.65
British Columbia (Canada)	
Edinburgh	0.35
City of Carlisle	0.40
Great Yarmouth	0.33
Kendal/Keswick	0.28
Towns and villages in Wales	0.18–0.47
UK	1.73

Source: Based on Archer 1982, Murphy 1985 and Pearce 1989

are paid for, is then distributed among various areas of the urban economy (e.g. as household income from employment, to local businesses or is paid to the government as taxes). The tourist expenditure then has an indirect effect on the tourism economy as secondary expenditure and the money continues to circulate through the economy and this process carries on. Thus, income which is re-spent by employers and employees as well as by government stimulates the economy once again.

The actual size of the multiplier reflects the expected economic benefit of tourism to the urban economy: the more self-sufficient a given town's economy, the greater degree of tourist revenue that is retained in the economy. It is widely acknowledged by tourism economists that the national multipliers are larger due to the greater propensity of the national economy to be self-sufficient compared to lower order economic systems (e.g. isolated rural areas). A range of tourism income multipliers reported in the literature are listed in Table 4.1.

Pearce (1989: 208) argues, that while values vary from place to place, there is a certain amount of consistency in similar areas. The higher value for Metropolitan Victoria in Canada may be attributed to the greater degree of interdependence in the regional economy and ability to retain expenditure in a diverse economic system (Var and Quayson 1985).

In contrast, employment multipliers are more difficult to operationalise due to problems in establishing the relationship between employment and its role in tourist expenditure. Employment does not necessarily expand as tourist expenditure increases because it depends on the state of the local economy, the nature of the tourism activity and degree of change in demand. Thus employment multipliers are only an indication of possible full-time employment which may result. Yet it is

Table 4.2 The economic impact of tourism on Merseyside: workforce per £100,000 turnover in selected businesses

Business type	Direct workforce	Secondary workforce	Total
Hotels and guest house	8.3	1.7	10.0
Rented self-catering	19.2	0.9	20.1
Restaurants	6.7	1.1	7.8
Shops	3.6	0.4	4.0
Attractions	8.7	1.6	10.3

Source: Murphy (1985)

not just the number of jobs created, but the type and quality resulting from tourism which are important (Mathieson and Wall 1982). For example, DRV Research (1986) examines the economic impact of tourism in Merseyside and provides data on employment (Table 4.2 summarises the findings).

As Table 4.2 shows, leakage of expenditure in the hotel and guest house sector reduces the beneficial effects on the hotel and guest house sector compared with the rented self-catering sector. Nevertheless, the accommodation sector is labour-intensive compared with other aspects of the tourism economy. However, it is apparent that urban tourism produces three types of employment:

- Direct employment in tourism establishments;
- Indirect employment in the tourism supply sector;
- Induced employment or additional employment as locally-employed residents spend the money earned from the results of tourism-related income circulating in the urban economy.

Although there are a range of useful studies which examine the technical aspects associated with different types of multipliers (e.g. Archer 1987) and their role in economic theory, one can summarise the significance of multipliers in the analysis of the economic impact of urban tourism thus:

- Multiplier analysis helps researchers to measure the present economic performance of the tourism industry and the effect of short-term changes in demand on the urban tourism economy;
- Multipliers may be used to assess the effects of public and private sector investment in urban tourism projects, and who are likely to be the main beneficiaries;

- Multipliers are frequently used to estimate the impact of tourist expenditure on tourism enterprises within cities together with the effect on direct, indirect and induced forms of employment and income.

Case study 5

The economic impact of urban tourism in Wellington, New Zealand

This case study develops and illustrates some of the principles and concepts developed in relation to the assessment of the economic impact of urban tourism within one capital city. Wellington is an interesting example of a large city which is poised to expand its tourism economy in the 1990s once a major new tourism-related project is completed – the National Museum of New Zealand Project. However, to examine the case of Wellington, it is useful to discuss some of the tourism demand and supply issues to place the study in a tourism context.

Tourism in Wellington: demand and supply issues

Tourism research in New Zealand has, to a certain extent, over-looked the role of urban areas and their potential for tourism. Yet urban areas are important generators of both domestic and inter-national tourism. Patterns of international tourist visits in New Zealand are linked to the location of the country's two main tourist 'gateways' – Auckland and Christchurch (Pearce 1987a). While the New Zealand Tourist Department's published statistics on international tourism highlight this relationship, the conse-quences for urban tourist activity patterns have not been ade-quately researched, with a number of exceptions (see Pearce 1987b). Research has tended to focus on the dispersion of tourist activities from these gateways and their geographical distribution throughout the country (Pearce and Elliot 1983; Forer and Pearce 1984). Consequently, the significance of capital city tourism has been neglected as other urban destinations such as Auckland, Christchurch, Queenstown and Rotorua have formed the focus

Case study 5 (*continued*)

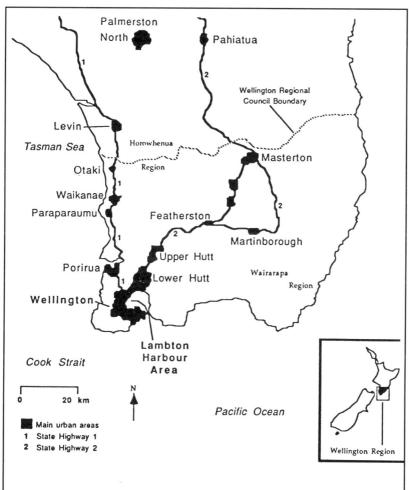

Figure 4.5 The location of Wellington

of research in terms of tourist activities. This is supported by Bywater (1990) who has argued that Wellington is a 'secondary' destination in terms of international and domestic tourism (Figure 4.5).

However, the scale of tourism demand in 1990 resulted in 1.1 million domestic and 253,000 overseas visits, which generated

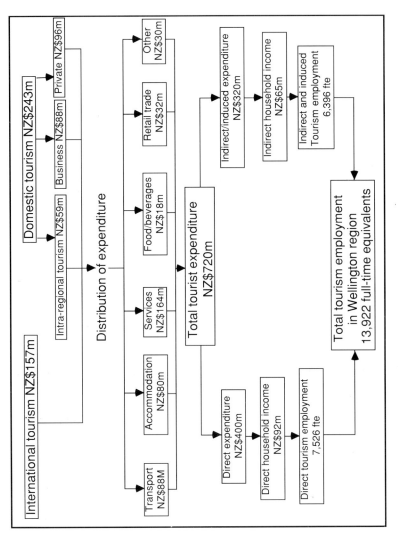

Figure 4.6 The economic impact of tourism in Wellington in 1990

Case study 5 (*continued*)

visitor expenditure of NZ$400.3 million for the urban economy. As Figure 4.6 shows, domestic and international tourist expenditure has a range of economic impacts. Although insufficient data exist to calculate income and employment multipliers for Wellington, it is notable that the direct, indirect and induced effects of tourist expenditure are apparent (Figure 4.6). Tourist motivation for visiting Wellington is partly related to its pivotal and strategic position for land, air and inter-island transportation networks and as a political and cultural centre. This has enabled the city to develop business tourism related to administrative functions of government and the location of many corporate headquarters in the Wellington region which have also generated business tourism. Recent visitor statistics suggest that among international tourists, 53 per cent visit the Wellington region for a holiday, followed by 21 per cent visiting friends and relatives (VFR) and 16 per cent for business with 10 per cent for other reasons (Wellington Regional Council 1991). Among domestic tourists, 38 per cent visit the Wellington region for VFR, 29 per cent for business, 18 per cent for a holiday and 15 per cent for other reasons (Wellington Regional Council 1991). In spatial terms, 70 per cent of domestic tourists' overnight stays are concentrated in the Wellington metropolitan area (Figure 4.5) compared with 95 per cent among overseas visitors. Among the domestic tourists, the wider geographical spread in patterns of visiting and overnight stays are accounted for by their distribution in the Wairarapa and Horowhenua region (Figure 4.5) with its natural environment appeal (e.g. mountains, coastline, rivers and valleys) which attracts unstructured outdoor activities among visitors. Nevertheless, it is central Wellington which has been the main beneficiary of tourism growth, since the majority of business class hotels are located in the 'downtown' area. But tourist use of serviced accommodation in Wellington is mainly short-stay in duration, since non-business travel tends to be based on VFR or transit tourists passing through en route to and from the South Island.

Tourism in central Wellington and its hinterland is based on a

Case study 5 (*continued*)

limited range of attractions and it lacks a variety of purpose-built tourist attractions and year-round events to encourage visitors to include Wellington on their New Zealand itinerary. Although the Wellington region is promoted as the 'Heart of New Zealand', its competitive advantage as a destination located on the international tourist circuit between Auckland and the South Island has not been fully recognised. This is, in part, due to the absence of high order facilities and attractions for tourists to meet the wide ranging needs of visitors. Consequently, the region is not realising its full tourism potential. It is in this context that the National Museum of New Zealand Project is significant. It is a notable project, being the largest state-funded tourism project in progress in New Zealand at a time of declining state involvement in tourism planning and development. It is also likely to provide a major boost to the city's tourism economy.

The National Museum of New Zealand Project

The Museum Project is a major feature associated with the redevelopment of Wellington's former port area. At its peak in the 1960s, Wellington's port was a major focus of economic activity along the city's waterfront. Following the demise and relocation of Wellington's port facilities in the 1970s, 20 ha of land and buildings became redundant on Wellington's waterfront. Although there were discussions and plans for revitalising the waterfront area in the 1970s, it was during the 1980s that Wellington Harbour Board realised the area's commercial and tourism potential if it were comprehensively redeveloped. The Lambton Harbour Development Project (LHDP) was established in 1987 as a partnership between the Wellington Harbour Board and Wellington City Council following parliamentary approval for a joint venture. This was closely followed by a national government's plans to develop a new National Museum (hereafter Museum Project) as one of the key attractions on the waterfront redevelopment. The project was estimated to have a capital cost of NZ$179 million (at 1985 prices) although this has subsequently been increased to NZ$280 million.

Case study 5 (*continued*)

Although the actual commercial development of the Museum Project is separate from the LHDP 'Concept Plan' for the waterfront, it will form the dominant tourism attraction on the waterfront. Future projects planned for the waterfront area include parks, plazas, squares, tourist facilities, shopping complexes, an international hotel, residential and commercial projects (e.g. offices). What forms of funding are available to develop the Museum and what are the principles guiding its development?

The funding, development and planning of the Museum Project were based on a report in 1985 by the National Museum Project Team *Treasures of the Nation: National Museum of New Zealand – A Plan for Development*, which was set up to review the future of the existing National Museum building, opened in 1936. The Project Team report, highlighted the role of the state in funding museums, the arts, heritage and culture. The state is a major contributor to the preservation, conservation and marketing of the nation's heritage, through the Ministry of Arts and Culture. The existing National Art Gallery and Museum are major components of state expenditure and a long-term financial commitment has also been made in relation to the new Museum Project. Given the level of support, one has to question the government's motives for funding the new Museum Project at a time when support for tourism-related activities has been directed towards the private-sector taking a leading role in development issues. Although it is widely acknowledged that the Museum project may assist in promoting the nation's cultural heritage and identity, its economic role was enshrined in the National government's view that the:

> Close interrelationship of arts and cultural activity with social and economic development . . . are necessary ingredients for economic development. There is a strong argument for the government's involvement in the arts and cultural area on economic grounds alone.
>
> (Department of Internal Affairs 1989:iii)

The Museum plans to open in 1998. The scale of the project may have considerable immediate and long-term economic benefits

Case study 5 (*continued*)

from tourism development in Wellington. These can be summarised as follows:

• An extension of the length of stay of international visitors in
  Wellington and New Zealand;
• An increase in GDP of up to NZ$21 million by the year 2025;
• A high potential rate of job creation as every NZ$100 million of
  tourist expenditure currently contributes to 2,930 direct and
  indirect tourist related jobs;
• The Museum Project is expected to employ 150 consultants and
  1,000 construction workers during the design and construction
  phase;
• The Museum Project will employ 260 staff and a further 100
  auxiliary staff once it is fully operational;
• By 1998, 440 extra jobs are expected to be generated by
  Museum-related activities, rising to 750 by the year 2010. The
  highest forecasts of jobs likely to be created by the year 2010
  have suggested up to 1,400 extra jobs may be created.

The expectation is that the Museum Project could have a direct
tourism benefit of NZ$23.3 million in 1999–2000, thereby provid-
ing a net addition to GDP from tourism expenditure of NZ$14
million in 1999–2000. These monetary benefits are also, of course,
complemented by educational and cultural benefits. The Museum
experience will be memorable and it will have important implications for heritage tourism in Wellington in the 1990s. The
Museum Project could be used to create a theme to unify tourism
promotion and marketing in the Wellington region based on urban
heritage and cultural tourism. For Wellington City Council and the
Regional Council it is an opportunity to develop a quality tourism
experience for discerning visitors.

The social and cultural impact of urban tourism

In recent years there has been a recognition by academics and community groups that the development of tourism in urban areas not only

leads to economic impacts, but also results in less visible and more intangible effects (Murphy 1985). Whilst economic impacts may be measured and quantified to identify financial and employment effects, social and cultural impacts on visitors and host communities in urban areas are often only considered when tourism development leads to local opposition. For example, in London's Central Tourism District, the effect of hotel development and tourism development in the late 1960s and 1970s, promoted by grant assistance from the English Tourist Board, resulted in the imposition of local authority planning restraints. These were a response to local community opposition to the urban nuisances and impacts of tourists on the locality (Eversley 1977; Page and Sinclair 1989). Therefore, it is important to understand the types of social and cultural impacts which result from tourism to try and avoid negative effects and conflicts in urban areas, between the host community and visitors. Otherwise the 'tourist experience' may be tainted by underlying conflicts and an unwelcoming attitude towards tourists which will ultimately erode the destination's popularity and competitive position. What is meant by the social and cultural impact of tourism?

According to Fox (1977), cited in Mathieson and Wall (1982: 133):

> The social and cultural impacts of tourism are the ways in which tourism is contributing to changes in value systems, individual behaviour, family relationships, collective lifestyles, safety levels, moral conduct, creative expressions, traditional ceremonies and community organisations.

These they identify as 'people impacts', impacts due to the effect of tourists on host communities and the interaction between these two groups. In other words, the analysis of social and cultural impacts of urban tourism involves the analysis of:

- *The tourist*, especially his or her demand for services, their attitudes, expectations and activity patterns within cities;
- *The host*, particularly their role and attitude towards the provision of services for tourists and their concerns for the impact of visitors on the traditional way of life in the locality;
- *The relationship between tourists and hosts*, and the type of contact which occurs between these two groups and the outcome for each group.

The most notable study to analyse these relationships is Smith's (1989) *Hosts and Guests: The Anthropology of Tourism* which contains an

Table 4.3 Types of tourists and their adaptation to local norms

Type of tourist	Numbers of tourists	Adaptation to local norms
Explorer	Very limited	Accepts fully
Elite	Rarely seen	Adapts fully
Off-beat	Uncommon but seen	Adapts well
Unusual	Occasional	Adapts somewhat
Incipient mass	Steady flow	Seeks Western amenities
Mass	Continuous influx	Expects Western amenities
Charter	Massive arrivals	Demands Western amenities

Source: Based on V.L. Smith (1989) cited in Pearce (1989)

interesting range of studies of the effect of imported tourist culture on host communities. For example, V.L. Smith (1989) notes that the type of tourist visiting a destination is an important precondition for their ability to adapt to local norms. Table 4.3 indicates, that while certain cultural, linguistic and educational barriers inhibit the interaction and integration of tourists into a local community, this varies according to the volume of visitors and their expectations. Although this typology has less importance to large urban areas and integrated resort complexes where visitors are effectively segregated from the local community, the expectations of service provision is a critical factor.

UNESCO (1976) focuses on the nature of tourist/host relationships where mass tourism develops which is significant for urban destinations with their capacity to absorb large numbers of mass tourists due to the diversity of attractions and activities available for visitors. UNESCO (1976) recognises that the host/guest relationship is:

Transitory in nature

This is because most tourist visits to urban areas are short in duration and are also artificial if spent in a hotel where non-local staff are employed who are usually expected to speak the language of visitors.

Limited in time and space

A situation which is especially so when the visitor is on a short break to an urban area. This often leads to distinctive forms of visitor behaviour. For example, visitors may seek to maximise the time available by high spending an activities and tourist services. The geographical concentration of tourist accommodation and attractions in the tourism business district (TBD, see Chapter 3) may also isolate the visitor from interaction with local residents even though they experience the effects of tourist congestion in shopping areas used by visitors in the peak season.

Often lacking in spontaneity

This is particularly true of relationships in an urban context. Where package and organised itineraries are used by tourists, these lead to formal, commercialised and contractual relationships between the tourist and service providers, removing the opportunity for spontaneous interaction between visitors and the tourist service worker.

Unequal and unbalanced

For the tourist, the experience of an urban destination is one based on an image of the place as a novel and exciting opportunity. Yet for the tourist worker, it is often a routine, mundane and regulated experience. There are often material differences between the affluence of visitors and the spending patterns and the relatively low levels of remuneration of workers undertaking tourism service tasks. Such relationships may lead to resentment among workers and residents in extreme cases. Pearce (1989) provides a range of specific social and cultural impacts based on research in Spain by Figuerola (1976) which can be modified to incorporate the effects on the host population in urban areas which includes the following.

Migration

This is the impact on the population structure of urban areas due to rural and urban migration to secure employment in service industries with the prospect of higher income levels than from rural occupations. This may often modify the age and sex structure of the destination.

Occupational structure

This covers the transformation of the occupational structure of the urban area, especially with the increasing emphasis on qualifications and language skills for managerial occupations and the demand for low paid and unskilled female labour for seasonal employment in hotels, attractions and the hospitality sector.

The transformation of political values

This is the situation where urban lifestyles among tourism workers replace more conservative rural attitudes with a greater disposition towards a new way of life. Social values also change as high levels of population turnover limit the opportunities to develop long-term social relationships. This is also complicated by the seasonal patterns of employment and the long hours and shift systems. However, for young temporary workers, this may be a positive attraction with the opportunity to live in a more cosmopolitan environment.

Changes to the social and moral behaviour of the host population

This impact is a controversial and much debated one in the context of prostitution, religion, crime and gambling. In the case of prostitution, tourism in urban areas does not necessarily lead to its development but may change its nature. Nevertheless, it displays a distinctive urban form in tourist cities (see Ashworth *et al.* 1988). The issue of religion, however, is more complex to analyse as some forms of urban tourism have developed for spiritual reasons (see Chapter 2). In other circumstances, the Church has exploited tourism by charging admission to cathedrals, shrines and churches. Likewise, the literature on urban tourism and crime is inconclusive as to whether tourism stimulates an increase in crime against visitors. Gambling, while not directly related to urban tourism development in most countries, has led to the expansion and fame of destinations such as Las Vegas, Monte Carlo and Atlantic City. Governments have examined its potential to revitalise declining tourist resorts and to stimulate economic activity, employment and tax revenue as in the case of New Zealand (Leiper 1990).

Native language

The use of native language appears to experience a decline in urban areas once migrants gain employment in hotels, and where face to face contact with tourists requires the use of international languages such as French and English (see White 1974).

Impact of the culture of the host population

This impact, is the 'behaviour as observed through social relations and material artefacts . . . [and] . . . in a deeper anthropological sense, includes patterns, norms, rules and standards which find expression in behaviour, social relations and artefacts' (Mathieson and Wall 1982: 158) since culture attracts visitors to urban destinations. Examples of the attraction of culture for urban tourists includes the arts, music, history and heritage, architecture, leisure activities and festivals. Not surprisingly, certain cities have developed cultural strategies to promote these attributes (e.g. Glasgow, Sheffield and Liverpool in the UK) since culture is viewed as a symbol of civility in urban living and a necessary feature to attract the new generation of professional workers to cities (see Page 1993a). However, the exploitation of urban culture may help in urban revitalisation but the local culture may be commodified, packaged and distorted in the pursuit of mass tourist consumption. Such criticisms have been levelled at the 1980s heritage centres developed in cities such as the Canterbury Tales (Canterbury), the Jorvik Viking Centre (York) and White Cliffs Experience (Dover) (see Chapter 3) which turn local history and heritage into a form of entertainment.

Patterns of consumption

Lastly, urban tourism may require residents to modify their own patterns of consumption due to inflationary pressures induced by mass tourism. Many of these impacts have been observed in the literature on the social and cultural impact of tourism, and a range of methodologies have been developed to analyse these impacts.

Analysing the social and cultural impact of urban tourism

As research on the impact of tourism has developed, different methodologies have been proposed to analyse the social and cultural impact (Smith 1989). The most commonly used approach is the social survey technique which examines the analysis, the attitudes and feelings of residents by means of closed and open-ended questions. For example, a recent visitor survey by Oxford City Council *et al.* (1992) employed this technique, using a sample of households and surveys undertaken at the resident's house to gain a representative survey of all districts. While a wide range of studies have been undertaken on the social impact, few have considered the cultural implications of urban tourism. For this reason, attention focuses on two studies by Doxey (1976) and Bjorklund and Philbrick (1975).

Doxey's Index of Tourist Irritation (Irridex)

Doxey (1976) developed his 'Irridex' to illustrate how the interaction of tourists and residents may be converted into different degrees of irritation. Using observations from the West Indies and Canada, Doxey (1976) argued that residents responses will change in a predictable manner, passing through four stages – euphoria, apathy, annoyance and antagonism (Figure 4.7). Doxey's (1976) index assumes that large numbers of visitors cause tensions and ultimately leads to antagonism. Yet it overlooks situations where such numbers of visitors do not ultimately lead to this situation (e.g. Garland and West 1985). It is also a unidirectional model that does not permit destinations to pass back to a situation where annoyance may be reduced by sensitive visitor management schemes. Garland and West (1985: 35) place resident irritation with tourists in context as 'host irritation with the presence of tourists in Rotorua is just that – irritation, and then only among small proportions of residents'. More recently Ap and Crompton (1993) proposed an alternative model (Figure 4.8) to assess resident attitudes to tourism while Lankford and Howard (1994) examined a multiple item tourism impact scale to assess this issue.

In contrast, Bjorklund and Philbrick's (1975) model of host attitudinal/behavioural responses to tourism suggests that a matrix characterises the attitudes and behaviour of the groups/individuals towards tourism (Figure 4.9). It suggests that attitudes reflect an active or passive approach and a negative or positive attitude towards tourism. Such a framework has a number of features which are useful in understanding the social impact of tourism in a locality. Firstly, it can accommodate the diversity of the community and different interests of the local population, including the attitudes of community groups, public providers/administrators, entrepreneurs and residents. Secondly, it does not assume that residents and the local population will progress through a series of stages. The framework is dynamic and allows for different individuals/groups to be located at various points on the matrix depending on their views on tourism. However, as Butler (cited in Mathieson and Wall 1982: 139–40) notes, 'the majority of the population is likely to fall into the two passive categories, either silently accepting tourism and

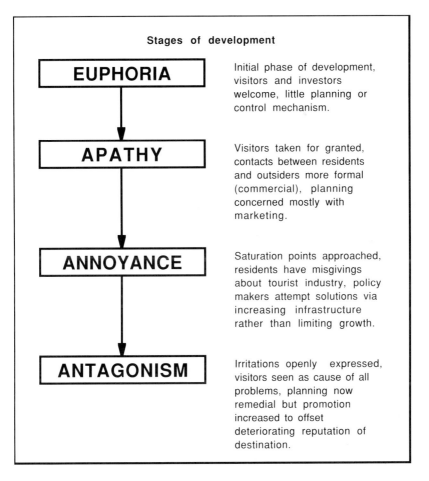

Stages of development

EUPHORIA	Initial phase of development, visitors and investors welcome, little planning or control mechanism.
APATHY	Visitors taken for granted, contacts between residents and outsiders more formal (commercial), planning concerned mostly with marketing.
ANNOYANCE	Saturation points approached, residents have misgivings about tourist industry, policy makers attempt solutions via increasing infrastructure rather than limiting growth.
ANTAGONISM	Irritations openly expressed, visitors seen as cause of all problems, planning now remedial but promotion increased to offset deteriorating reputation of destination.

Figure 4.7 Doxey's Irridex index of resident attitudes to tourism

its impacts because of the benefits it brings or because they can see no way of reversing the trend'.

One of the most useful studies to illustrate the social and cultural (as well as the economic and environmental) impact of urban tourism is Cant's (1980) study of Queenstown, New Zealand. Although it is now rather dated, the study examines a small town of 1,759 inhabitants which received up to 180,000 visitors a year. As part of a UNESCO project, the study examined the impact of tourism as viewed by

Embracement:	Residents eagerly welcome tourists.
Tolerance:	Residents show a degree of ambivalence towards tourism (there were elements of tourism they liked or disliked).
Adjustment:	Residents adjusted to tourism, often by rescheduling activities to avoid crowds.
Withdrawal:	In this context, residents withdrew temporarily from the community.

NB: All four strategies are likely to be adopted concurrently, since in any community there are going to be different reactions to tourism. The strategies and behaviour adopted by individuals and groups of residents need to be viewed in relation to thresholds and tourism impacts.

Figure 4.8 Resident attitudes to tourism (after Ap and Crompton 1993)

residents in the host community, which was complemented by structural interviews and small discussion groups. Although the consensus of the community was that it had not suffered from the impact of tourism development, a number of specific pressures existed:

- The pace of life had become much quicker;
- Some of the population adapted to the new pace of life and others withdrew from situations which did not suit them;
- There was a narrow range of low cost entertainment of a suitable nature for local families;
- Pressures associated with the number of people and vehicles in the central area of Queenstown in the peak season.

In addition, the study noted the existence of:

- A more transient population, making it more difficult to establish stable social relationships;
- High costs associated with the provision of public utilities reflected in the increase in property rates.

Even so, most households in Queenstown felt, on balance, that they were materially better off because of the changes induced by tourism. The study also considers attitudes to further tourism development with households more cautious about endorsing uncontrolled expansion in

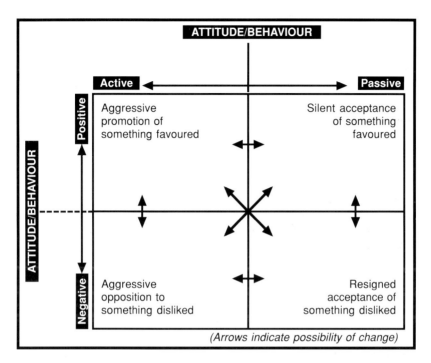

Figure 4.9 Attitudinal/behavioural attributes to inter-cultural perception based on Bjorklund and Philbrick (after Murphy 1985)

the future. Their consensus was that previous expansion in tourism 'had been too rapid and that future growth should be slower and more carefully planned' (Cant 1980: 96).

The environmental impact of urban tourism

The environmental dimension is assuming a growing significance as a research area in tourism studies. Dowling (1992) provides a useful synthesis of how interest in the relationship between tourism and the environment has developed over the last forty years.

In the 1950s it was viewed as being one of coexistence. . . . However, with the advent of mass tourism in the 1960s, increasing pressure was put on natural areas for tourism developments. Together with the growing environmental awareness and concerns of the early 1970s the relationship was perceived to be in conflict. During the next decade this view was endorsed by many others . . . at the same time a new suggestion was emerging that the relationship could be beneficial to both tourism and the environment.

(Dowling 1992: 33)

The recent concern for a sustainable approach towards tourism development, to ensure its long-term viability as an economic activity, is reflected in the recent government task force in the UK, formed in 1990 to find solutions to the impact of tourism on the environment (English Tourist Board/Employment Department 1991). The task force was charged with establishing the scale and nature of environmental problems induced by mass tourism at major tourist sites. It was also required to draw up guidelines on how such problems were to be addressed while maintaining the resource-base for tourism activities. The study examines case studies of historic towns, heritage sites and resort areas which fall within the remit of urban tourism and notes common problems resulting from tourism, including: wear and tear on the urban fabric; overcrowding and social and cultural impacts between the visitors and local communities. The recent development of the *Journal of Sustainable Tourism* also reflects the increasing awareness that tourism needs to develop in harmony with the environment in a symbiotic manner.

Shaw and Williams (1992) provide a useful insight into the environmental implications of tourism development for urban areas. They report on the existing view within the literature that tourism–environment impacts have been viewed along a continuum where impacts may be minimal or positive in inner city areas, but assume a growing negative impact as one moves through a range of other tourism environments from old coastal resorts to urban historic areas to natural coastal and rural areas. They argue that in some urban environments, where past industrial processes have damaged the environment (e.g. former inner city and dock areas), tourism can actually enhance the environmental quality (Department of the Environment 1990). This is particularly the case where tourism is used to regenerate entire inner city districts and redundant spaces in cities (Law 1993).

Nevertheless, it is widely acknowledged that research on the environmental impact of tourism has generally neglected urban areas, although if purpose-built tourist resorts are considered as a form of urban tourism, then these localities have received a specialised treatment in the tourism literature. Much of the concern has been on *after the event* studies which consider the consequences of coastal resort development, such as that along the Mediterranean coastline or newly developed South East Asian beach resorts. Here the emphasis has been on the environmental damage and consequences of development, as the landscapes have been modified to meet the needs of the tourism industry, with urban development resulting from the economic needs of the industry to concentrate activity in urban agglomerations. Herein lie the main problems in assessing the environmental impact of tourism:

• Baseline information is needed on the environment prior to, and during the development of tourism, and;
• The impact attributable to tourism has to be identified and separated from non-tourism impacts, but this is less than straightforward due to the complex interrelationships that exist between different activities within urban areas.

One useful methodology used by environmental scientists and geographers to assess the future impact of specific tourism projects is EA which, as mentioned earlier, requires the establishment of a baseline study to monitor the effects of specific tourism projects (e.g. the impact of the Channel Tunnel on the environment in and around the main rail terminus at Waterloo and wider afield in London – see Page and Sinclair 1992 for a discussion of some of the likely effects of tourism). In view of the specialised nature of this environmental methodology and its increasing use in relation to major tourism projects, a number of good reviews and examples exist which explain how it is undertaken and its methodological basis (see Page 1992; Goodenough and Page 1994; Green and Hunter 1992) which need not be discussed here.

Mathieson and Wall (1982) offer a number of insights into the environmental problems associated with tourism in resort areas which are also relevant for other urban areas. The impacts are related to:

• Architectural pollution due to the effect of inappropriate hotel development on the traditional landscape;
• The effect of ribbon development and urban sprawl in the absence of planning and development restrictions (e.g. the resorts of Buggiba and Quawra on the island of Malta have now merged, forming one zone of continuous urban tourist development);

- The resort infrastructure becomes overloaded and breaks down in periods of peak usage;
- Tourists become segregated from local residents (though this may not necessarily be a problem);
- Good quality agricultural land may be lost to urban tourist development due to the inflationary effect on land prices which encourages land owners to sell to developers;
- Traffic congestion may result in urban resort areas (see Schaer 1978);
- Pollution of the local ecosystem from sewage, litter and too many visitors in the peak season may also pose serious problems for the destination.

Even where integrated tourist development occurs in a planned manner (e.g. Disneyland in California) many environmental problems remain as a permanent cost for developing tourism. Green and Hunter's (1992) assessment of environmental impacts caused by tourism provides a useful insight into the specific environmental impacts associated with tourism. Table 4.4 summarises some of the impacts which shows that urban tourism *may* lead to changes in the:

- Urban environment and its physical characteristics;
- Visual impact of the environment;
- Requirements for urban infrastructure;
- Urban forms;
- Restoration of specific features in the historical and cultural environment;
- Competition from other urban destinations, possibly leading to a decline in the quality of the urban environment.

How do we assess whether the urban environmental quality for visitors has been eroded to such an extent that the long-term viability of tourism is threatened? One useful concept used by researchers is 'carrying capacity'.

Carrying capacity

Mathieson and Wall (1982: 21) describe carrying capacity as 'the maximum number of people who can use a site [or area] without an unacceptable alteration in the physical environment and without an unacceptable decline in the quality of the experience gained by visitors'. Such a concept has been used to measure the capacity for tourism in

Table 4.4 The impact of tourism on the urban environment

1 The urban environment
 - land lost through development which may have been used for agriculture
 - change to the hydrological system

2 Visual impact
 - expansion of the built area
 - the effect of new architectural styles
 - population growth

3 Infrastructure
 - overloading the urban infrastructure with the following utilities and developments:

   - roads
   - railways
   - car parking
   - the electricity grid
   - waste disposal and water supply

 - provision of new infrastructure
 - additional environmental management measures to accommodate tourists and adapt areas for tourist use

4 Urban form
 - changes to the land use as residential areas see hotels/boarding houses develop
 - alterations to the urban-fabric from pedestrianisation and traffic management schemes to accommodate tourists
 - changes to the built environment lead to contrasts in the quality of the urban areas used by tourists and residential areas

5 Restoration
 - the reuse of redundant buildings
 - the restoration and preservation of historic sites and buildings

natural and man-made tourism environments, making it suitable for use in an urban context. While the literature on carrying capacity has been extensively reviewed in other studies and need not be reiterated here, three principle elements can be discerned in an urban context. According to van der Borg and Costa (1993: 7) the tourist carrying capacity in urban areas comprises the following three elements.

The physical (or ecological) carrying capacity

This is the limit at which the number of visitors can be accommodated at maximum stress. Beyond this threshold, the cultural, historical and built environment is irreparably damaged by tourism.

The economic carrying capacity

This is the limit beyond which the quality of the tourists' experience of the urban area falls and makes it less attractive to visit as a destination;

The social carrying capacity

This is the number of visitors a city can absorb without adversely affecting the other social and economic activities in the city which underpin its rationale for existence. These components of the carrying capacity of sites or areas have become notoriously difficult to calculate. For example, what degree of environmental modification is acceptable to tourists before the visitor experience is affected? Cynics argue that the carrying capacity can only be established retrospectively, once it has been exceeded. Nevertheless, research by Canestrelli and Costa (1991) and van der Borg (1991) has attempted to establish the environmental impact of tourism in Venice using this approach.

Case study 6

The environmental impact of tourism in Venice

Venice is an internationally renowned tourist destination and a fine example of a small historic city, with its cultural antiquities and highly acclaimed fifteenth century Renaissance art. Venice is located on a series of islands in a lagoon, and is the capital of the Veneto region of Italy (Figure 4.10), which has experienced massive economic growth since the 1960s. However, the historic city of Venice experienced continued population loss during this period, dropping from 175,000 in 1951 to 78,000 in 1990. The age and condition of many of Venice's buildings are under constant threat. The environment in Venice is suffering from:

- A sinking ground level;
- A rising sea level;
- Pollution of the lagoon in which it is located;
- Atmospheric pollution.

One can also add to a further category to these environmental problems – tourism.

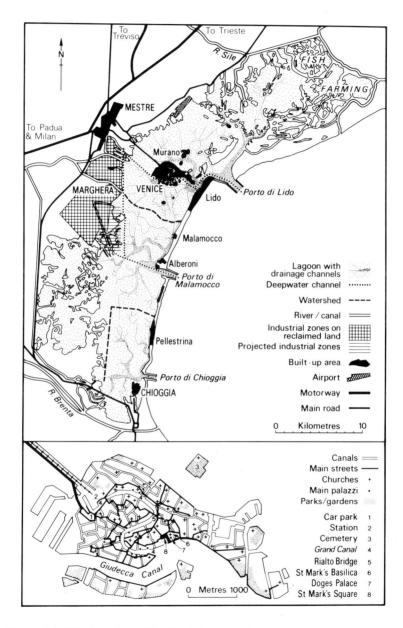

Figure 4.10 The location of Venice (after King 1987, reproduced by kind permission from Paul Chapman Publishing)

Case study 6 (*continued*)

As a tourist destination, visitor arrivals have developed from 50,000 tourists spending 1.2 million bednights in the historic city of Venice in 1952. By 1987 these figures had risen to 1.13 million tourist arrivals and 2.49 million bednights. These visitor numbers are swelled by a large day-visitor market from other parts of Italy, especially the Adriatic beach resorts and Alpine areas. In 1987, the day tripper market was estimated to be 4.9 million visitors providing a total market in excess of 6 million visitors a year. While the demand and supply of urban tourism in Venice is extensively documented by van der Borg (1991), and van der Borg and Costa (1993), it is Canestrelli and Costa's (1991) attempt to calculate the carrying capacity using a mathematical model – linear programming – which offers a number of insights into the carrying capacity of Venice as a tourist destination.

Venice's carrying capacity

To assess the carrying capacity of the historic centre of Venice, Canestrelli and Costa (1991) established:

- The historic centre of Venice comprises 700 ha, with buildings protected from alterations by government legislation;
- The resident population and extent of daily commuting into and out of the city;
- The optimal use level of the destination using a range of variables such as supporting facilities (e.g. hotels, restaurants and parking spaces) and those variables describing the nature of the users (e.g. categories of tourist);
- The local tourist-dependent and non-tourist dependent population in the locality and the theoretical relationship which exists between tourists and these two sub-groups. Each group also seeks to maximise their own position. For example, the tourist-dependant population will seek to push the tourist carrying capacity up as they derive economic benefits from visitor spending, but residents not dependent on tourism are likely to try and minimise the number of visitors to reduce the costs of tourism.

Case study 6 (*continued*)

Using a linear programming technique (see Canestrelli and Costa 1991 for full details of the mathematical model and its application), the optimal growth of Venice as a tourist destination was explored. According to Canestrelli and Costa (1991) the optimal carrying capacity for the historic city of Venice would be to admit *9,780 tourists* who use hotel accommodation, *1,460 tourists staying in non-hotel accommodation* and *10,857 day trippers* on a *daily basis*. One important consideration is that tourism demand is seasonal, although less so for urban destinations with their all-year-round attractions. Nevertheless, if the 4.1 million day trippers who visit Venice were evenly spread this would still amount to 11,233 trippers a day. In fact research has estimated that an average of 37,500 day trippers a day visit Venice in August. Canestrelli and Costa (1991) argue that a ceiling of *25,000 visitors a day* is the maximum *carrying capacity* for Venice. This has important implications for the envionment and its long-term preservation if the carrying capacity is being exceeded. Obviously, the ecological and economic carrying capacity are likely to have slightly different values, but the 25,000 threshold provides an indication of the scale of tourism that is desirable in an ideal world. Yet the reality of the situation is very different: van der Borg and Costa (1993) observe that in 1987, on *156 days a year* this number was exceeded. On 22 occasions *40,000 visitors a day* visited Venice and on *6 days the visitor numbers exceeded 60,000*. So what are the implications for the future?

According to a variety of tourism forecasts produced by van der Borg (1992) for the year 2000, the critical threshold of *25,000 visitors will be exceeded on 216 days* and on *7 days the visitor numbers will exceed 100,000* if the current growth rate in arrivals continues. In fact when 100,000 visitors fill the city, the local police close the bridge connecting the historic centre with the mainland for safety reasons. But the large volume of visitors which descend on Venice each year not only exceeds the desirable limits of tourism for the city, but also poses a range of social and economic problems for planners. As van der Borg observes:

Case study 6 (*continued*)

> The negative external effects connected with the overloading of the carrying capacity are rapidly increasing, frustrating the centre's economy and society . . . excursionism [day tripping] is becoming increasingly important, while residential tourism is losing relevance for the local tourism market . . . [and] . . . the local benefits are diminishing. Tourism is becoming increasingly ineffective for Venice.
>
> (van der Borg 1992: 52)

Thus, the negative impact of tourism on the historic centre of Venice is now resulting in a self-enforcing decline as excursionists, who contribute less to the local tourism economy than staying visitors, supplant the staying market as it becomes less attractive to stay in the city. Ironically, changing the attitude of the city's tourism policy-makers is difficult: it is heavily influenced by the pro-tourism lobby while hotel owners have sought to get the city council to restrict the booming eastern European day trip market which contributes little to the tourism economy. A number of positive measures have been enacted to address the saturation of the historic city by day visitors including:

- Denying access to the city by unauthorised tour coaches via the main coach terminal;
- Withdrawing Venice and Veneto region's bid for EXPO 2000.

Even so, the city continues to promote the destination thereby alienating the local population. A range of positive steps are needed to provide a more rational basis for the future development and promotion of tourism in the 1990s (see van der Borg 1992 for more details).

Clearly, Venice is a small historic city under siege from a new marauding army in the late twentieth century: the tourist and excursionist. In this case, tourism *has not* been a stimulus for urban growth, but has actually contributed to urban decline as residents have continued to leave. The excessive numbers of day trippers have also led to a deterioration in the quality of the tourist experience. This case study is significant in that it highlights the

Case study 6 (*continued*)

> prevailing problems affecting many historic cities around the world, especially those in Europe. But it takes political will to embark on a decision-making process which will address the pressures posed by tourism in Venice.

The carrying capacity of any tourist city needs to be carefully examined and if quantitative techniques, such as linear programming, help to establish an independent and authoritative basis for future planning, then they are a useful starting point in helping to reach a symbiotic balance between tourism and the urban environment. Otherwise a situation may develop which is characterised by conflict. The management of the environment of tourist cities is equally as important as in sensitive rural environments even though urban areas have attracted less attention among researchers. The conclusions of the *Tourism and the Environment: Maintaining the Balance* report indicate that in some environments, their recommendations for the management of tourism (Table 4.5) may offer a way forward although the particular requirements of each urban location need to be considered to develop an appropriate solution for each city.

Conclusion

This chapter has shown that the impact of tourism on urban destinations is far more complex than has hitherto been considered in the literature. Identifying the complex relationship between the costs and benefits of tourism in different cities is far from straightforward, with the economic benefits tending to overshadow the social, cultural and environmental impacts. Even the case study of Venice illustrates that researchers tend to focus more on the economic and social carrying capacity of cities than the more complex environmental dimensions of tourism impacts. The tendency for many city authorities to hail tourism as a solution to their many economic problems may be short-term expediency, as unplanned tourism development can bring as many problems as it purports to solve. Hall's (1970: 445) prediction that 'the age of mass tourism is the biggest single factor for change in the great capitals of Europe – and in many of smaller historic towns and cities too – in the last 30 years of this

Table 4.5 The management of tourism–environment problems

Key issues

1 Improved management information, including:
   - Visitor surveys
   - Site surveys (to assess carrying capacity)
   - systematic monitoring

2 Effective co-ordination, including:
   - a partnership approach to tourism
   - a greater emphasis on tourism development action programmes (TDAPs)
   - Town centre management schemes

3 Adequate resourcing, including
   - a greater integration of the public and private sector in funding tourism projects

Practical management approaches

These include:

   - the assessment of capacity
   - tourist-transport management
   - marketing and information provision
   - conservation and adaptation of tourist activities to suit the environment
   - a greater concern for design principles and the control of tourism development
   - a greater involvement of the local community (e.g. community planning)

Source: Modified from English Tourist Board/Employment Department (1991) *Tourism and the Environment*

century' still remains a valid assessment of the situation now facing many urban areas. In fact many small historic cities are now facing so many pressures from urban tourism that they are taking radical steps to try and limit tourism development and visitor numbers, often under the guise of sustainable development. As Chapters 6 and 7 will show, marketing and visitor management strategies are key issues for many locations seeking to reduce the overwhelming impact of mass tourism. In the UK the English Tourist Board and Employment Department's (1990) *Tourism and the Environment: Maintaining the Balance* report documents many of these problems although they are not just confined to small historic towns and cities. It is clear from the issues discussed in this chapter and the detailed case studies, that tourism planning and development needs to be carefully considered if the benefits of tourism are to be maximised and the problems minimised. For this reason, the next chapter considers the issue of tourism planning in urban areas and the objectives and goals which public sector planners have to meet in the context of tourism.

Questions

1 What are the problems associated with tourism impact analysis in urban areas?
2 To what extent can multiplier analysis be used to calculate an approximate measure of tourism's economic impact on a city?
3 'The environmental impact of urban tourism is impossible to assess due to the absence of a workable research methodology'. Discuss.
4 How should Venice develop its tourism industry in the 1990s?

Further reading

Since this is a large chapter covering a range of impacts, the following references will be of help for specific impacts:

Ap, J. and Crompton, J.L. (1993) 'Residents strategies' for responding to tourism impacts', *Journal of Travel Research* 32(1): 47–50.

This is a very useful article which causes one to rethink the arguments put forward by Doxey and should be read in combination with P. Pearce's article listed below.

Archer, B. and Cooper, C. (1994) 'The positive and negative impacts of tourism', in W. Theobald (ed.) *Global Tourism: The Next Decade*, Oxford: Butterworth-Heinemann: 73–91.

This is an up to date, though somewhat general, discussion of the impact of tourism.

Glasson, J. (1994) 'Oxford: a heritage city under pressure', *Tourism Management* 15 (2): 137–44

This provides a good overview of the range of impacts facing a small historic city – Oxford.

King, R. (1987) *Italy*, London: Harper & Row.

This contains a very good insight into the range of problems facing Venice.

Mathieson, A. and Wall, G. (1982) *Tourism: Economic, Physical and Social Impacts*, London: Longman.

Although this is a dated book, it still provides one of the most comprehensive reviews of the impact of tourism.

Oxford City Council, Thames and Chiltern Tourist Board and Oxford and District Chamber of Trade (1992) *Oxford Visitor Study 1990–91: Final Report*, Oxford: Oxford Centre for Tourism and Leisure Studies, Oxford Brookes University.

This contains a survey on the social impact of tourism in Oxford, focusing on residents' views.

Pearce, D.G. (1989) *Tourist Development*, London: Longman.

This book contains a good analysis of the impact of tourism in the context of tourism development and should be read in conjunction with Mathieson and Wall (1982).

Pearce, P. (1994) 'Tourism-resident impacts: examples, explanations and emerging solutions', in W. Theobald (ed.) *Global Tourism: The Next Decade*, Oxford: Butterworth-Heinemann: 103–23.

This is an up-to-date assessment of the social and cultural impact of tourism.

Williams, P. and Gill, A. (1994) 'Tourism carrying capacity management issues', in W. Theobald (ed.) *Global Tourism: The Next Decade*, Oxford: Butterworth-Heinemann: 174–87.

This is a good up-to-date analysis of the concept of carrying capacity and its management implications for tourism.

5
The management and planning of urban tourism

Introduction

For urban tourism to operate in an efficient and organised manner, its existing and future development needs to be viewed in a systems framework to understand the inputs and outputs, even if some of the linkages between elements are rather tenuous (see Getz 1986; Haywood 1992). By understanding the relationships which exist between the inputs and outputs within the urban tourism system, it is possible for policy-makers and planners to influence elements within the urban system, and to take action to ensure that the benefits accruing from tourism are not outweighed by its costs. Since tourism development is extensively documented in the literature, and the conflicts and effect of the development cycle on urban tourism are dealt with in Haywood (1992) and Pearce (1989), these do not feature in this chapter. The development of tourism in cities does, however, have important implications for urban management and planning. While some destinations have flourished with little formal management and planning, the long-term consequences of failing to plan for the future development of urban tourism has often led to insurmountable problems for some localities. A failure to plan for tourism could result in tourism becoming an unwieldy and unmanageable phenomenon which is virtually impossible to control. Thus, the process of urban management and planning is an important prerequisite for the effective functioning of the tourism system in cities which are predisposed towards tourism development (Haywood 1992).

Urban tourism destinations exist and function in a constantly chang-ing business environment as tourism is a dynamic and ever-changing economic activity. For this reason, it is necessary for planners and managers in the public and private sector to understand how different inputs   in
the urban system will affect the existing and future 'tourism experience' (the output). However, Leiper (1990) argues many tourism systems are 'open', meaning that they are affected by environmental factors and managers play a smaller part in controlling the system: the urban tourism system is no exception to this. Thus, urban managers and planners need to constantly assess the city's position as a tourist destina-tion in the changing business environment of the 1990s to take immedi-ate and strategic action to ensure the locality retains its competitive position *vis à vis* other destinations. Clearly, the competitive nature of individual businesses in the private sector is a matter for entrepreneurs. Individual businesses, through efficient planning and management, will contribute to the long-term economic well being of the city, if the different interest groups involved in tourism liaise and cooperate with each other. If city managers and planners are able to take a strategic and holistic view of the city's ever-changing leisure product and monitor its performance in the context of the product life cycle (Cooper 1992), they may be able to recognise how the destination is changing and what measures are required to manage and plan for the future prosperity of the tourism economy. Consequently, tourism planning fulfils an import-ant function in urban areas (see Table 5.1) as it is one component of the wider management of urban tourism.

This chapter focuses on the management and planning of urban tourism, by examining the rationale for these activities and the organisa-tions responsible for these functions. The relationship between planning and tourism is also considered and the planning process as it applies to urban tourism is reviewed. Different approaches to urban tourism planning are also discussed, emphasising the feasibility of sustainable tourism planning. This is followed by a case study of tourism planning in Canterbury to illustrate the planning process in practice together with the need for a visitor management strategy, when tourism saturates small historic cities.

Table 5.1 The five purposes of tourism planning

According to Mill and Morrison (1985), the five main reasons for tourism planning are to:

1 Identify alternative approaches to:
   (a) Marketing
   (b) Development
   (c) Industry organisation
   (d) Tourism awareness
   (e) Support services and activities

2 Adapt to the unexpected in
   (a) General economic conditions
   (b) The energy supply and demand situation
   (c) Values and lifestyles
   (d) Fortunes of individual industries
   (e) Other factors in the external environment

3 Maintain uniqueness in:
   (a) Natural features and resources
   (b) Local cultural and social fabric
   (c) Local architecture
   (d) Historical monuments and landmarks
   (e) Local events and activities
   (f) Parks and outdoor sports areas
   (g) Other features of the destination area

4 Create the desirable, such as a:
   (a) High level of awareness of the benefits of tourism
   (b) Clear and positive image of the area as a tourism destination
   (c) An effective industry organisation
   (d) High level of cooperation among individual operators
   (e) Other objectives

5 Avoid the undesirable, such as in:
   (a) Friction and unnecessary competition between individual tourism operators
   (b) Hostile and unfriendly attitudes of local residents toward tourists
   (c) Damage or undesirable, permanent alteration of natural features and historical resources
   (d) The loss of cultural identities
   (e) The loss of market share
   (f) The stoppage of unique local events and activities
   (g) Overcrowding, congestion, and traffic problems
   (h) Pollution
   (i) High seasonality
   (j) Other factors

Source: Based on Mill and Morrison (1985: 363–4)

Urban management and planning: its purpose and role in cities

According to C.M. Hall:

> Planning for tourism occurs in a number of forms (development, infrastructure, promotion and marketing), a number of structures (different government organisations) and a number of scales (international, national, regional, local and sectoral).
>
> (Hall 1991: 98)

In the context of urban tourism, planning is undertaken at the local level, although one also has to recognise the significance of what is happening at other levels in the hierarchy of planning and national economic management. In urban areas, management and planning are often used as interchangeable terms, although it is important to recognise that:

- Government structures (e.g. city governments) are responsible for managing the urban system in particular localities, and;
- Planning is undertaken in urban areas to achieve many of the goals associated with urban management.

The management of systems

Leiper's (1990) research on tourism systems offers a number of useful insights into the process of managing systems. He argues that:

> Management can refer to a set of roles that people perform, and it can refer to the functions pursued in those roles. The functions are often listed as a condensed set of four: planning, directing, organising (which includes coordinating) and controlling . . . [which] . . . can be modelled in a systemic form which describes how the functions are integrated in practice. The coordination function refers to managers drawing on information, from sources such as planning and controlling, and applying that information, systematically to all managerial functions.
>
> (Leiper 1990: 256)

This is a useful definition of management and the role of planning as a management function which involves a wide range of structured activities by individuals, groups and organisations working towards established goals. In a general sense, many managerial functions involving people are undertaken within organisations (Handy 1993) and managers can influence the inputs, processes and outputs associated with the organisational system for which they are responsible. However, Leiper (1990) also cites the work of Carroll (1988) which considers that a wider range of functions are associated with management, including: planning, representing, investigating, negotiating, coordinating, evaluating, staffing and supervision. As Leiper (1990: 257) acknowledges 'one manager may perform all those functions; more commonly, teams of managers share overlapping responsibilities'. In the case of open systems, such as urban tourism, it is important for managers in organisations associated with planning and management to cooperate closely with other organisations and interest groups so that systemic relationships develop. Such relationships offer important advantages for all parties, with the ultimate aim of ensuring the system functions in an efficient manner.

The nature of urban management and planning

Urban management, often referred to as municipal management, has its origins in the growth of public administration, a feature enshrined in national legislation in many Western cities during periods of rapid urbanisation. In the UK, this period can be dated to the 1830s and 1840s with the requirements to manage the implications of the vast influx of people into cities during the Industrial Revolution. Much of the national legislation post-1840 was aimed at improving the quality of life in the urban environment, particularly in relation to public health, infrastructure and development. This was also accompanied by permissive legislation which provided a framework for municipal governments to undertake urban improvement projects and other activities to improve the quality of life (e.g. the establishment of urban parks as open spaces within cities – see Patmore 1983). Similar patterns of development can be traced in other countries during periods of rapid industrialisation where municipal governments were established to manage different aspects of the urban system (see Barlow 1991 for case studies in other countries).

The financial base of municipal government has remained the revenue it levies on its inhabitants, businesses and workers via rates and the subsidies it receives from central or regional government derived from direct or indirect taxation. In most democratic countries, municipal government is based on the involvement of the local population who elect representatives to represent the public interest in local government and direct the public administration towards the goals and objectives agreed by the ruling party. As Green (1975: 353) suggests, urban administration is 'a system of public organisational interactions, focusing on a single urban area (however defined) that results in the performance of essential/important services and/or functions'. It is through the functions of municipal government that the framework of the management and planning of urban areas is established. Sazanami (1984: 6) argues that urban management is based on the mobilisation of human and financial resources through government and non-government organisations to achieve societal goals. Thus, urban management is a broad term which encompasses the role of the municipal government and other non-government organisations (e.g. voluntary bodies) in the day-to-day operation, planning and management of the urban system. For example, McGregor (1993) discusses the role of the Art Deco Trust in planning and managing the built environment in the Art Deco city of Napier in New Zealand with its concern for urban heritage conservation.

Urban government organisations

Identifying the archetypal local government organisation responsible for managing the city is almost an impossible task, since most organisations develop in response to the local conditions. They do, however, have a common range of statutory functions (including planning) and a number of instruments available to manage the urban environment which may include the following:

- Public ownership of land;
- Legal regulation of private land ownership and tenure;
- Legal powers enshrined in national legislation to control private use and development of land;
- Powers to control urban nuisances (e.g. pollution);
- Provision of infrastructure, social housing and control of vehicles and transportation and recovery of the cost of provision from those benefiting from the provision;
- Direct provision of public services (e.g. waste collection) and powers to contract other services from the private sector;
- Taxation of private land ownership and development.

In other words, urban governments have *control of land use, public services* and *infrastructure provision*. Whilst the control of these activities is vested in the hands of managers within the local bureaucracy inside such organisations, one has to question the traditional view that such functions are undertaken by disinterested and neutral administrators under the watchful eye of elected policy-makers. The professional advice of administrators has to be viewed in the political context of the elected representatives and their particular ideologies. In any city, there will be interest groups and individuals seeking to further their own position. Thus, the management of urban areas and the decision-making process which influences the activities administrators undertake is one often associated with conflicting interests. As Devas and Rakodi (1993) observe, conflict in the management of urban areas may occur between competing political parties, between local and national government and between elected representatives and administrators. They also note that conflict may arise between agencies and within different departments in the same organisation as well as between the urban government and voluntary non-government organisations due to differences of ideology, policy or practice. Making informed judgements on the conflicting claims and establishing consensus, or making strategic trade-offs (Haywood 1992) on the precise action to take is a fundamental requirement of urban government (for more details on how organisations operate – see Handy 1993). So where does planning fit into the management of urban areas by municipal governments?

Planning as a statutory function in urban government

Urban planning (also referred to as town planning) has its origins in architecture and public health engineering which date back to the evolution of municipal government (P. Hall 1992). As Devas and Rakodi argue, such planning was primarily concerned with 'the orderly, aesthetic and healthy layout of buildings and land uses' as well as communications and infrastructure. They also argue that 'during the 1960s and 1970s, many town planners sought to adopt a more rational, systematic and comprehensive approach to planning and the evaluation of alternatives' (Devas and Rakodi 1993: 41). As a result, town planning recognises not only the need for physical planning (i.e. the growth and management of the physical environment) but also the need to achieve social and economic objectives in planning which are established through a political consensus. This also reflects the influence of national economic planning on local planning where urban governments have become concerned not only with the preparation of plans but also their implementation, requiring the deployment of scarce resources in relation to human need.

In recent years, the planning and management of urban areas in many Western countries (see D. Hall 1991 for a discussion of urban tourism in Eastern Europe) has seen a change in emphasis. For example, in the 1970s many city governments had an all-embracing role in the management of the city, with the private sector having a lesser role. The ideological position adopted by each city determined their position in the spectrum of possible approaches to urban management, though it largely depends on their view of the role of the state and the place of the individual in the urban system. The 1970s saw many cities taking a corporate view that they would embrace the welfare needs of its population, requiring the population to forego some individual freedom to choose the services they require. The 1980s have seen a response by many national governments which have introduced legislation to emphasise the freedom of the individual to choose the services and activities they require (see Ambrose 1992 for a discussion of the New Right's impact on planning). These changes have resulted from spiralling costs of urban management functions in the 1970s and 1980s (e.g. New York declared itself bankrupt as a municipal organisation in the 1980s), as the increased number of functions which cities embraced in the 1970s led to heavy costs for urban residents.

Changes in political ideology and the rise of monetarist policy in the late 1970s led to national government rationalising municipal and local governments, to reduce national and locally-based public expenditure. The result is that many urban authorities still retain a number of core functions in relation to management and planning, but are no longer the sole provider as private sector contractors are introduced through market-testing practices to reduce the cost of provision. A greater emphasis on a user-pay approach to urban services also characterises the municipal government in the 1990s. In large cities in the UK (e.g. London, Birmingham, Manchester and Sheffield), many functions of municipal authorities were restructured in the 1980s as strategic planning bodies with a holistic view of large metropolitan areas were abolished (see *Streamlining the Cities*, HMSO 1985; Eversley 1984; Thornley 1990).

In London this led to the abolition of the Greater London Council and the planning functions were transferred to a central government quango (the London Planning Advisory Committee) to advise central government and the thirty-two London boroughs. In effect, the London boroughs became responsible for preparing unitary development plans for their own local area. This led to major changes in the management of tourism in London (Grimnett 1984), as the London Tourist Board (LTB) assumed a greater responsibility for preparing tourism policy in the capital and the coordination of the public sector planning departments through its Borough Liaison Department. Although the LTB is funded by central government, via the English Tourist Board (Cooper 1987), it has no powers to plan since these powers rest with the London boroughs. Therefore, it is only able to advise the planning departments even though it is the only agency with a London-wide vision of tourism (Page 1989a). It really represents a piecemeal approach to planning. Since there is no political consensus among the London boroughs on the role of tourism in the their local areas, 'tourism planning and development in the capital is fragmented, reflecting the differing objectives and political views of the London boroughs' (Page and Sinclair 1992: 59). In 1994, the British government were also in the process of assessing the future shape of local government, with a view to abolishing county councils and their strategic functions and amalgamating local authorities (i.e. district councils) into larger units of administration. This would reduce the ability of cities to manage their local area and the tourism system because larger administrative units are divorced from the area which assumes the management and planning functions. As a result, services, planning and other statutory functions may not be as responsive to local needs without costly research and consultation. Again, the motivation for such action appears to be the reduction of public expenditure on local areas and a greater control by national government.

The relationship between planning and tourism

There is surprisingly little literature on planning for tourism in urban areas as 'the characteristics of urban tourism and its planning have been studied less than resort and outdoor recreation development' (Inskeep 1991: 236) with a number of exceptions (e.g. Jansen-Verbeke 1988, 1992). Much of the literature has been based on national and regional planning (Pearce 1989). There are a number of good studies which examine the development of tourism planning as a specialised area of research and its professional practice (e.g. Gunn 1988; Inskeep 1991), while Mill and Morrison (1992) discuss the development of tourism planning and its evolution from the 1960s in Europe, especially France, the UK and Ireland as well as in Canada in the 1960s and 1970s. They also note that the United States lags behind these countries. Pearce (1989) also offers a useful overview of tourism planning, noting its need to accommodate the dynamic nature of tourism processes and to review the situation every five years.

Cooper *et al.* highlight the rationale for tourism planning as:

> The development of tourism will not be optimal if it is left in the hands of private sector entrepreneurs, for they are primarily motivated by the profit and loss accounts. But on the other hand, if tourism development is dominated by the public sector then it is unlikely to be developed at the optimal rate from the economic point of view.
>
> (Cooper *et al.* 1993: 130)

This implies that tourism planning requires the coordination of the public and private sector to ensure a suitable balance is reached between the interests of each party. In fact Gunn (1988) argues that there are a number of foundation points for the development of an overall approach toward tourism planning:

- Planning can avert negative impacts and all agents and actors associated with tourism should be involved;
- Tourism is symbiotic with conservation and recreation; tourism planning should be pluralistic, incorporating economic, social and physical planning objectives;
- Planning is a political process and should recognise the effect of politics on the planning process;
- Tourism planning should be strategic, meaning that it should be capable of achieving desired objectives through the process of planning and management;
- Tourism planning should be integrative, meaning that planning at the city level should also attempt to incorporate the objectives of regional and national plans.

Gunn (1988: 241) suggests that 'most cities do not have the legal and organisational structures to plan for tourism's growth and development' a feature reiterated by Haywood (1992: 14). Most city plans do not refer to tourism. Planning for tourism is 'an amalgam of economic, social and environmental considerations' (Heeley 1981: 61) which affect tourism development and results in planning for aspects of tourism rather tourism planning as a separate activity in its own right. In the UK, urban governments have a statutory duty to plan for tourism as an economic activity with a land use outcome. Yet they have no obligation to be involved in the management and organisation of tourism beyond land use planning. Nevertheless, many cities are actively involved in urban tourism as Law notes:

> The principal actors within the organisation of tourism in cities may be drawn from either the public or private sectors. In addition to the local authority, the public sector may also include regional or national governments, development corporations, national and regional tourist boards, national museums and other semi-autonomous public organisations'.
>
> (Law 1993: 143)

This illustrates the wide range of interest groups associated with tourism in cities although:

> The local authority which [sic] is responsible for the city is the key actor in the local tourist industry. Its aim is to secure the benefits of tourism for the community, and it does this through its ability to control, co-ordinate and lead policy-making. In a democracy its policies are determined by politicians and reflect both the ideology of the ruling political party and the views of the public.
>
> (Law 1993: 144)

Table 5.2 provides an example of one such brief generated by the London Borough of Newham which sought to commission consultants to produce a tourism strategy as a basis for economic development. A number of approaches are advocated which highlight the appeal of using tourism as a basis for economic regeneration in areas with a range of inner city problems. This has followed the experience of 'difficult areas' in successfully establishing urban tourism (Buckley and Witt 1985).

The nature of urban tourism presents particular problems for planners as it:

> Typically presents special problems, such as competing demands for development of certain prime sites for hotels, offices, retail or residential uses, traffic congestion in central areas, which may be exacerbated by tourism development, and over-use of primary tourist attractions and perhaps their degradation by intensive use.
>
> (Inskeep 1991: 236–7)

However, this has to viewed in relation to the argument that:

Table 5.2 Preparing a strategy for tourism in the London Borough of Newham

---

1.1 OBJECTIVES OF THE STUDY

The London Borough of Newham is seeking to establish a strategy for tourism development, in the form of a clear action plan over a ten-year horizon, divided into short, medium and long-term phases. This approach underlines the need for a practical and workable programme which fits within the Council's own planning and service delivery framework.

In a review of the brief, the consultants have identified the following as the principal goals of the study:

- Establish a clear vision on tourism, in association with those departments who will be responsible for its promotion
- Harness tourism's potential for assisting urban regeneration
- Raise local incomes by increasing spending in the area
- Enhance the quality of life for residents and promote the Borough's cultural assets and diversity.

Since Newham is not a conventional tourist destination, within a London-wide context, the Borough is understandably cautious about the realisable economic and social benefits of tourism. Much of the potential gain from transport improvements is likely to arise over the long term, towards the end of the ten-year horizon and beyond. On the other hand, there is already modest activity on which the strategy can build and the prospects for growth are favourable.

1.2 APPROACHES TO TOURISM DEVELOPMENT

Tourism development can encompass a variety of development activity, including retail, catering, attractions, accommodation, and event planning. For the purposes of this study, 'tourist' will include visiting friends and relatives (VFRs), business travellers, and day leisure visitors to Newham.

Historically there are several broad ways of undertaking tourism developments:

Option 1 Creating major new attractions or other large tourist-related developments (which entail creating a market)

Option 2 Creating attractions or other tourist-related developments around existing magnets or concentrations of activity

Option 3 Developing smaller, typically discrete schemes, often based on existing facilities, and secured through existing policy instruments.

These approaches are not mutually exclusive. The first option, however, is likely to involve higher risk and in the event of failure could prove potentially damaging in terms of public support. There is also often a financial dilemma – if the development is 100% privately funded, benefits accruing to local residents may be minimal; if there is a requirement for significant public funding, it may not happen at all. In this study, the consultants would not dismiss possibilities under option 1, but would recognise that here needs to be good evidence of their expected market success, before pursuing them further.

In option 2, where new tourism developments are achieved by expanding on existing or planned nodes of activity, the risk of failure is substantially reduced. Because this option is likely to involve new development, it is important that it be of a high standard, which may prove more expensive than developments identified under option 3. Being more dependent on the completion of future developments such options are more likely to have medium to long-term potential.

Table 5.2 *(continued)*

Developments identified under option 3, are more likely to be feasible within the short term and be less costly to achieve, including town trails and the advantage of enhancing the quality of the environment for local residents. Generally, however, they are likely to have less significant impact on visitor spending.

The decision as to which opportunities should be followed will be based on an appraisal of Newham's existing tourism markets (primarily VFRs, business tourism, and day leisure tourism), an assessment of planned future developments, and after discussions with the Client to establish how tourism development can be linked to the Borough's policies and programmes, such as 'City Challenge'.

1.3 STUDY PROCESS AND OUTPUTS

The objectives identified in the brief have been encapsulated into three main stages of work:

Stage 1. Analysis and Market Appraisal
This entails an audit of existing attractions and tourism benefits, based largely on existing sources of information. Estimates based on existing data will be made in relation to:

* Visitors (types, origins and expenditures);
* Accommodation (available, used and weaknesses in supply);
* Attractions (characteristics and visitor numbers);
* Accessibility to the area (quality of transportation);

Stage 2. Synthesis and Strategy
From the stage 1 outputs, sensible scenarios of development potential can be developed which take into account natural growth and opportunities provided by new and improved transport links. The strategy emerging from this should identify and clearly report on separate development components, notably:

* Tourism associated with town centre regeneration – particularly the Stratford City Challenge area
* Tourism associated with the Docklands area of the Borough
* Accommodation – types of hotel, B&B, self-catering, and other accommodation which should be attracted or upgraded
* Major magnets or new attractions – conclusions on feasibility and priorities
* Locally rooted physical development, e.g. town/urban trails
* Locally rooted activities, e.g. street markets and events
* Wider linkage to East London, including association with existing and planned developments in neighbouring boroughs.

Stage 3. Implementation
The development concepts identified in stage 2 will be formulated into a plan which:

* Establishes targets and priorities;
* Sets out the tasks and identifies who performs them;
* Designs a monitoring mechanism;
* Establishes a review procedure.

Each of these tasks would involve discussions with relevant departments to ensure that workable programmes are identified.

Source: Berkeley Hanover Consulting, November 1992

Note: This is an extract from a much larger submission prepared as a tender for the London Borough of Newham.

Urban tourism, in addition to its basic economic benefits of generating income and employment, can be an important technique for helping to support urban facilities and services such as theatres and museums, helping to justify and paying for historic preservation and infrastructure improvements. . . .

(Inskeep 1991: 237)

How do planning organisations set about planning for urban tourism?

The planning process and urban tourism

Planning for tourism in any locality requires that certain procedures are followed (P. Hall 1992). The view that tourism planning is a specific process followed in various situations is advocated by Getz (1987: 3) who views it as 'a process, based on research and evaluation, which seeks to optimise the potential contribution of tourism to human welfare and environmental quality'. Murphy (1985: 156) (cited in Pearce 1989: 246) argues that tourism:

> Planning is concerned with anticipating and regulating change in a system, to promote orderly development so as to increase the social, economic and environmental benefits of the development process. To do this, planning becomes 'an ordered sequence of operations, designed to lead the achievement of either a single goal or to balance between several goals.

In other words, tourism planning at the local level (the city level), is a process with a number of clear stages. It considers social, economic and environmental issues in a spatial context (i.e. the city) and has regard to development, conservation, land use, the tourism industry and the local business environment and economy. In many cases tourism planning is undertaken as part of the statutory planning process in urban areas or it may be a specialised function undertaken by key individuals or a team in a tourism department of local government (if they exist). Alternatively it can be developed by tourism consultants for the public sector client where no expertise is available in-house.

Urban tourism planning may often appear as a subset of much larger tourism development plans. For example, the island of Malta's national tourism development plan contains a number of tourism planning zones based on urban areas (Horwath and Horwath 1989; Inskeep 1991).

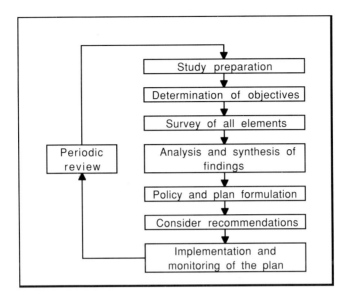

Figure 5.1 The tourism planning process

Similarly, in Ireland, Bord Fáilte's current development strategy for heritage tourism contains an element of urban tourism planning in relation to heritage towns, which act as honeypots (areas designed to accommodate a heavy concentration of tourists) (see Page 1994c,d for further detail). This feature is recognised by Heeley (1981: 61) in that:

> Overall planning objectives in tourism vary from encouragement to restriction, while planning tools range from grants and other incentives to development control schemes . . . [and] . . . tourism is not a self-contained policy area. It overlaps with policy fields such as transport, conservation, rural development, and so forth, so that only a small proportion of the sum total of plans affecting tourism are exclusively devoted to it.
>
> (Heeley 1981: 61)

Where tourism planning is undertaken in an urban context, the following process is normally followed (Figure 5.1) and a range of elements associated with urban tourism are examined (Figure 5.2). The planning process normally includes the following stages.

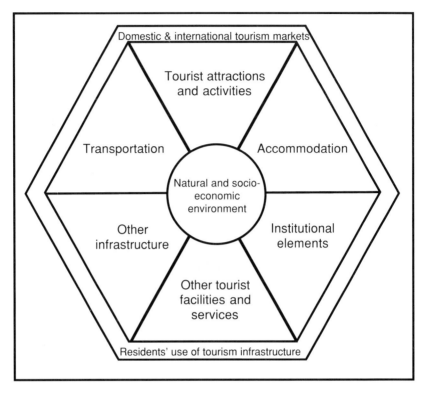

Figure 5.2 The elements of a tourism plan

1 Study preparation

This is where the planning authority based within the local government organisation takes a decision to proceed with the study and the terms of reference and organisation of the study are outlined. It is also the case that the local planning authority may not be the only organisation involved in the decision to undertake a plan.

Heeley (1981) notes that a number of public agencies may be active in a given locality and that while the urban authority is the statutory organisation which undertakes the planning function, other bodies such as regional planning authorities also have an input in the decision to proceed. For example, in the case of Wellington in New Zealand, the Wellington Regional council is responsible for the entire district while the City Council is responsible for the city. Yet it was the regional authority's interest in tourism that produced the first strategy document for the Wellington area, with a focus on the city (see Page 1993a). This also illustrates the importance of integration in the planning process.

2 Determination of objectives

This describes the main purpose of initiating the study, such as to encourage the development of urban tourism to derive tangible economic and environmental benefits for the city as well as benefiting the host population through employment generation and the support of a wider range of services for the local population and visitors.

3 Survey of all elements

This commonly refers to an inventory of the existing range of tourism resources and the state of development as well as the nature of the tourism economy. This will require the collection of data on both the demand for urban tourism (e.g. the characteristics of visitors, travel patterns and trends) and supply of tourism resources (e.g. attractions, accommodation, facilities, infrastructure, the structure of the local tourism economy and the environment) as well as an assessment of the availability of investment and capital for future development. The range of public and private sector organisations with an involvement in tourism also needs to be identified.

For example, Industry Science and Technology Canada (1991) provides an inventory of studies evaluating tourism in three major Canadian cities (Montreal, Toronto and Vancouver) which summarises the nature of the tourism product in each locality based on existing data, though such studies rarely reach the public domain. Increasingly, the role of the host population and social and cultural issues are being incorporated in relation to the local community's views where planning seeks to adopt a community approach (Murphy 1985).

4 Analysis and synthesis of findings

This refers to the process of analysng the information generated from the survey stage to provide the basis for the formulation of the plan. The data are often analysed to assess a wide range of issues and Cooper *et al.* (1993: 135) note that four commonly used techniques are: asset evaluation, market analysis, development planning and impact analysis (see

Cooper *et al.* 1993 for more detail). Such information is used to establish possible policy options for urban tourism.

5 Policy and plan formulation

This involves the interpretation of the information from the previous stage to provide a range of possible development options or scenarios for urban tourism. The usual procedure is to construct a draft development plan based on tourism policy options. According to Acernaza (1985), tourism policy determines the direction and actions which need to be taken to achieve certain goals. The policy stage is often viewed as the underlying framework or guidelines for the plan.

Acernaza (1985: 60) (cited in Pearce 1989) argues that there are three elements evident in most tourism policies: visitor satisfaction, environmental protection and ensuring there are adequate rewards for developers and investors. A range of alternative policies are usually considered and the policy options which offer a wide range of tourism objectives for the city are then incorporated in relation to the goals and objectives set out in the study preparation stage.

6 Consideration of recommendations

This is the point at which the full tourism plan is put forward to the planning committee of the urban authority for internal scrutiny and comment. Discussions normally take place between the individuals or team preparing the plan and the planning committee and other interested parties may be consulted.

In many local authorities responsible for planning, the draft plan then undergoes a period of public consultation and this enables both the general public and tourism interests to comment on the plan and to suggest alterations. Once this procedure is completed, the plan will be approved by the planning committee and the final plan is produced.

7 The implementation and monitoring of the plan

This is where the plan is put into action, a feature which is normally considered as an ongoing process by the planning team. Legislation may be required to control certain aspects of development which will be needed to implement certain aspects of the plan.

The planning team will also need to recognise the political implications of implementing certain aspects of the plan. It is often the case that changes in the political complexion of the elected representatives may cause changes to the priorities when implementing the plan. For example, if an investment programme has been specified and the elected representatives feel a new priority exists, programmes may be altered or frozen if public funds are limited. This illustrates the importance of programming large capital investment projects such as roads, coach parks and other infrastructure in a development programme over a five-year period as resources usually outstrip the available budget.

This is often complemented by an action plan which normally incorporates specific actions needed to achieve objectives in the plan on a staged basis. Again, budgetary estimates are usually needed to illustrate what options are available given limited resources.

As well as implementing the plan, it is also important to monitor the plan closely to assess whether the objectives are being met. This is an ongoing process used to inform both the planning committee and the tourism industry on the progress of the plan during its five-year period of operation. The monitoring is a useful mechanism for assisting the planning authority to make minor adjustments to the timing, phasing and budgetary requirements of the plan for it to achieve its stated objectives.

8 Periodic Review

This refers to the process of reporting back on the progress of the plan once it has run its course and the study preparation stage will often be initiated again. It is widely acknowledged that the implementation stage of the plan is one of the most critical stages. The failure of the plan at this stage can often result from:

- The failure to generate interest from developers;
- An inability to introduce the necessary legislation to control the land development process;
- A failure to coordinate the public and private sector so that disagreement or misunderstandings cause 'bottlenecks' in the supply of services and facilities which ultimately affect the leisure product and tourist experience. This may cause the plan to miss its targets;
- A lack of public sector funding to implement the plan fully;
- Inadequate infrastructure and transport provision;
- The inability to recognise the public opposition to tourism develop-

ment which can cause delays or the failure of the plan depending on the degree of opposition.

However, tourism plans are based on certain approaches to the situation prevailing in each city or town.

Approaches to urban tourism planning

According to Getz (1987) there are four traditions to tourism planning: boosterism, an economic-industry oriented approach, a physical–spatial approach and a community-oriented approach. As Getz (1987: 5) observes 'the four traditions are not mutually exclusive, nor are they sequential . . . [but they are] . . . a convenient way to examine the different and sometimes overlapping ways in which tourism is planned'. Each of these approaches is extensively documented in the literature (e.g. Getz 1986, 1987; C.M. Hall 1991) and only a brief mention is required here since other categories can be added, particularly the sustainable approach to tourism planning. Table 5.3 summarises the basic principles associated with the four approaches noted by Getz (1987). For this reason, the emphasis here will be on a fifth approach – the sustainable approach to urban tourism planning.

Sustainable tourism planning

The sustainable approach to tourism and development is evident from a wide range of publications now appearing with 'sustainable' in their title (see the *Journal of Sustainable Tourism* and Page 1994b for a more detailed discussion). Sustainability, with its concern for the long-term future of resources and the effects of economic development on the environment may also cause cultural and social disruption to established patterns of living and individual life styles. This has led to calls for human activities which minimise and harmonise these impacts in relation to the interests of the local population. In the context of urban tourism planning, sustainable development is based on many of the principles set out in the World Commission on the Environment and Development (the Brundtland Commission) report (1987) which C.M. Hall (1991: 109) argues is concerned with 'equity, the needs of economically marginal populations, and the idea of technological and social limitations on the ability of the environment to meet present and future needs'. Urban tourism planning which seeks to develop a sustainable approach will need to implement many of these principles.

Table 5.3 Approaches to urban tourism planning

Boosterism

This is a simple approach whereby tourism is viewed as a positive attribute for a place and the residents. Objects in the urban environment are promoted as assets for tourism development without any concern for the impact, almost constituting a 'form of non-tourism planning' (C.M. Hall 1991: 103). Local residents are not included in the planning process and the carrying capacity of the region is not given adequate consideration. As Getz (1987: 10) notes 'Boosterism is still practised . . . by two groups of people: politicians who philosophically or pragmatically believe that economic growth is always to be promoted, and by others who will gain financially by tourism'.

The Economic-Industry Approach

This is a widely used approach adopted by many cities who see tourism as an industry which can yield economic benefits *vis à vis* employment generation and development opportunities. The concept of tourism as an export for the urban system and marketing is used to attract visitors who are likely to be the highest spenders. Economic goals taken precedence over social and environmental goals, with the visitor experience and satisfaction level seen as key objectives.

The Physical–Spatial Approach

This is based on the land-use tradition of geography and planners with a rational approach to planning the urban environment. Tourism is viewed in a range of contexts but the environmental dimension is recognised as well as the critical issue of the carrying capacity of tourism resources within the city. Different planning strategies based on spatial principles are used such as concentrating visitors in key areas or their dispersion to avoid over-concentration and conflicts. However, one criticism of such approaches has been their neglect of the social and cultural impact of urban tourism.

The Community Approach

This approach is epitomised in the seminal work by Murphy (1985) which argues for the maximum involvement of the local community in the planning process. It argues that traditional 'top-down' planning models where the planners set the agenda need to be modified to incorporate the needs and wishes of the local community in the decision-making and planning process. In other words, community tourism planning recognises the significance of socially acceptable guidelines for tourism development. The approach seeks to emphasise the importance of social and cultural benefits for the local population together with a range of economic and environmental considerations (see Murphy 1985 for a fuller discussion). Haywood (1988) acknowledges the practical problems of implementing such plans, particularly the political nature of the planning process, as public partnership is often reduced to tokenism in reality. However, the principle of community planning is based on tourism as a 'successful and self-perpetuating industry . . . [which] . . . needs to be planned and managed as a renewable resource industry, based on local capacities and community decision-making' (Murphy 1985: 153).

A recent study by Grenier *et al.* (1993) argues that the growth of environmentalism, sustainable development and ecotourism (Cater and Lowman 1994) offers a niche for urban planning. Yet as C.M. Hall (1991) acknowledges there are practical problems in adopting such an approach. For example, the term sustainability often implies an infinite time scale whereas urban planning usually works on a five-year time span. The diverse nature of the tourism industry's composition sometimes makes coordination of different interest groups difficult. It can complicate sustainable tourism planning as decisions taken by the wide range of small tourism businesses in urban areas may run contrary to the objectives of the tourism plan. Dutton and Hall (1989) note that this inhibits the synchronisation of policy and practice and may impede sustainable development objectives. Nevertheless, Dutton and Hall (1989) do identify six mechanisms which may help in achieving a realistic sustainable approach to tourism planning so that:

1 Tourism planning should be cooperative and based on integrated control systems, to foster cooperation and mutual concern for increased benefits from such an approach;
2 Industry coordination mechanisms are to be developed;
3 Consumer awareness of sustainable and non-sustainable options needs to be raised, including the benefits of visitor management;
4 Producer awareness of the benefits of sustainable tourism planning is to be promoted;
5 Strategic planning supersedes conventional planning approaches, requiring all interested parties to make firm commitments to sustainable objectives;
6 There is a greater concern for the planning requirements for a quality tourist experience, with a view to the long-term sustainability of the tourism product, while enhancing the attraction of the urban destination.

However, one of the main problems in achieving a sustainable tourism plan that can be implemented is the tourism industry's failure to fully embrace such principles in their operation. Ashworth points out that the:

Tourism industry is tackling the criticisms being made of it, not the problems that cause the criticisms. If there is no resource or environmental problem, then it does not need to be defined nor do solutions need to be found. The problem is seen as one of promotion, and

promotion is what the tourist industry is especially good at. Buying off the grumblers with a few 'commitments' and 'mission statements . . . is easier than the alternative [of sustainable tourism planning].
(Ashworth 1992b: 327)

Ashworth's (1992b: 327) cynicism that 'the alternative is to think the unthinkable, which may mean setting actual norms for environmentally damaging activities and actual sustainable targets for specific activities, sites, towns or regions' is well placed since any tourism plan which embraces sustainable principles will need to radically rethink the way the industry operates and its effects on the urban environment. To develop a sustainable tourism plan in an urban context may require planners and the tourism industry to make a commitment to implement a plan which could conceivably require potential tourists to engage in other forms of activity, or in extreme cases it could ask tourists: 'please go somewhere else' (Ashworth 1992b: 327). This is a feature that no industry-sector representatives are likely to endorse, to reduce pressure on sensitive urban tourism environments.

The practice of tourism planning in an urban context, is illustrated in the case study of Canterbury (UK).

Case study 7

Tourism planning in a small historic city – Canterbury

Canterbury is a small historic city in the UK, which has developed from a long tradition of tourism dating back to the medieval period, and pilgrimages to the shrine of Thomas à Becket in Canterbury Cathedral. The city's rich and varied heritage is reflected in the forty-two ancient monuments and 1,570 listed buildings within the city, together with a variety of archaeological sites. Such relict features have proved to be an important determinant of the form and layout of the town (Figure 5.3), and since the 1970s, Canterbury City Council (CCC) pioneered a successful conservation scheme for the historic town centre. As such, Canterbury is a fine example of a historic walled city with its city centre enclosed within the town walls. The city also contains three World Heritage Sites:

Case study 6 (*continued*)

- Canterbury Cathedral
- St Martin's Church
- St Augustine's Abbey.

As a tourist destination, surprisingly little is known about the impact of tourism in the town, as well as the long-term consequences of tourist development on the local population, economy and the appeal of the city to visitors. Existing knowledge of tourism is largely confined to locally derived tourism statistics and data sources generated by CCC. For example, the only major publicly available source of information is the 1975 tourism survey which examined the volume and characteristics of tourism and its impact on the city (the survey can be viewed as part of the survey stage of plan formulation). It concluded that the City received an estimated 1 million visitors a year, subsequently corroborated by national tourism data and estimates of the volume of tourism to other towns on the overseas 'tourist circuit' (see Pearce 1987a).

The survey, based on a limited sample of 600 visitors found that 45 per cent were from overseas, with sightseeing, history and the built environment the most important reasons for visiting. It was estimated that tourist spending contributed £6.8 million to the economy, increasing to £8.5 million through a multiplier value of 1.25. These estimates suggest that in 1975, 2,500 full time job equivalents were generated by tourism in Canterbury, though the absence of a detailed economic impact model for the town limited any detailed analysis of where tourists spent their money.

In 1985, a further tourism survey was undertaken which included a count of visitors to the Cathedral and the Visitor Centre together with interviews with tourists and an assessment of levels of hotel occupancy. The results show that the socio-economic profile of visitors to Canterbury were typically day-trippers in the 35–54 age group, drawn from social classes A, B and C1 in most cases. The number of visitors was estimated at 1 million day visitors and half a million staying visitors, representing a 50 per cent increase on 1975. The most recent estimates of the throughput of visitors to Canterbury Cathedral are between 2.25 and 2.5

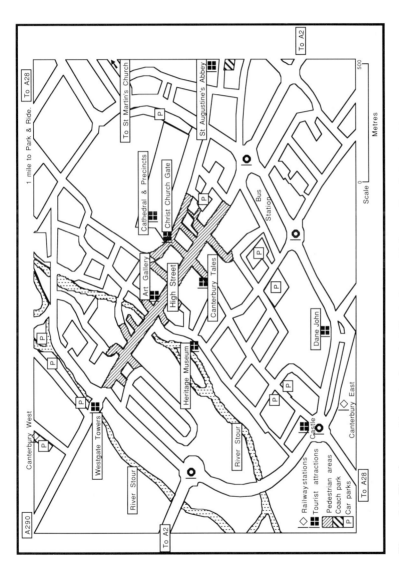

Figure 5.3 The form and layout of central Canterbury with its medieval street pattern

Case study 6 (*continued*)

million, forming one of the largest visitor attractions in the County of Kent. At the time of writing, CCC were still in the process of analysing the 1991 tourism survey of 2,500 visitors, which means estimates of the economic impact of tourism are still based on the 1985 survey. However, CCC estimates that tourism generates £45 million for the local economy, supporting in excess of 3,700 jobs and approximately 14 per cent of the local workforce.

Managing and planning for tourism in Canterbury: the city plan

Various agencies, such as Kent County Council and the South East England Tourist Board, each have an input into strategic planning for tourism in the town, although the day-to-day management and planning is based within the planning department of CCC. Their responsibilities also include policy formulation and the implementation of the local plan. The City's local plan is part of a wider district plan for the entire region (Canterbury and the coastal towns of Whitstable and Herne Bay and the surrounding villages). However, Canterbury city receives a prominent place in the plan and the situation with respect to tourism is set out in an accompanying background paper (Canterbury City Council 1991a).

The policies established and implemented in the local plan are listed in Table 5.4 and are based on decisions taken in 1983 and subsequently reaffirmed and modified in 1987 and 1992 by the Economic Policy Committee of CCC. It is clear that no detailed tourism plan exists for the entire city, being integrated within the existing local plan under the heading of 'business and tourism'. The policies which have shaped the component in the local plan were refined in the 1990s to recognise the action required to address the problems associated with tourism in the city which include:

• A gradual erosion of the historic fabric of the city due to heavy use by tourists;

Table 5.4 Tourism policies in Canterbury

The following marketing policies for tourism were adopted by Canterbury City Council in 1983:

1 To encourage and promote the international and national tourism significance of the city of Canterbury; to encourage improvements to the quality of its fabric, amenity and service; and to introduce appropriate methods of visitor management to spread the benefits of tourism.

2 To encourage each area to identify itself as an important part of the whole district and to make a major contribution to the area's tourism activity by developing and promoting Whitstable and a national and regional 'heritage' venue, and Herne Bay as a regional and local 'leisure' venue and rural areas and local 'amenity' venues.

3 To encourage wider local understanding of the values of a healthy tourist economy; to co-ordinate all local initiatives in reviewing and developing local tourist/amenity provision; and to ensure that the entire district profits from its natural and commercial tourist provisions and potential.

In 1991 the Council proposed refinements to the existing principles used to guide tourism planning in Canterbury in the 1990s:

1 It is Canterbury's international duty to care for the World Heritage sites.

2 Positive effects [should] be made to maintain the volume and value of tourism at a level which continues to support conservation and the cultural life of the city.

3 Visitor management measures [should] be introduced to alleviate problems of congestion for visitors to the city and residents and local people [should] be involved in devising those measures.

4 Greater emphasis [should] be given to explaining the benefits of tourism to the local people, seeing their views on tourism and encouraging them to be proud to display their city to others.

5 Efforts [should] continue to be made to increase the numbers of staying visitors to Canterbury and its district by encouraging the provision of more accommodation, better provision of sports and leisure facilities, continued investment in visitor attractions and provision of information about the district.

6 Policies and proposals in the local plan [should] be sufficiently flexible to allow the emerging strategy for tourism and new trends in tourism to be accommodated during the plan period.

However, the Council recognises that 'very few of the measures suggested above can be accommodated through the local plan process and require a separate marketing and visitor management strategy'.

Source: Modified from *Canterbury District Local Plan: Background Paper No. 3 – Tourism.* Canterbury City Council (1991: 1 & 10–11)

Case study 6 (*continued*)

- Traffic congestion due to the location of city car parks in or near the town centre and the location of the A28 which takes cross town traffic near to the City walls;
- Insufficient and inadequate parking facilities for coaches;
- The geographical concentration of tourists at major heritage sites in the town (especially the Cathedral) and the high street;
- A lack of quality serviced tourism accommodation;
- A dearth of novel and stimulating tourist attractions;
- A poorly situated Visitor Information Centre;
- The saturation of the High Street at peak times when flows of up to 39,000 people/day occur.

The local plan recognises some of these problems and is based on the following principles:

- Conservation and restraint;
- Economic development, and;
- Enhancing and improving the local environment.

Not surprisingly, the local plan emphasises the principles of restraint needed to address these problems related to tourism and other economic activities as:

- The protection and conservation of the historic character of Canterbury;
- The geographical containment of the city to maintain it as a desirable place to live, work, shop and visit;
- The control of land use within the city, to control traffic and to enhance in-town shopping with a park and ride scheme to reduce traffic congestion in the city;
- The control of traffic within the city embodied in the PARC plan (the CCC Park and Ride Strategy), using park and ride to switch people from cars to public transport and through other mechanisms such as the pricing of car parking to deter in-town parking.

Nevertheless the CCC local plan does acknowledge that 'tourism supports conservation measures in Canterbury and contributes to

Case study 6 (*continued*)

the cultural life of the City . . . [and] in recognising the pressures caused by tourism the City Council proposes to develop further a visitor management strategy for Canterbury in conjunction with local businesses and people' (Canterbury City Council 1991b: 29).

Towards a visitor management strategy in Canterbury in the 1990s

At the time of writing, plans are being developed to establish a visitor management strategy and plan for Canterbury as part of the Canterbury City Centre Initiative (CCCI) (Canterbury City Council 1993). It is based on a partnership of CCC, local businesses, representatives of the regional tourist board and Kent County Council. A steering group has been established to direct the programme, based on a partnership between an educational institution and the local planning department with a research fellow to liaise between the two bodies. This initiative recognises that action is needed to address the severe visitor saturation now occurring in the City which is having a detrimental impact on local residents – many now choose to shop out of town at peak times to avoid the tourists. The visitor management programme has now received budgetary approval from the main funding bodies (i.e. CCC, the regional tourist board and local businesses). It reflects the cooperation of different organisations in the town with an interest or involvement in tourism, and the objectives of the CCCI are shown in Table 5.5. As research is an integral part of the proposed strategy for managing tourism (Figure 5.4), a specialist team is monitoring specific projects in an impartial and independent manner. This closely follows the principles of tourism planning discussed above and recognises the need to monitor the programme.

However, since tourism is a politically sensitive issue in Canterbury, decision-making is often tempered by local opposition which illustrates the need for a local survey of resident attitudes. In a small historic city such as Canterbury, visitors concentrate at the key nodes in the town centre (see Figure 5.3).

Case study 6 (*continued*)

Table 5.5 The objectives of the Canterbury City Centre Initiative

The City Centre Initiative should:

1 Enable local people to use their own town centre more easily;

2 Promote Canterbury as a 'package', i.e. Cathedral, shops, attractions, restaurants, new leisure facilities, theatre;

3 Ensure the provision of high quality facilities for all visitors arriving or leaving by car, coach, rail and local bus services;

4 Ensure that visitors have the information they need for an enjoyable stay in Canterbury City Centre;

5 Ensure that visitors are aware of the opportunities to purchase locally available goods and services;

6 Provide a coordinated strategy for managing parties of school children;

7 Ensure that visitors are aware of the management measures designed to enhance their enjoyment of Canterbury City Centre;

8 Minimise the physical impact of tourism on residents and workers in Canterbury City Centre;

9 Encourage visitors to spend at least one night in the Canterbury district;

10 Persuade British Rail to improve train services to Canterbury;

11 Monitor the cleaning of public toilets and streets;

12 Ensure that local people are encouraged to support Canterbury by shopping there;

13 Ensure that people are aware of how to use the parking strategy in Canterbury effectively;

14 Encourage events and festivals in the town centre for local people and visitors.

Source: Canterbury City Council (1993)

The immediate need of any attempt to address the over-concentration of visitors in the town is to find a mechanism by which to disperse visitors and manage the day trippers within the town. Therefore any visitor management strategy will need to recognise the need to:

• Appoint a visitor manager and relocate the town's car park so that a scheme of hosting and guiding parties of visitors (shepherding), based on the successful scheme developed for

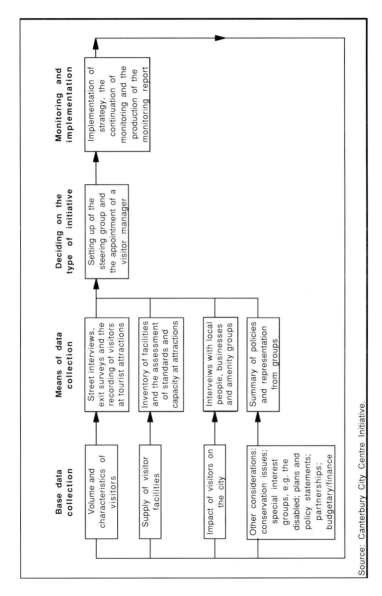

Base data collection

Volume and characteristics of visitors

Supply of visitor facilities

Impact of visitors on the city

Other considerations: conservation issues; special interest groups, e.g. the disabled; plans and policy statements; partnerships; budgetary/finance

Means of data collection

Street interviews, exit surveys and the recording of visitors at tourist attractions

Inventory of facilities and the assessment of standards and capacity at attractions

Interviews with local people, businesses and amenity groups

Summary of policies and representation from groups

Deciding on the type of initiative

Setting up of the steering group and the appointment of a visitor manager

Monitoring and implementation

Implementation of strategy, the continuation of monitoring and the production of the monitoring report

Source: Canterbury City Centre Initiative.

Figure 5.4 Framework for establishing and monitoring Canterbury's Visitor Management Plan

Case study 6 (*continued*)

---

visitors to Canterbury Cathedral, is set up and to ensure it is capable of being implemented;

- Establish the thresholds for tourist use of existing resources in terms of their carrying capacity to ensure the ambience of the town is not further eroded (Table 5.6 examines a range of techniques used to assess visitor numbers and visitor flows in visitor management schemes);
- Address the congestion arising from cross-town traffic, by positively routing vehicles to avoid the town centre and introducing further traffic calming measures in the city centre;
- Enhance and implement the PARC scheme and to remove in-town car parking for all but the disabled and those people with mobility difficulties;
- Take a positive decision not to market Canterbury to day-trippers (Ashworth and Tunbridge 1990 call this de-marketing a destination);
- Examine the feasibility of radical measures such as the charging of entrance to visitors to Canterbury Cathedral;
- Enhance the management of the town centre by developing sites across the city as alternatives nodes of activity, to address the congestion and over-use through leisure shopping and sight-seeing;
- Introduce a public awareness campaign to overcome local opposition to tourism through the provision of meetings and educational initiatives to highlight the positive benefits of tourism for the city.

Above all, effective visitor management requires the visitors' values and behaviour to be influenced (McArthur and Hall 1993) as well as altering the patterns and activities visitors undertake. Although these principles are by no means exhaustive, their implementation is perhaps more important than developing a lengthy visitor management plan that never moves beyond the planning stage. The implementation of even the most basic principles listed above would be a good start to managing tourism in a city overwhelmed by visitors, though research will be an important element

Table 5.6 Techniques for determining visitor numbers and profiles in a visitor management scheme

Techniques	Forms
Determining quantity of visitors	
Counters	• Counters for vehicles, turnstiles, doorways and tracks (compressed air tubes, pressure pads, spring-loaded switches, and infra-red beams). • Observations of numbers and/or group size
Administrative	• Bookings • Visitor books • Receipts and income • Number of enquiries and amount of information (publications) distributed
Impact assessment	• Noting vehicle tracks, trampling, amount of waste and resource consumption (e.g. wood and water)
Determining profile of visitors	
Observation	• Visitor flow diagrams • Type and order of visitor experience • Timing experience • Recording use of facilities (individual or photographic e.g. video and audio-time-lapse or motion/sound triggered) • Recording behavioural characteristics (as above)
Computers	• Programmes that record visitor choices made on interactive devices
Surveys/interviews	• Written, oral, and behavioural
Focus groups	• Selected small groups in lengthy discussions
Polling	• Phone, post and personal
Visitor numbers and profile	
Extrapolation from other sources	• Numbers at neighbouring sites • Past studies • General number of enquiries and complaints (written and verbal)

Source: Based on McArthur and Hall (1993: 257)

Case study 6 (*continued*)

> here to monitor the success of various measures. The *Tourism and the Environment* report acknowledged that:
>
> Historic towns are a more complex environment than individual heritage sites and cater for many kinds of people . . . [including visitors and residents]. . . . This makes it difficult to disentangle the pressures caused by visitors from pressures caused by other groups and a few towns have carried out detailed analysis to enable this to be done.
>
> (English Tourist Board/Employment Department 1991)
>
> The management of tourism by Canterbury City Council and other agents in the steering group face a difficult task in the 1990s in seeking to strike a delicate balance between managing tourism and the economic needs of the locality now that tourism is assuming a growing role in the local economy.

Berkhout *et al.* (1991) argue that the absence of planning and management for urban tourism has led to the current level of problems facing many popular destinations besieged by visitors. They advocate a computer-aided management model for tourism to calculate the actual limits to growth in destinations, in the same vein as van der Borg and Costa (1993). However, where they differ from these authors is that they suggest what level of investment is needed to facilitate further growth. Their methodology may offer a number of useful options for urban tourism planning, helping interested parties to identify what comprises a workable tourism plan and how to achieve planning goals with clear resource implications and options for growth in the form of a development strategy and action plan. But without action to address the problems facing tourism planners in cities such as Canterbury, it is clear that such locations may not be worth visiting in the 1990s. Thus, destinations facing saturation tourism could fall victim to the vicious circle that has beset Venice (see Case Study 6), where conflict dominates the political agenda for tourism.

Conclusion

This chapter has shown that the planning of urban tourism is often subsumed within the wider concept of urban planning. Though as Haywood argues:

More emphasis [should] be placed on tourism as a means of developing cities rather than merely a form of development in cities. To accomplish this objective tourism will have to become a more mainstream urban planning topic in which numerous social, environmental as well as economic implications require consideration.

(Haywood 1992: 18)

The management of urban tourism is now growing in significance as the tourism industry in many cities reaches a stage of maturity and requires long-term planning to ensure that short-term economic returns do not jeopardise the future sustainability of tourism. Yet 'to understand tourism in an urban context much urban research is required. Until such time as data is available, it is still possible to develop appropriate strategic and structural mechanisms so that tourism can develop and become a fundamental part of the healthy development of cities' (Haywood 1992: 18). The planning of tourism follows a lengthy process from the decision to develop a tourism plan through to its implementation. It is evident that the entire process of tourism planning is embroiled in urban politics, particularly the decision-making process related to the prioritisation of scarce public resources. Where the political complexion of elected representatives changes, there is potential for discontinuity in the political priorities for tourism planning and development. In large cities such as London, local areas have differing views of tourism which can make the coordination and agreement of priorities for city-wide planning virtually impossible. Likewise, a lack of agreement between the public and private sector agencies involved in planning may also militate against attempts to develop community-based and sustainable approaches to tourism planning (Haywood 1989). Nevertheless, some degree of planning is required to manage the complex nature of the urban tourism system to ensure its integration into the city system as well as the regional and national economic system.

There appear to be differing views on the use of urban tourism as a planning tool to stimulate economic development (e.g. the economic–industry approach). While research by Law (1993) emphasises the benefit of harnessing urban tourism as a tool for regenerating the inner city areas of large cities, Inskeep is more cautious arguing that:

> Tourism should not be seen as a panacea for inner city redevelopment and small town revitalisation. Not all places have the resources for tourism, nor would there likely be sufficient numbers of tourists to visit.
>
> (Inskeep 1991: 237)

These sentiments are also echoed by Leslie (1989) in the context of Northern Ireland. Such concerns emphasise the importance of the survey, analysis and synthesis of findings stages in the process of urban tourism planning to ensure that there is a realistic opportunity for tourism to develop.

Yet where urban tourism is a viable development option, or it is part of a well-established tourism economy, planning is a necessary process to retain a healthy tourism product and environment in which tourism can flourish. Quite often, the planning and development of tourism in urban areas is accompanied by highly visible strategies to market and promote the attributes of the locality. For this reason, the next chapter examines the role of marketing and promotion associated with urban tourism.

Questions

1 Why do cities need to plan and manage economic activities such as tourism?
2 How has urban planning evolved since 1945? Does tourism feature in post-war urban planning?
3 How does one go about preparing a tourism plan for an urban area? What steps and processes would you follow?
4 To what extent can towns and cities develop sustainable tourism plans? Is the term sustainable simply used as a fashionable phrase to make tourism planning appear community-oriented and environmentally-sensitive?

Further reading

van der Borg, J. (1992) 'Tourism and the city: some guidelines for a sustainable tourism development strategy', in H. Briassoulis and J. van der Straten (eds) *Tourism and the Environment: Regional, Economic and Policy Issues*, Dordrecht: Kluwer Academic: 121–31.

This is a good chapter of a little known book which examines different tourism development strategies which are available to city planners.

Hall, P. (1992) *Urban and Regional Planning*, London: Routledge, third edition.

This seminal study forms a good starting point for those interested in urban planning and its development since 1945, and also contains a good range of examples of how cities have approached the issue of planning.

Hall, C. M. (1991) *Tourism in Australia: Impacts, Planning and Development*, Melbourne: Longman Cheshire.

This is a very useful text which examines the planning process in relation to tourism in Australia.

Haywood, K. M. (1992) 'Identifying and responding to challenges posed by urban tourism', *Tourism Recreation Research* 17(2): 9–23.

This is a good article to consult on urban tourism and has a useful section on planning. However, the most valuable aspect of the article is its extensive bibliography which has a very good list of books, articles, reports and monographs for the researcher.

Healey, P. and Shaw, T. (1993) 'Planners, plans and sustainable development', *Regional Studies* 27(8): 769–77.

This is a good article which looks at the issue of sustainability and the planning process.

Inskeep, E. (1991) *Tourism Planning: An Integrated and Sustainable Development Approach*, New York: Van Nostrand Reinhold.

Inskeep, E. (1994) *National and Regional Tourism Planning*, London: Routledge.

These two studies by Inskeep are by far the most comprehensive and accessible publications on tourism planning. They are based on the author's experience as a practitioner and consultant to the World Tourism Organization.

Murphy, P. E. (1994) 'Tourism and sustainable development', in W. Theobald (ed.) *Global Tourism: The Next Decade*, Oxford: Butterworth-Heinemann: 274–90.

Pearce, D. G. (1989) *Tourist Development*, London: Longman, second edition.

This is by far the most authoritative study on the process of tourism development and the role of planning to control the tourism development process.

6
Marketing urban tourism: place-marketing

Introduction

In the 1980s, there was a resurgence of municipal interest in the promotion and advertising of cities as desirable and unique places for tourists
to visit, a tradition that dates back to the nineteenth century (Brown
1985). This is an important feature of urban management and planning
to facilitate the development of urban tourism by selling the city as a
product to customers (the tourists and visitors). This process of 'place-
marketing' or 'city-marketing' is now gaining increasing attention within
the tourism and marketing literature (e.g. Ashworth and Voogd 1988,
1990a, b; Goodall 1990; Madsen 1992; Neill 1993; Gold and Ward
1994). The process of place-marketing reflects a:

> New paradigm (that is a new approach) structuring the way the
> complex functioning of cities is viewed . . . [as] . . . many urban
> activities operate in some kind of a market . . . in which a planned
> action implies an explicit and simultaneous consideration of both the
> supply-side and the demand-side . . . [and] . . . such an approach has
> implications for not only the way the cities are managed.
>
> (Ashworth and Voogd 1988:65)

A consideration of place-marketing is a natural extension of the process
of urban management and planning, which requires public authorities to
consider the market context and competitive position of the city, especially in terms of tourism and leisure markets.

The significance of this new paradigm is the recognition within the tourism literature that tourists select particular place-products (i.e. destinations) in their holiday decision-making process, often on the basis of limited knowledge of the destination and available options (see Kent 1990). As Goodall (1990: 260) observes, the holiday may be as much the place as the place is the holiday for the tourist. In contrast, the various businesses and organisations associated with tourism focus on specific aspects of the place-product (e.g. an attraction or facility). The organisation charged with marketing the city will tend to adopt a composite view of the city and its place-product in selling the destination to potential visitors. This also illustrates one of the major problems associated with the marketing of places: place-marketers adopt a composite view of the place-product with little real understanding of the diversity of the services and products being sold by the tourism industry within the locality. This can lead to a more generalised image of the urban tourism destination and the way in which it is constructed and sold to visitors by agencies responsible for marketing and promotion. Recent research by van der Borg (1994) examines the brochures produced by tour operators for 144 European cities to illustrate the supply of European urban tourism products by operators. He emphasises that nineteen of the most popular cities, mainly capital cities, feature prominently in the brochures produced across the EC (Table 6.1). Such research implies that both tour operators market cities to specific market segments, and the competitive pricing of such products is examined elsewhere (Clewer *et al.* 1992). In view of the existing knowledge of how cities are marketed and how products are priced by tour operators, this chapter focuses on urban tourism marketing by city-wide agencies and the way in which destinations are promoted as place-products. The significance of place-marketing is examined as is how cities differ from other products which are marketed. The basic purpose of place-marketing is used to illustrate the context in which tourism place promotion exists. A discussion of the conceptual basis of place-imagery and the way in which such images are transmitted to people is followed by a brief discussion of how the image is communicated using different marketing tools. To end, the preconditions for successful place-marketing are reviewed and the implications are considered.

It is important to stress that within the confines of one chapter, there is insufficient space to undertake a detailed review of place-marketing, and its development as an area of academic research and practical application. For this reason, readers are directed to the numerous

Table 6.1 The supply of urban destinations in various European countries offered in tour operators' summer 1993 catalogues. Places featured/not featured in the brochures available in each country.

City	NL	DE	FR	GB	BE	DK	IT
Aachen (DE)	X	X	.	.	.	.	.
Aberdeen (GB)	.	.	.	.	.	X	.
Aix-en-Provence (FR)	.	.	.	X	.	.	.
Amsterdam (NL)	X	X	X	X	X	X	X
Ankara (TR)	.	.	.	.	.	X	.
Antalya (TR)	.	.	.	.	.	X	.
Antwerp (BE)	X	X	.	.	.	.	.
Athens (GR)	X	X	.	X	X	X	X
Bamberg (DE)	.	X	.	.	.	.	.
Barcelona (ES)	X	X	X	X	.	X	X
Bardolino (IT)	.	.	.	X	.	.	.
Basle (CH)	X	X	.	.	.	.	.
Baveno (IT)	.	.	X	X	.	.	.
Belfast (GB)	X	.	.	.	.	.	.
Bergen (NO)	.	.	.	.	.	X	X
Berlin (DE)	X	X	X	X	X	X	.
Berne (CH)	X	.	.	X	.	.	.
Biarritz (FR)	.	.	.	X	.	.	.
Billund (DK)	X	.	.	.	.	.	.
Birmingham (GB)	X	.	.	.	.	X	.
Blankenberge (BE)	X	.	.	.	.	.	.
Bologna (IT)	.	X	.	.	.	.	.
Bolzano (IT)	.	.	X	.	.	.	.
Bonn (DE)	X	.	.	.	.	.	.
Bordeaux (FR)	X	X	.	X	.	.	.
Bremen (DE)	X	X	.	.	.	.	.
Brescia (IT)	.	.	X	.	.	.	.
Brighton (GB)	X	.	.	.	.	.	.
Bruges (BE)	X	X	.	X	.	.	.
Brussels (BE)	X	X	.	X	.	X	X
Bucharest (RO)	.	X	.	.	.	X	.
Budapest (HU)	X	X	X	X	X	X	X
Cannes (FR)	X	X	.	X	.	X	.
Chester (GB)	X	.	.	.	.	.	.
Citta di Castello (IT)	.	.	.	X	.	.	.
Cologne (DE)	X	X	.	X	.	X	.
Como (IT)	.	.	X	X	.	.	.
Copenhagen (DK)	X	X	.	X	X	.	X
Cordoba (ES)	.	X	.	.	.	.	.
Cork (IE)	X	.	.	.	.	.	.
Davos (CH)	X	.	.	.	.	.	.
Dijon (FR)	.	X	.	.	.	.	.
Dresden (DE)	X	X	.	.	.	X	.
Dublin (IE)	X	X	X	X	X	X	X
Dusseldorf (DE)	X	X	.	.	.	X	.

Table 6.1 *(continued)*

City	NL	DE	FR	GB	BE	DK	IT
Edinburgh (GB)	X	X	X	.	.	X	X
Erfurt (DE)	.	X	.	.	.	.	.
Florence (IT)	X	X	X	X	X	X	.
Frankfurt (DE)	X	X	.	.	.	X	.
Freiburg (DE)	X	X	.	.	.	.	.
Gdansk (PL)	.	X	.	.	.	.	.
Geneva (CH)	X	.	.	X	.	X	.
Genf (CH)	.	X	.	.	.	.	.
Ghent (BE)	X	X	.	X	.	.	.
Gibraltar	.	.	.	X	.	X	.
Glasgow (GB)	X	.	.	.	.	X	.
Gothenburg (SE)	X	X	.	.	.	.	.
Granada (ES)	.	X	.	.	.	.	.
Graz (AT)	X	X	.	.	.	.	.
Hamburg (DE)	X	X	.	.	.	X	.
Hanover (DE)	X	X	.	.	.	X	.
Hasselt (BE)	X	.	.	.	.	.	.
Heidelberg (DE)	X	X	.	X	.	.	.
Helsinki (SF)	.	X	.	.	.	X	X
Innsbruck (AT)	X	X	X	. X	.	.	.
Interlaken (CH)	X	.	.	X	.	.	.
Istanbul (TR)	X	X	X	X	X	X	X
Izmir (TR)	.	X	.	.	.	X	.
Karlsbad (DE)	.	X	.	.	.	.	.
Kiel (DE)	.	X	.	.	.	.	.
Kiev (CIS)	.	X	.	.	.	X	.
Knokke (BE)	X	.	.	.	.	.	.
Koblenz (DE)	X	.	.	.	.	.	.
Krakow (PL)	.	X	.	.	.	.	.
Lausanne (CH)	X	.	X	.	.	.	.
Leipzig (DE)	X	X	.	.	.	X	.
Leuven (BE)	X	.	.	.	.	.	.
Linz (AT)	X	.	.	.	.	.	.
Lisbon (PT)	X	X	X	X	X	X	X
Locarno (CH)	X	.	.	.	.	.	.
London (GB)	X	X	X	.	X	X	X
Lucerne (CH)	X	.	.	X	.	.	.
Luebeck (DE)	.	X	.	.	.	.	.
Lugano (CH)	X	.	.	.	.	.	.
Luik (BE)	X	.	.	.	.	.	.
Luxembourg (LU)	X	.	.	.	.	X	.
Lyons (FR)	X	X	.	.	.	X	.
Maastricht (NL)	X	.	.	.	.	.	.
Madrid (ES)	X	X	X	X	X	X	X
Malaga (ES)	X	.	.	.	.	X	X
Manchester (GB)	X	.	.	.	.	X	.
Marseilles (FR)	X	.	.	.	.	.	.

Table 6.1 *(continued)*

City	NL	DE	FR	GB	BE	DK	IT
Mechelen (BE)	X	.	.	.	.	.	.
Mestre (IT)	.	X	.	.	.	.	.
Milan (IT)	X	X	.	X	.	X	.
Monte-Carlo (MC)	X	X	.	X	.	X	.
Montreux (CH)	X	.	.	.	.	.	.
Moscow (CIS)	X	X	X	.	X	X	X
Munich (DE)	X	X	X	X	.	X	.
Namur (BE)	X	.	.	.	.	.	.
Naples (IT)	X	X	X	.	.	.	.
Nuremberg (DE)	X	.	.	.	.	.	.
Newcastle (GB)	X	.	.	.	.	.	.
Nice (FR)	X	X	.	X	.	X	.
Oslo (NO)	X	X	X	.	.	X	X
Ostend (BE)	X	.	.	.	.	.	.
Palermo (IT)	.	X	.	.	.	.	.
Paris (FR)	X	X	X	X	X	X	X
Perugia (IT)	.	.	.	X	.	.	.
Pisa (IT)	.	X	.	.	.	X	.
Pono (PT)	X	X	.	.	.	X	.
Potsdam (DE)	X	X	.	.	.	.	.
Prague (CS)	X	X-X	X	X	X	X	.
Reykjavik (IS)	.	X	.	X	.	X	.
Riga (Latvia)	.	.	.	.	.	X	.
Rome (IT)	X	X	X	X	X	X	.
St Gallen (CH)	X	.	.	.	.	.	.
St Petersburg (CIS)	X	X	X	.	X	X	X
Salamanca (ES)	.	.	X	.	.	.	.
Salzburg (AT)	X	X	.	X	.	.	.
San Gimignano (IT)	.	.	.	X	.	.	.
Seville (ES)	X	X	.	X	.	X	X
Sienna (IT)	X	X	.	X	.	.	.
Sofia (BG)	.	X	.	.	.	.	.
Stenin (PL)	.	X	.	.	.	.	.
Stockholm (SE)	X	X	X	X	.	X	X
Strasbourg (FR)	X	X	.	X	.	.	.
Stresa (IT)	.	.	X	X	.	.	.
Stungart (DE)	X	X	.	.	.	X	.
Talloires (FR)	X	.	.	X	.	.	.
Tallin (Estonia)	.	.	.	.	.	X	.
The Hague (NL)	.	X	.	.	.	.	.
Thessaloniki (GR)	.	X	.	.	.	X	.
Toledo (ES)	.	X	X	.	.	.	.
Torshavn (SE)	.	.	.	.	.	X	.
Toulouse (FR)	X	.	.	X	.	.	.
Tours (FR)	X	.	.	X	.	.	.
Trier (DE)	X	.	.	.	.	.	.
Trondheim (NO)	.	.	.	.	.	X	.

Table 6.1 *(continued)*

City	NL	DE	FR	GB	BE	DK	IT
Turin (IT)	X	X	.	.	.	.	.
Valencia (ES)	X	X	.	.	.	X	.
Venice (IT)	X	X	X	X	X	X	.
Verona (IT)	X	X	.	X	.	.	.
Vienna (AT)	X	X	X	X	X	X	X
Vilnius (Lithuania)	.	.	.	.	.	X	.
Warsaw (PL)	X	X	.	.	.	X	.
Weimar (DE)	.	X	.	.	.	.	.
York (GB)	X	.	.	.	.	.	.
Zagreb (YU)	.	X	.	.	.	.	.
Zurich (CH)	X	X	.	X	.	X	.

Key

AT	=	Austria
BE	=	Belgium
CH	=	Switzerland
CIS	=	Commonwealth of Independent States (former Soviet Union)
DE	=	Germany
DK	=	Denmark
ES	=	Spain
FR	=	France
GB	=	Great Britain
GR	=	Greece
HU	=	Hungary
IE	=	Republic of Ireland
IT	=	Italy
NL	=	Netherlands
NO	=	Norway
PL	=	Poland
PT	=	Portugal
SE	=	Sweden
TR	=	Turkey
YU	=	Former Yugoslavia

X	=	Featured in brochures
.	=	Not featured in brochures

Plate 6.1 British Tourist Authority Sales Manual for Brazil 1990–91: This illustrates the icons used to attract overseas visitors to the UK, appealing to popular images which visitors associate with London (reproduced by kind permission from the British Tourist Authority Photographic Library)

journal articles (e.g. Ashworth and Voogd 1988; Madsen 1992), books (Ashworth and Voogd 1990a) and edited collections of papers (e.g. Gold and Ward 1994) for more detail on the wider application of place-marketing to achieve objectives other than tourism promotion.

Place-marketing: a conceptual framework

The term place-marketing (Madsen 1992), selling places (Burgess 1982) or geographical marketing (Ashworth and Voogd 1987) in an urban context is based on the principle that the city is a place-product which can be marketed and promoted to potential customers. Even so, certain critics have questioned its role in the local authority planning (Clarke 1986). In 'marketing terminology, a customer purchases the core product (set of valued attributes) by acquiring the tangible product' (Ashworth and Voogd 1990a: 69–70). This is based on the premise that marketing is a process whereby individuals and groups obtain the types of products or goods they value (Kotler and Armstrong 1991). These goods are created and exchanged through a social and managerial process which requires a detailed understanding of consumers, their wants and desires so that products can be effectively and efficiently delivered.

Within marketing, three key areas exist:

- Strategic planning
- Marketing research
- The marketing mix

and each area is significant in the process of communicating the place product to the urban tourist.

Strategic planning

Within any business or company, there is a need to provide some degree of order or structure to its activities and to think ahead. This is essential if companies are to be able to respond to the competitive business environment in which organisations operate. For this reason, a formal planning process is necessary which is known as 'Strategic Planning'. According to Kotler and Armstrong (1991: 29), strategic planning is defined as 'the process of developing and maintaining a strategic fit between the organization's goals and capabilities and its changing marketing opportunities'. Businesses need to be aware of their position in the wider business environment and they will respond to competition and new business opportunities within an organised framework. Therefore, strategic planning is undertaken by organisations involved in place-marketing to review where they want to be in the future regarding the city's market position. Strategic planning will often lead to the formulation of a marketing strategy to assess how an organisation will achieve its goals using certain actions.

Marketing research

This process is one which is often seen as synonymous with market research but, as the following definition by Seibert (1973) implies, in reality it is a much broader concept as 'marketing research is an organised process associated with the gathering, processing, analysis, storage and dissemination of information to facilitate and improve decision-making'. It incorporates various forms of research undertaken by organisations to understand their customers, markets and business efficiency. The methods used to investigate different aspects of a company's business ultimately determine the type of research under-taken. Six main types of research can be identified:

1 *Market analysis and forecasting*, which is used in marketing planning to measure and project market volumes as well as the market share and revenue generated by different segments.
2 *Consumer research*, which is used to segment and position a product within a market. It can involve quantitative assessment of consumer profiles and qualitative assessment of consumer needs as illustrated in Chapter 2.
3 *Products and price studies*, which are used to formulate the pricing and presentation of products. These are often used to test consumer demand for new products and price sensitivity to the products.
4 *Promotion and sales research*, which is used to assess the efficiency of the marketing communication process. For example, consumer response to advertising and media may be examined as well as sales promotion.
5 *Distribution research*, which is used to assess the degree of effi-ciency in the distribution of goods and services such as the stocking of brochures in retail outlets and distributor awareness of the product.
6 *Evaluation and performance monitoring studies*, which are used to

examine the overall success in the marketing process and often involve assessing consumer satisfaction.

A number of good introductions to marketing research are available and more recent books on tourism research are recommended as preliminary reading on this topic (e.g. Veal 1992). Marketing research allows the company to keep in touch with its customers to monitor needs and tastes which are constantly changing in time and space. In terms of place-marketing, marketing research will be a useful activity to understand the type of place-image which is likely to appeal to potential tourists. However, the actual implementation of marketing ultimately depends on the 'marketing mix'.

The marketing mix

The marketing mix is 'the mixture of controllable marketing variables that the firm [or company] uses to pursue the sought level of sales in the target market' (Kotler, cited in Holloway and Plant 1988: 48). This means that for any organisation responsible for place-marketing, there are four main marketing variables which it needs to harness to achieve the goals identified in the marketing strategy formulated through the strategic planning process. These variables are:

1 *Product formulation*, which is the ability of a company or organisation to adapt to the needs of its customers in terms of the services it provides. These are constantly being adapted to changes in consumer markets.
2 *Price*, is the economic concept used to adjust the supply of a service to meet the demand, taking account of sales targets and turnover.
3 *Promotion*, is the manner in which a company seeks to improve customers' knowledge of the services it sells so that those people who are made aware may be turned into actual purchasers. To achieve promotional aims, advertising, public relations, sales and brochure production functions are undertaken within the remit of promotion. Not surprisingly promotion often consumes the largest proportion of marketing budgets.
4 *Place*, this refers to the location at which prospective customers may be induced to purchase a service – the point of sale.

As marketing variables, production, price, promotion and place are normally called the 'four Ps'. These are incorporated into the marketing

Plate 6.2 British Tourist Authority promotional literature: this illustrates the appeal of the monarchy, regal pomp and splendour and the urban attractions associated with such images (e.g. Windsor Castle, the Houses of Parliament and Buckingham Palace). (reproduced by kind permission from the British Tourist Authority Photographic Library)

Plate 6.3 Winchester Visitor Guide 1994 (reproduced by kind permission from Winchester City Council)

process in relation to the known competition and the impact of market conditions. Thus, the marketing process involves the continuous evaluation of how a business operates internally and externally and it can be summarised as 'the management process which identifies, anticipates and supplies customer's requirements efficiently and profitably' (UK Institute of Marketing, cited in Cannon 1989).

In place-marketing, the 'place has a certain amount of resources (infrastructure, houses, castle, parks, people, museums, etc). It is only through an interpretation of these resources that a place product and a place image' (Madsen 1992: 633) are derived. This involves organisations engaging in each of the three areas of marketing activity. Consequently, the process of place-marketing requires urban managers and planners to engage in:

• Product development to improve the physical resources of the city;
• The promotion of the city as a place by producing and enhancing people's image of the city as a place to visit.

As Madsen (1992: 633) observes 'the promotion of a place-image becomes a matter of commodifying it through a rigorous selection from its many characteristics'. What is the basis of such an approach within marketing?

The concept of place-marketing: marketing influences

The science of marketing has evolved from the practices of the private sector with its pursuit of profit and exchange of goods and services. Ashworth and Voogd (1990a) explain that the concept of place-marketing is an amalgam of three different traditions in marketing: marketing in non-profit organisations, social marketing and image marketing.

Marketing in non-profit organisations

The conceptual basis of the change in emphasis in marketing from a private sector profit-led approach to one where non-profit perspectives were also emphasised, can be traced to an influential publication by Kotler and Levy (1969). They showed that public and semi-public agencies (which are responsible for public services and cities) had different objectives to the private sector. The implication for place-marketing is that public authorities are not necessarily motivated by direct financial profit when conducting marketing. Nevertheless, it still requires such organisations to identify who their markets and consumers are. These ideas were subsequently developed in the marketing literature by Kotler and Zaltman (1971), Kotler (1972) and Lovelock and Weinberg (1984). At the same time, Ashworth and Voogd (1988: 67) acknowledge that 'it was appreciated that ideas were as marketable a commodity as physical products, and that the objective of the marketing exercise could be logically extended from the influencing of purchasing behaviour to wider aspects of human behaviour'. This led to the emergence of two other schools of thought within marketing: 'social marketing and the 'concept of image marketing'.

Social marketing

According to Kotler (1982: 16) social marketing 'is aimed at enhancing the consumer's and society's well-being' in the immediate and long term. This is seen as one way for organisations to broaden their concept of marketing so that the behaviour of consumers can be influenced in ways other than those connected to their direct purchasing behaviour, a feature Kotler (1982: 193) observes as 'seeking to increase the acceptability of a social idea'. More recently this has been termed 'attitudinal marketing', with the aim of seeking to alter or influence the attitudes or behaviour of those people targeted through the marketing process. Clearly this has an immediate application to place-marketing by encouraging people to think about a place and its product in a certain way.

Image marketing

The concept of the marketable image (Kotler and Mindak 1978) developed in the 1960s where the images of politicians were promoted using public relations with little reference to their policies. This confirmed that marketing could be undertaken with a vaguely defined product with the aim of 'manipulating the behavioural patterns of selected audiences' (Ashworth and Voogd 1990a: 20). Thus, an image can be marketed without a tangible physical product (Fines 1981) and in combination with the ideas of non-profit marketing and social marketing, the process of place-marketing can be undertaken.

The process of place-marketing

The process of place-marketing is described by Ashworth and Voogd as one:

> Whereby urban activities are as closely as possible related to the demands of targeted customers so as to maximise the efficient social and economic functioning of the area . . . [which] . . . can be applied at many spatial scales and thus city marketing can be viewed as part of a broader geographical marketing alongside regional or even national marketing.
>
> (Ashworth and Voogd 1988: 68)

This involves the recognition of the relationships that exist between customers and producers, requiring an understanding of the spatial and organisational structure of the city in relation to its product. It also requires an understanding of the demand for the product in terms of the characteristics, market behaviour and needs of its customers. In a marketing context, these relationships are normally achieved through the 'marketing mix'.

In terms of city-marketing, Ashworth and Voogd (1988: 68) note that 'it is appropriate to develop a geographical marketing mix that is distinctly spatial'. As part of the process of marketing, cities need to devise a strategy in which policy towards marketing the city is outlined. As discussed in Chapter 5, strategy and plan formulation is an important and lengthy process and also needs to be applied to marketing the city. Kotler *et al.* (1993: 18) argues that 'place marketing at its core embraces four activities:

- designing the right mix of community features and services
- setting attractive incentives for the current and potential buyers and users of its goods and services
- delivering a place's products and services in an efficient, accessible way
- promoting the place's values and image so that potential users are fully aware of the place's distinctive advantages'.

This requires a policy and Ashworth and Voogd (1988: 69) identify four types commonly used. These are:

1 A consolidation or defensive policy, whereby the existing range of services are maintained for current consumers;

2 A quality-oriented policy, whereby the effort is placed upon enhancing a better quality of facilities for consumers;
3 An expansionist policy, whereby towns and cities with an attractive
   portfolio of historic buildings or resources (e.g. Dunedin in New
   Zealand) seek to develop a marketing strategy to promote urban
   heritage tourism;
4 A diversification policy, whereby new markets are targeted for a new
   range of services it is providing, such as Sheffield's cultural and sport
   strategy following the infrastructure that was available following the
   World Student Games (Roche 1992).

Who is responsible for place-marketing?

Local authority marketing

In many cities, this is one additional function adopted by the local
municipal authorities. This is a relatively recent feature for many such
bodies which is reflected in what has been termed 'minimal marketing',
the belief that the product actually sells itself without promotion.
However, there are examples of 'aggressive marketing' where cities
have over-invested without regard to the market. In the case of urban
heritage tourism marketing in the UK, Ashworth and Voogd (1988)
argue that a balanced approach to place-marketing is needed so that
policies are appropriate to the particular demand in each city (Table
6.2).

An effective marketing strategy for a city will include the following
stages.

Auditing the market

This is the systematic analysis of the market position of a city in relation
to its external environment, including issues which cannot be influenced
by planning, and internal issues within organisations. This is often
expressed as a 'strengths, weaknesses, opportunities and threats analysis' (SWOT analysis). The external audit will help to shape the policies
required to shape the product to meet the needs of users. For example,
how do users perceive the city and its products? Have past policies met
the needs of users and how effective is the current organisation and
management of the city and resources to deliver these products?

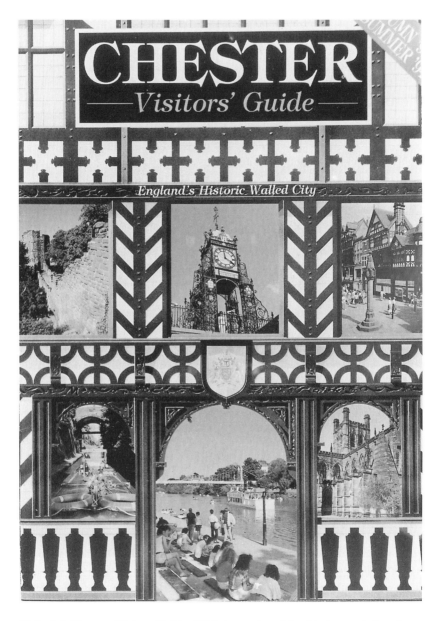

Plate 6.4 Chester Visitor Guide 1994 (reproduced by kind permission from Chester City Council)

Plate 6.5 Exeter Visitor Guide 1994 (reproduced by kind permission from Exeter City Council)

Table 6.2 Urban heritage marketing strategies

Demand characteristics	Marketing strategy	Possible UK example
Full demand	Maintenance marketing	York/Chester
Latent demand	Developmental marketing	Lincoln
Negative demand	Conversional marketing	Wigan
No demand	Stimulational marketing	Leicester
Faltering demand	Remarketing	Scarborough
Over-full demand	(Selective) de-marketing	Bath/Oxford/Canterbury

Source: Based on Ashworth and Voogd (1988: 70)

Identifying the target market

This is done by using market segmentation, a process discussed at length in Chapter 2. This may also incorporate information on the spatial behaviour of users and the consumer decision-making process on the consumption of product within the city;

Identifying the qualities of the city

Complex quantitative multi-criteria evaluation techniques such as competition analysis and potency analysis (see Ashworth and Voogd 1990a: 53–64 for a detailed discussion) are used to establish how the city's product compares to other cities.

Developing and shaping the city product

A process carried out to meet the needs of the market.

Constructing the image of the city

This is the image to be transmitted to the target market through the process of promotion. This may require extensive efforts in relation to image building. The application of these principles to selling cities as urban tourism destinations raises one important question: Can places be sold for tourism? (Ashworth and Voogd 1990b). To examine this contention, it is useful to consider a number of issues such as whether a tourism destination is a product and whether the tourist is a place customer, drawing on the seminal study by Ashworth and Voogd (1990b).

Marketing urban tourism places

The city as a tourism place-product

The discussion of tourism supply issues in Chapter 3 highlights the concept of the city as a leisure product which is a bundle of products consumed by the tourist as part of their urban tourism experience. The issue here is whether these can be sold as a commodity, even though many elements of the tourist experience are services (see Edgett and Parkinson 1993 on the marketing of services). The fundamental difference between a marketable service or good compared to a tourism destination is the way in which it is consumed. The service or good is purchased and consumed directly by the tourist. The place-product is rather more complex to understand as Jansen-Verbeke (1988) notes in her concept of the 'tourist recreation product' (TRP). The TRP is both a complex product representing the city as well as being the commodities of which it is composed (Ashworth and Voogd 1990b: 7). Furthermore, Ashworth and Voogd (1990b) also note the following issues which affect the extent to which a tourist destination constitutes a product:

Definition

Defining and delimiting a tourist city as a product (Ashworth 1987) poses practical problems in terms of the spatial extent of the city as well as more complex conceptual issues. For example, urban tourism destinations contain both facilities and attractions as well as other elements which are both the product and the containing context for the bundle of products;

Variations and permutations

Many aspects of the services and products sold to the tourist are consumed as packages which are determined by the producer of the services or the intermediaries in the tourism industry. This means that the destination marketing agencies are unable to market a precise product in view of all the possible permutations and variants available to the tourist;

Plate 6.6 Kent County Council Visitor Guide to Kent 1994 (reproduced by kind permission from Kent County Council)

Plate 6.7 Heart of England Tourist Board Visitor Guide, 1994 (reproduced by kind permission from the Heart of England Tourist Board)

Boundaries

The scale at which the city is marketed to tourists is often arbitrarily constructed, since local government boundaries may not reflect the real range of experiences or products available to the tourist. For example, in London Docklands the marketing of tourism has not been integrated with the wider promotion of the city by the London Tourist Board though the recent evidence suggests that LDDC is undertaking joint promotions with the British Tourist Authority to attract foreign visitors to the region;

Multi-selling

Cities marketed by local authorities may be multi-sold, meaning that the city as a product is simultaneously sold to different customers with different needs and motives for visiting, unlike the marketing of goods. For example, the tourist-historic city (see Ashworth and Tunbridge 1990) may be sold to one group of tourists while at the same time, the city may be marketed as a desirable location for leisure shopping. This can lead to planning or resource conflicts if physical planning does not recognise the potential conflicts that may arise from multi-selling the city product. Furthermore, assuming that the tourist is a place customer also requires some qualification as since:

- The tourist is a sophisticated consumer, with different and varied patterns of behaviour which need to be recognised and analysed. Research by Crompton (1979) is interesting in this context as it found that individual tourists' perception of the same product can vary. This needs to be recognised in dealing with tourists as customers;
- The tourist product is not only multi-sold but multi-bought and therefore the product is being simultaneously consumed by tourists, residents, workers, shoppers and other visitors. Each of these users need to be recognised so that the product can be targeted to each group. Ashworth and Voogd (1990b: 11) argue 'the tourist is logically a place consumer but the identification and measurement of this market will pose particular difficulties' as the tourist can only usually be identified at the point of consumption.

How is the city sold to tourists and how is the image of the city produced?

Selling the city to tourists

Kotler *et al.* (1993) view the selling of the city to tourists as one of four broad strategies to attract visitors, residents, industry and to increase their exports. These are: image marketing, attractions marketing, infra-structure marketing and people marketing. A wide range of actors are involved in this process (e.g. local actors such as the local authority, regional actors and national agencies such as the Civil Service), although in the context of tourism, it is their overall contribution to place improvement and image promotion that is important. For example, the development of festivals and special events (Getz 1991) and hallmark events may make an important contribution to the image of a destination. Getz (1991) shows that in the case of Baltimore, urban development initiatives and fairs were combined with the work of the Baltimore Office of Promotion and Tourism to stage special events to attract visitors and residents back into the downtown area after riots in 1968. It is this type of activity that illustrates the significance of public and private sector partnerships between the agents in Table 6.3, and points to the significance of urban tourism organisations in selling the city to visitors.

Urban tourism organisations

According to Law (1993), the marketing and promotion of cities was traditionally a function undertaken by firms in the private sector. Yet as Queenan (1992) shows, local authorities in British and German cities have taken a lead role in both the development and promotion of urban tourism. This has also been followed by coordination and liaison to develop public–private sector partnerships. For example, in the USA the organisation and management in large cities has been the function of 'a central tourist agency which may be public, quasi-public, non-profit or private' (Kotler *et al.* 1993: 219). In smaller US cities this function may be undertaken by the chambers of commerce, though as Law (1993) shows, a large promotional budget is available in large tourist-oriented cities with Las Vegas deemed to be among the best financed and most aggressive. In the case of Las Vegas, it has an annual budget of $81 million to operate its tourist and convention agency while in San Francisco the budget amounts to $9 million, followed by Atlanta ($8 million) and San Diego ($6 million). The public and private sector funding of these tourist organisations is based on a variety of sources, typically through local room taxes on tourist accommodation and membership fees from affiliated organisations and advertising revenue from promotional literature. To maintain a high profile in tourism marketing overseas, many convention bureaux attend trade shows where they market their products in promotional literature, such as the annual World Travel Market in London and similar events in Europe.

In the case of Las Vegas' tourist and convention bureau, it operates as a quasi-government organisation – The Las Vegas Authority. In contrast, San Francisco's Convention and Visitor Bureau operates as a non-profit corporation as does the Atlanta Convention Bureau. The San Diego Convention and Visitor Bureau is a hybrid organisation somewhere between the Las Vegas and San Francisco model, being a quasi-public body which operates on a non-profit basis.

Law (1993: 150) notes that 'most of these organisations cover the entire metropolitan area rather than just the central city. This makes sense, since boundaries are irrelevant to the tourist' and the products within the urban area. However, the case of the London Tourist Board illustrates (see Chapter 5) they are mainly marketing organisations with little power to plan and develop tourism. Thus, 'their rationale is that by concentrating the marketing resources of the public and private sectors there will be a greater impact than would occur if each firm attempted its own advertising' (Law 1993: 151). In the UK and Europe, local authorities make a large contribution to the funding of urban place marketing, although private sector membership fees play a major role (see Law 1993 for a more detailed discussion of their findings). The scale of North American city marketing for tourism is massive compared to the UK budgets for cities such as Glasgow (£2.2 million), Greater Manchester Bureau (£0.5 million) and Birmingham (£1.4 million) (Touche Ross 1991). In France, Lyon receives 70 per cent of its budget from the local authority with a budget similar to its UK counterparts. Thus, the North American attitude towards urban tourism marketing appears to be more proactive and is worthy of further discussion.

Urban tourism marketing in North American cities

Pearce (1992: 43) notes that 'government tourist organisations . . . associated with city government . . . [have] . . . attracted little attention yet available evidence suggests that in monetary terms they may be as important as State Tourism Organisations (STO)'. For example, the United States Travel Services (1978) survey of American cities with a population exceeding 100,000 found that expenditure from travel, tourism and convention programmes (to attract conferences and exhibitions – see Law 1993) was almost $54 million for 102 cities (compared to a total STO budget of $53 million in 1976). It is interesting to note that in the case of the Atlanta Convention and Visitor Bureau, its $8.1 million budget for 1988 received 61 per cent of its funding from a public room sales tax. Although somewhat dated, the US Travel Service (1978) 'remains the most comprehensive source of information on city, government involvement in travel and tourism' (Pearce 1992: 43). Of the 142 cities responding to the survey:

• About half stated they contracted out their tourism activities to agencies (e.g. convention and visitor bureaux and chambers of trade);
• Nearly 16 per cent dealt with tourism activities through their offices and units;
• 16 per cent indicated that they were not involved in promoting urban tourism.

The activities which these organisations undertook included:

• Production of information materials;
• Administration of the tourist bureau and the maintenance of public facilities;
• National and regional advertising, promotion and public relations;
• Convention planning and technical assistance (in larger cities);
• A hotel/motel reservation system in some cities;
• Tourism research.

In addition, approximately 50 per cent of cities reported that they undertook activities in partnership with the private sector (e.g. advertising, promotion, familiarisation tours and the development of packages). Although certain cities are relatively new to place promotion for tourism, many emphasise the need for coordination and liaison (Frank 1985), and well-developed visitor and convention bureaux (see Drake 1985). Where city governments have become involved in urban regeneration projects and tourism features as a component (e.g. Baltimore, Philadelphia, Boston, Charleston, New Orleans and San Francisco), they are able, in some cases, to coordinate the funding and resources needed to develop facilities and attract tourists.

Urban tourism marketing in other cities

Pearce's (1992) seminal study also documents the extent of urban tourism marketing by tourist organisations in cities outside of North America. For example, Munich City Tourist Office had a budget of DM 23.3 million in 1989, with 40 per cent of its income derived from the city council and the remaining amount generated from self-funding activities. Only 9 per cent of its budget was directly allocated to marketing, and the Tourist Office has no formal links with the private sector tourism industry, though it did have opportunities for informal exchanges. The characteristics of the Munich City Tourist Office include:

- The employment of 140 people (and 150 guides/hostesses);
- The operation of visitor services including information offices, arranging accommodation, guides and concert bookings;
- The operation of a convention bureau;
- The production and distribution of promotional material;
- Press and public relations work;
- The promotion and organisation of festivals and events (e.g. the Oktoberfest beer festival);
- Participation in trade shows, seminars and exhibitions.
- In conjunction with Heidelberg, the city has a representative in New York to deal with the tourism wholesalers and the Press;
- It does not undertake market research of its own, relying on that generated by DZT (the Federal Statistic Office), other agencies and the tourism industry.

In the Netherlands, the tourism promotion by the VVVs (Vereniging voor Vreemdelingen Verkeer) is well established in three largest cities; Amsterdam, Rotterdam and The Hague. The characteristics of the Amsterdam VVV are that:

- It runs as a corporation with a board of directors. Of the thirteen directors, three are nominated by the city; three by the chamber of commerce; seven are elected by its membership (Pearce 1992: 128);
- In the 1980s it had 900 members from a cross-section of the tourism industry;
- Its annual budget in 1989 was fl1.8 million generated by member's contributions, subsidies from the city and Chamber of Commerce and self-generated revenue;

- The staff comprises ninety in the peak season, staffing two visitor information centres in the city (and a motorway kiosk);
- fl1.3 million were spent on marketing Amsterdam in 1989 with the aim of making 'target groups aware that Amsterdam is an excellent choice for business and recreational tourism throughout the year' (Pearce 1992: 128);
- It commissions research, such as the KPMG (1993) study of tourism in European cities.

In the context of New Zealand, Pearce (1992) notes the characteristics of Auckland's promotion as the country's main gateway. Tourism promotion is undertaken by Tourism Auckland, a regional organisation, established in 1987 as a non-profit organisation and funded by Auckland Regional Authority. Its principal features were that;

- It is administered by an eleven-member board, with industry and local government representatives;
- It is staffed by five people and has ninety members;
- In 1990–91 Tourism Auckland's income was under NZ$40,000 and 50 per cent of this was from an Auckland Regional Council grant; the rest is generated from membership fees and other activities;
- The organisation's aim is 'to be the focal point for the promotion of tourism in Auckland which best serves the economic and social needs of our members and the people of Auckland' (Pearce 1992: 173);
- Pearce (1992: 173) suggests that the organisation 'is still trying to establish its identity and role within the region';
- Its promotional efforts are directed towards events and conventions;
- Research findings are disseminated to members but it does not undertake primary research;
- It manages two self-funded visitor centres at Auckland Airport;
- It participates in trade shows in Melbourne and Sydney;
- Other visitor servicing is supported by the activities of the city councils (see Page 1993b for a discussion of these roles in Wellington);
- No formal links exist between Tourism Auckland and the Auckland City Council's funded Auckland Visitor Centre, although some joint promotion and liaison does take place.

It is clear from these examples that in some cases, a lack of integration in the activities of tourism organisations promoting urban areas leads to competition and duplication of efforts. Even so, the North American examples suggest that urban tourism markets, especially the business travellers attending conventions, are being aggressively targeted due to the economic impact they generate for the city economy (Kotler *et al.* 1993). The type of tourism organisations which market and promote urban tourism vary immensely as the examples above show. Even so, they all have a common purpose, to raise visitor awareness of the positive attributes of the destination. For this reason, attention now turns to the way in which such organisations develop and promote an image of their destination and the conceptual basis of such activities.

The conceptual basis of place-imagery

In the marketing of places for tourism, their complex array of features and facilities mean that it is only possible to consider a small component of the total place-product. The result is the place-image which involves the bringing together of the product and customer in the marketing process so that the exchange occurs, which in this case is the image. As Ashworth and Voogd (1990a: 77) note, this requires an understanding of 'how individuals perceive and react to their external environment and the way social behaviour is influenced by, and in turn itself influences, attitudes towards places'. This enters the realms of environmental psychology, behavioural sociology and geography. Although what follows is a simplification of a highly complex process, it does illustrate some of the principles associated with the way in which places and images are perceived.

According to Ashworth and Voogd (1990a: 79) images are 'projected through a set of cultural codes. These are then transmitted through a variety of channels, which in itself implies some interference, distortion or loss of information'. These messages are received by individuals from external sources and decoded and used in the construction of images. According to Haynes (1980) people do not have identical images of the world around them because information about the places they visit is subjected to 'mental processing'. This processing is based on the information signals which the real world sends out and is received through our senses (sight, hearing, smell, taste and touch). This part of the process is known as perception (see Figure 6.1). As our senses can only take in a small proportion of the total amount of information received, the brain sorts the information and relates it to the knowledge, values and attitudes of the individual through the process of cognition. The outcome of the perception and cognition process is the formation of a mental image of a place, meaning that people develop images which are an individual's representation of reality. The significance of this process of image construction is that people base decisions and their actions on what they think reality is and so visitors can be influenced to visit urban areas by the images portrayed through the marketing and advertising of individual cities. The result of tourists' views of the localities they visit and the location of specific attractions and facilities in the 'tourist city' may also be embodied in 'mental maps' and images of the tourism environment (see Walmesley and Jenkins 1992 for more detail). In the coding and decoding of the messages which contribute to the construction of images, a range of tools are used to portray images through advertising and marketing. These include *significant* objects which are used to signify feelings and states of mind. For example, in the advertising of London Docklands, Burgess and Wood (1988) decoded the advertising messages and identified the following signs:

- Iconic signs (icons which represent features of the place such as Big Ben and Tower Bridge to represent London – see Plate 6.1; also see Plates 3.2 and 3.3);
- Indexical signs (features which imply a 'casual relationship to the receiver such as traffic sounds suggest a busy street scene' Ashworth and Voogd 1990a: 79);
- Symbolic signs (where objects may illustrate a wide range of activities by association with a state of mind or particular lifestyle). For example, Plate 6.2 illustrates the appeal of urban heritage attractions for overseas visitors to the UK seeking to experience the pageantry and heritage associated with the monarchy.

These depend upon recognising the cultural values of the receivers and illustrate the need to target specific tourism markets where symbolic signs will create an image which appeals to the life style of potential visitors. Each of these phases of transmitting an image, and the tools used to construct the messages inherent in the image, reflect the importance of the:

- Projection phase
- Transmission phase
- Reception phase.

This is a continual process and one needs to recognise that the receiver is not a passive element in the process as the development of image marketing suggests. In the case of tourism, the complex motives for

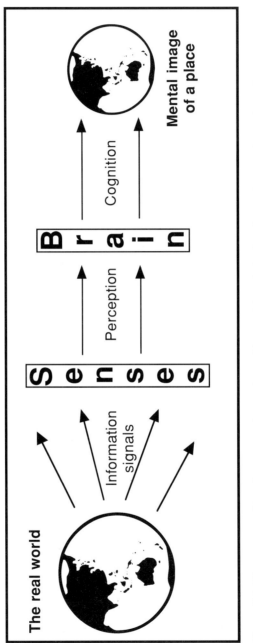

Figure 6.1 The process of tourism perception and cognition and its role in forming an image of an urban place

tourist travel (P. Pearce 1982) means that the tourist is selecting a destination based on limited information, often without personal experience of the destination. For example, Winchester Tourism portray an image of discovering the city by car which is surrounded by countryside, hoping to attract first-time visitors (see Plate 6.3). Therefore, researchers need to understand not only the decision-making process associated with choosing a holiday destination (Kent 1990), but the features they stress in their image of place. How are the images of places transmitted by tourism organisations?

Transmission of urban place images

The communication process, whereby organisations transmit images to tourists, is based on the use of different mediums to portray their image. Having identified the target market, the organisation has to decide on the medium they wish to use, a feature often constrained by budgetary considerations. For example, the tools available to influence the tourists are:

- Advertising
- Direct marketing
- Sales promotion
- Public relations
- Personal selling.

Research by Ashworth and de Haan (1986) looks at the role of tourist information centres as a medium, which only transmitted information to 16 per cent of tourists visiting Norwich. The tourist use of printed information also reveals a low level of market penetration for brochures and leaflets. Commercial and city-specific guide books are also used by a small proportion of respondents who actually select the destination after receiving the information. For example, Plates 6.3, 6.4, 6.5 and 6.6 highlight a range of examples of recent image advertising by towns and cities in the UK seeking to attract the urban tourist using the historic landscape and features of interest within each locality. Plates 6.5 and 6.6 are particularly interesting in this respect because they emphasis urban attractions despite being aimed at a wide range of potential visitors.

Whilst the findings of Ashworth and de Haan (1986) may be rather discouraging for city promotion activities, they can influence intermediaries and their decision to market tourism services in an urban destination (Buck 1988). For this reason, the precise communication channel used in city tourism promotion will depend upon the markets one seeks to reach, and how such organisations seek to influence the tourists' purchasing behaviour. In the case of Chester, Exeter, the Heart of England, Kent and Winchester, holiday guides or guide books are distributed through direct mail, in response to reader advertisements in popular magazines around the period December to February. This is the period at which most tourism analysts believe individuals and families take the decision to book their next long or short vacation in the UK. Thus, the guides seek to influence tourist decision-making at this critical time. The different marketing mixes used to promote a city's tourism attributes may have a compounding effect, by reinforcing early messages which tourists receive and associate with a particular place. This may also affect their decision to purchase a product on arrival where additional promotion influences the purchaser. Even so, research suggests that much of the information which bombards the potential or actual tourist is normally discarded.

The selection of an appropriate type is a formidable task. For example, in the United States, there are 11,238 magazines, 482 newspapers, 9,871 radio stations and 1,220 television stations (see Kotler *et al.* 1993 for a discussion of the possible media types which can be used to promote urban tourism).

Communicating the image

Having decided on the medium for promoting an image, work can proceed on the design an image. For a place image to be effective, Kotler *et al.* (1993) state that it must meet the following criteria:

- It must be valid and not based in fantasy;
- It must be realistic;
- It needs to be believable;
- It should be simple;
- Above all it should have appeal;
- It should be distinctive to differentiate the city from other destinations while emphasising the unique characteristics of the place.

To achieve these goals, place image makers utilise a wide range of tools, remembering how images are projected and transmitted. These include:

Table 6.3 The Great British Cities Marketing Group Project

The Great British Cities Marketing Group Project was established in 1984, comprising thirteen English towns (Birmingham, Coventry, Bradford, Leicester, Nottingham, Leeds, Newcastle, Manchester, Liverpool, Stoke-on-Trent, Portsmouth, Plymouth and Southampton) who set out to change their image. Each city contributed £10,000 into a joint marketing budget which was match funded by the English Tourist Board. The Project targeted the domestic short-break market by filling spare capacity in business hotels at weekends. In 1986, a 'Great English Cities' brochure was produced, with 800,000 distributed through travel agents. A target of 10,000 bookings for 1986 was exceeded with 15,000 bookings. In 1987 Hull joined the consortium, followed in 1988 by Glasgow, Dundee, Cardiff and Swansea. The brochure was then relaunched as the 'Great British Cities'. In 1989, the eighteen cities joined with British Rail to gain access to a larger market with wider circulation in travel agencies. A direct-sell holiday company (British Heritage Tours) also feature the cities in its 'A Grand Tour: An Explorers Guide to Great British Cities' brochure.

Each city developed its own logo, slogan and brand as the following list shows:

City	Slogan/organisation brand
Birmingham	The Heart of England
Bradford	A surprising place
Cardiff	Cardiff Tourism
Coventry	The City in Shakespeare Country
Dundee	City of Discovery
Glasgow	Its Miles Better
Hull	City of Hull
Leeds	Yorkshire's City for Variety
Leicester	Right at the Centre
Liverpool	City Resort
Manchester	Right at the Heart of Things
Newcastle	A Warmer Welcome
Nottingham	City of Legend, Lace, Literature and Life
Portsmouth	Flagship of Maritime England
Plymouth	A Great Place: A Great Base
Southampton	Great weekends start here
Stoke-on-Trent	The City that fires the imagination
Swansea	Wales Maritime City

Slogans, themes and positions

Slogans are used to embody the overall vision of the place. In contrast, themes are more versatile, flexible and able to create a new image of the place. Lastly, image positioning may be used to locate the place in relation to an equally successful competitor. A range of examples are illustrated in Table 6.3.

Visual symbols

Here prominent features in the urban landscape are used to create a memorable image in the tourist's mind (e.g. Red Square in Moscow, the Eiffel Tower in Paris and canals in Amsterdam) (see Kotler *et al.* 1993: 154–5 on the visual image strategies used to market cities);

Events and deeds

These are used to influence potential audiences over time, such as the former Soviet Union's use of ballet and gymnastics during visits to the USA to influence public opinion and to improve knowledge and understanding of their country. In some cases, cities seek to alter a negative image by promoting positive attributes (or in some cases by building on the negative attributes). It is also possible to discern some cities using icon marketing to improve a negative image. A good example of the success in removing the negative features of a place is Glasgow, with its social and economic problems. Through urban regeneration, imaginative marketing (e.g. 'Glasgow Miles Better') and its role in harnessing the arts as a European City of Culture in 1990, the city transformed itself as a desirable place to visit (Neill 1993). In fact Neill argues that:

> Examples of re-imaging in UK cities through the mobilisation of the arts and cultural industries, local heritage and physical renewal centred on the city centre are not hard to find. Newcastle upon Tyne boasts image building initiatives with marketing and product development blending in the appointment of a major international advertising agency to create a strong positive image for the city, projecting the promotion of culture in the city and the hosting of important events with additional tourist spin-off.
>
> (Neill 1993: 596)

Yet the promotion of a city's image should not be divorced or seen as a cheap form of place-marketing. Product development and a thorough assessment of the target markets is needed if the process of image promotion is to be fully integrated into the management of the city. Place promotion for tourism will not act as a panacea for ridding a city of urban problems. These need to be addressed as part of the overall planning process as place-marketing is not a quick fix to 'sell what the city has' while overlooking existing problems.

Towards successful place-marketing: organisational and managerial issues

Place-marketing is a sophisticated and complex process if undertaken in a systematic manner and Ashworth and Voogd (1990a) conclude their seminal study, *Selling the City* with a number of preconditions for success in place-marketing:

- Place marketing is interpreted in different ways and means different things to planners, public relations agencies, marketers and academics. Often, new administrative structures have to be devised to integrate the work of different public and private sector interests so that place-marketing is viewed as a coherent management process.
- A holistic view of place-marketing is needed so that is not broken down into small elements which are applied *ad hoc* depending on the views of urban managers. Like the tourism planning process, place-marketing needs to be seen as an ongoing process.
- Appropriate organisations are needed which can undertake the place-marketing process, though as Pearce's excellent (1992) review of tourist organisations suggests, there is no suitable model to fit the requirements of every city in its pursuit of place-marketing.
- Quite often private sector experience is needed to operationalise the place-marketing process, as private sector firms usually have the practical skills of marketing goods and services. Yet this raises a problem for the public sector planning organisation whereby it needs to understand the role of marketing and the market place. It does offer a new way of viewing the city and this creates opportunities for public–private sector partnerships to effectively promote urban tourism destinations.

Conclusion

This chapter examines some of the theoretical and practical issues associated with the marketing of urban tourism destinations by the public sector. Clearly, the private sector performs its own marketing function to sell individual products and services. Yet at a city-wide level, marketing is now being recognised as a powerful tool to harness some of the city's actual, perceived or imagined attributes which are combined in an image of the place as a tourist destination. There is nothing new about the practise of place-marketing; Victorian and Edwardian seaside resorts were undertaking place-promotion to attract domestic tourists

(Brown 1985). What is new, is the sophisticated manner in which large, multi-functional cities are now being re-imaged to sell both their tourism, locational, residential and business features as part of the place-marketing competition which cities are engaging in. Perhaps this is part of a growing realisation among city managers that cities need to compete more aggressively to promote their localities in national and global tourism markets. Whatever the different motives of individual cities in marketing their locality, one thing is certain: urban tourism is big business in many North American, European and Australasian cities which explains why more and more urban managers are realising that this is a major activity to undertake. Yet attracting visitors to cities also places an onus on destinations to think of imaginative ways in which to manage the urban tourism experience. For this reason, the final chapter considers the management of the urban tourism experience in the 1990s and the issue of quality.

Questions

1 What aspects of marketing science have contributed to the development of place-marketing?
2 How would you develop a place-marketing strategy for a small historic city and a large industrial city?
3 What type of tourism organisation would you establish to market a city? What degree of private/public sector involvement would you wish to achieve?
4 Outline the prerequisites for a successful action plan to market a city which is about to open a convention centre.

Further reading

Ashworth, G.J. and Voogd, H. (1990) *Selling the City*, London: Belhaven.

This is a difficult but useful study which is a good basis for those seeking detailed information on place-marketing and a range of tourism and non-tourism examples.

van der Borg, J. (1994) 'Demand for city-tourism in Europe: tour operators' catalogues' *Tourism Management* 15(1): 66–9.

This is a useful survey of the supply of urban tourism place-products by European tour operators and their emphasis on capital cities.

Gold, J. and Ward, S. (eds) (1994) *Place Promotion: The Use of Publicity and Public Relations to Sell Cities*, Chichester: Wiley.

This is a good up-to-date assessment of place-marketing.

Haynes, R. (1980) *Geographical Images and Mental Maps*, London: Macmillan.

This is a good introduction to the process of perception, cognition and the formation of place-images.

Lim, H. (1993) 'Cultural strategies for revitalising the city: a review and evaluation', *Regional Studies* 27(6): 589–95.

This is a good discussion of the way in which some cities have used cultural strategies to re-image themselves. It also has a good discussion of the literature.

Madsen, H. (1992) 'Place-marketing in Liverpool: a review', *International Journal of Urban and Regional Research* 16(4): 633–40.

This is a useful review of the literature and the way in which Liverpool has been re-imaged and the following article also provides a good comparison:

Neill, W. (1993) 'Physical planning and image enhancement', *International Journal of Urban and Regional Research*, 17(4): 595–610.

Pearce, D.G. (1992) *Tourist Organisations*, London: Longman.

This is an excellent study which contains a good deal of information on marketing and promotion activities by urban tourist organisations.

7
Urban tourism in the 1990s: managing the tourist experience

This book set out to highlight the potential of urban tourism as a neglected, but important, area for tourism research, emphasising the value of a systems approach to examining the relationships which exist between different elements of the tourism product. A systems approach to urban tourism has the advantage of distinguishing between the production and consumption of urban tourism products and services. It is clear that urban tourism is now gaining a greater recognition in the *tourism* (Pearce 1987a; Ashworth 1989, 1992a; Haywood 1992), *geographical* (Law 1993; Shaw and Williams 1994), *sociological* (Roche 1992), *marketing* (Ashworth and Voogd 1990a), *economics* (Clewer *et al.* 1992), *planning* (Ball and Metcalf 1992), *social psychological* (Walmesley and Jenkins 1992) and *management* literature (Haywood and Muller 1988; van der Borg and Costa 1993). Yet this growing interest in urban tourism has not led to a more holistic view of the processes, patterns and development of cities as tourism destinations. A systems approach helps one to understand the relationships between the development, operation and management of urban tourism so that the role of the tourist and the tourist experience receive a more integrated treatment.

Within an introductory book such as this, it is impossible to present a comprehensive review of urban tourism. Hence the systems approach is used to define the scope and extent of the book. Topics such as the development process have been deliberately omitted from this synthesis due to the constraints of space and the existence of specialised studies which consider it in the context of urban tourism (Pearce 1987a; 1989; Shaw and Williams 1994). Even so, major gaps still exist in our knowledge of urban tourism, particularly in underdeveloped and developing countries (Watts 1987) and in the Pacific Rim (C.M. Hall 1994). Not surprisingly, the focus of the book is on the existing literature which is largely North American or Eurocentric in outlook. Even so, a number of innovative studies exist (e.g. Crick 1992; D. Hall 1992a) while in Eastern Europe the literature is based on a limited number of studies (D. Hall 1991). Each of these areas will continue to offer a useful context for urban tourism research where data exist.

Although a systems approach highlights the importance of the inputs to the system in terms of production and consumption, the output (the tourist experience) has only received a limited treatment in most chapters. For example, in Chapter 1 the multidisciplinary nature of urban tourism research and theoretical contributions to its study are outlined and the tourist experience is introduced as an output. Chapter 2 develops the tourist experience concept a stage further while Chapter 3 illustrated the products and elements which can influence the experience. The impact of tourism has a profound effect on the tourists' experience and there is a growing demand from local communities and business for urban management and planning to control the effects of tourism. Planning and managing the tourism industry and destinations within cities needs to go hand in hand with the targeted marketing of visitors, without losing sight of the tourists' experience. It is in this context that interdisciplinary research has a real role to play in encouraging researchers to collaborate and focus on specific problems such as how to manage the tourism system to optimise visitor satisfaction, and to integrate the growing body of knowledge on urban tourism so that the tourist experience can be seen as a central feature. A more holistic view is needed, whereby public–private partnerships are fostered and academic researchers contribute to the design, analysis and synthesis of research to monitor the tourist experience. Such partnerships are a way forward to address the multi-faceted problems associated with tourism in many large cities and small historic towns and cities. The saturation of historic places by uncontrolled mass tourism cannot easily be addressed by developing a sustainable or community tourism plan. In many towns and cities radical action is needed to address the issues contributing to the problem, such as limiting visitor numbers at peak times. Yet while the tourist saturation of towns and cities is now becoming a major issue for many destinations, place-marketing continues to promote towns and cities as destinations with a reputation for service quality. What is service quality in urban tourism?

Service quality and urban tourism

The competitive nature of urban tourism (Woodside *et al.* 1989) has meant that cities have responded to tourist demands for higher standards of comfort, reliability, courtesy and quality in their tourist experience. As Clewer *et al.* (1992) note, certain urban visitors (e.g. the German market) have higher expectations of service quality than others. Yet the literature on service quality readily acknowledges that developing a definition or concept of quality is difficult because of the intangible nature of services as products which are purchased and consumed. For urban tourism, assessing quality in the tourist experience is even more complex than for other tourism services such as transport (see Page 1994b) because three fundamental issues need to be considered. First, place-marketing generates an image of a destination that may not be met in reality due to the problems of promoting places as tourist products (see Chapter 6). The image promoted through place-marketing may not necessarily be matched in reality through the services and goods which the tourism industry delivers. As a result, the gap between the customers perception of a destination and the bundle of products they consume is reflected in their actual tourist experience, which has important implications for their assessment of quality in their experience. Secondly, the urban tourism product is largely produced by the private sector either as a package or a series of elements which are not easily controlled or influenced by the place-marketer. Thirdly, there is a large range of associated factors which affect a tourist's image of a destination such as less tangible elements like the environment and the ambience of the city which may shape the outcome of a tourist experience (Haywood and Muller 1988). As a result, the customer's evaluation of the quality of the services and products provided is a function of the difference ('gap') between expected and perceived service (Parasuraman *et al.* 1985). It is in this context that the concept of service quality is important for urban tourism. As already mentioned, there is no universal definition of quality in relation to tourism and service provision, but Gilbert and Joshi (1992) present an excellent review of the literature, including many of the concepts associated with service quality. In the case of urban tourism, it is the practical management of the gap between the expected and perceived service that requires attention by urban managers and the tourism industry. In reviewing the service quality model of Parasuraman *et al.* (1985), Gilbert and Joshi (1992: 155) identify five gaps which exist between:

- The expected service and the management's perceptions of the consumer experience (ie what they think the tourist wants) (Gap 1);
- The management's perception of the tourists needs and the translation of those needs into service quality specifications (Gap 2);
- The quality specifications and the actual delivery of the service (Gap 3);
- The service delivery stage and the organisation/providers' communication with the consumer (Gap 4);
- The consumers perception of the service they received and experienced, and their initial expectations of the service (Gap 5).

Gilbert and Joshi (1992) argue that the effective utilisation of market research techniques could help to bridge some of the gaps for:

Gap 1 by encouraging providers to elicit detailed information from consumers on what they require (see Page *et al.* 1994 for a discussion of this in the context of urban parks);

Gap 2 the management's ability to specify the service provided needs to be realistic and guided by clear quality standards (eg what is the maximum length of time a tourist should expect to wait to enter a tourist attraction?);

Gap 3 the ability of employees to deliver the service according to the specification needs to be closely monitored and staff training and development is essential: a service is only as good as the staff it employs;

Gap 4 the promises made by service providers in their marketing and promotional messages need to reflect the actual quality offered. Therefore, if a city's promotional literature promises a warm welcome, human resource managers responsible for employees in front-line establishments need to ensure that this message is conveyed to its customers;

Gap 5 the major gap between the perceived service and delivered service should be reduced over time through progressive improvements in the appropriate image which is marketed to visitors, and the private sector's ability to deliver the expected service in an efficient and professional manner.

Such an approach to service quality can be applied to urban tourism as it

Table 7.1 Factors to consider in evaluating the urban tourism experience

- the weather conditions at the time of visit
- the standard and quality of accommodation available
- the cleanliness and upkeep of the city
- the city's aesthetic value (i.e. its setting and beauty)
- the tourists' personal safety from crime
- accessibility of attractions and points of interest in the city
- the extent to which local people welcome visitors in a warm manner
- the ability of tourism employees to speak foreign languages
- the range of cultural and artistic amenities
- the ambience of the city environment as a place to walk around
- the level of crowding and congestion
- the range of nightlife and entertainment available
- range of restaurants and eating establishments in the city
- the pleasurability of leisure shopping
- the price levels of goods and services in the city
- the level of helpfulness among local people
- the adequacy of emergency medical care

Source: modified from Haywood and Muller (1988)

emphasises the importance of the marketing process in communicating and dealing with tourists. It is clear that the process of information exchange considers the perceptions of the marketer and consumer. This approach also provides a framework for formulating strategies and appropriate action to close the gaps between the service provider and consumer (e.g. Lewis 1987). To obtain a better understanding of this area, Haywood and Muller (1988) identify a methodology for evaluating the quality of the urban tourism experience. This involves collecting data on visitors expectations prior to, and after their city-visit by examining a range of variables (see Table 7.1). Such an approach provides a better appreciation of the visitation process and they argue that cameras may also provide the day-to-day monitoring of city experiences.

By viewing service quality in a systems framework, it may be possible to develop a greater degree of control in the tourists' experience of urban areas, by managing their activities and contact with businesses in the city. Yet this is not as straightforward as it may seem. Chapter 5 emphasises the issue of politics at the local level in city government and the need to reach consensus on the action to be taken. But as Jansen-Verbeke (1989) found, tourism is no longer the well-defined responsibility of a single branch of a municipal government organisation. She argues that the urban core of a city is viewed as both a recreational environment and tourism resource, which nearly every branch of urban government influences in some way. This highlights the importance of the two responses now being adopted by cities in Europe to manage towns which are discussed below. Nevertheless, for individual businesses in the public and private sector who wish to implement quality controls in their service operations, they often choose to pursue a strategy of quality as an integral feature of their organisation. This not only requires a more sophisticated approach to recognising customers' needs, if total quality management (TQM) is pursued (see, for example, Oakland 1989; Dotchin and Oakland 1992), but also necessitates a TQM philosophy. A TQM philosophy needs to be integrated in all the activities of an organisation rather than simply being added at the end of the production cycle. Individual measures which companies may adopt are:

• A greater awareness of quality assurance (QA) and TQM;
• Improvements to quality processes and procedures (possibly leading to certification to BS5750 in the UK – see Callan 1992);
• Customer care programmes to enhance service delivery, recognising both internal and external customers to the organisation;
• Communicating clearly to existing and potential customers the services provided, service standards and improvements being made.

Both Normann (1984) and Groonroos (1988) argue that embracing service quality as part of a corporate culture can enhance the appreciation of good service and the importance of being customer-led. It may also enhance employees' esteem and commitment to an organisation where achievement is rewarded. However, Speller and Ghobadian (1993a) are critical of attempts to use QA and TQM as 'window dressing', where organisations fail to deliver service improvements. In addition, they criticise those organisations that claim to be customer-led but fail to listen to their customers, as well as inertia among managers who are unwilling to change the culture of organisations. In any event, service quality is a complex area for organisations to address, particularly in delivering quality and consistency in tourism services to ensure the tourist experience is favourable. One outcome of a satisfactory tourist experience is that visitors may promote the destination to friends and relatives by word of mouth. In this context, it is notable that Gilbert and Joshi (1992: 164) argue that future research on quality management will need to focus on 'developing more sensitive instruments and measurements of consumer service quality perceptions and establishing the usefulness of segmenting consumers on the basis of their service quality perceptions'.

At a city-wide level, there is growing evidence that North American and European cities with large visitor numbers, which are exceeding their carrying capacity, are developing two specific responses.

1 Town Centre Management Schemes

The aim of Town Centre Management Schemes is to improve the built environment of the city (Wells 1991), exemplified by the measures discussed in Chapter 5, to ensure a more user-friendly environment (see Table 7.2 for a list of Town Centre Management schemes in the UK). In some cases, Town Centre Management Schemes receive a large number of tourists associated with visits to attractions and leisure shopping which the scheme seeks to address. For example, Murphy (1980) examines the role of land use planning as a mechanism used in towns to redirect tourism development and to reduce visitor congestion. In North America, the Mainstream Programme is a good example of a town centre management initiative. As Table 7.3 shows, even small towns such as Ayr in Scotland view a Town Centre Management scheme as an opportunity to promote the town as a tourist destination.

2 Visitor Management Schemes

Visitor Management schemes are set up to manage tourism as a result of the effect of the volume of visitors on sensitive urban environments such as small historic cities. Visitor management schemes are a relatively recent and specialised development in Europe and may be of interest for cities in other parts of the world. For this reason, it is useful to focus on the techniques used in visitor management, and their application to one scheme in Stratford-upon-Avon. This develops many of the points raised in Chapter 5 in the case study of Canterbury which outlined the scope and range of tourism-related problems which exist in many small historic cities.

Visitor management: addressing tourist saturation and the impact on the tourist experience

Graefe and Vaske (1987) recognise that tourism quality is a multifaceted concept and that various factors impact upon the tourist experience.

Table 7.2 Town centre management schemes in the UK in 1993

Ayr	Falkirk	Maidstone
Barry	Feltham (London)	Nantwich
Bath	Fife	Newport
Belfast	Glasgow	Nottingham
Birmingham	Gosport	Oxford
Blackburn	Gravesend	Paisley
Bracknell	Greenwich (London)	Peckham
Bradford	Hamilton	Reading
Bristol	Harlesden	Reigate
Cardiff	Harlow	Rochdale
Chester	Hastings	Sheffield
Chingford (London)	Hemel Hempstead	Southend
Coventry	Herne Bay	Stirling
Crawley	Horsham	Stockton-on-Tees
Crewe	Ilford	Stratford (London)
Cwmbran	Ipswich	Wandsworth
Darlington	Kilmarnock	Wembley
Derby	Leeds	Willesden
Dumfries	Linlithgow	Woking
Eastbourne	Liverpool	Wolverhampton
Edinburgh	Llanelli	Wood Green
Epsom	Macclesfield	York

Source: Data derived from the Association of Town Centre Managers

Table 7.3 Ayr Town Centre Management Initiative 1993

Ayr Town Centre Management Initiative was formed as a public/private sector partnership in June 1993 as a company and its objectives are:

- To promote Ayr Town Centre as a retail, commercial, entertainment and tourist centre to Ayr residents and further afield;
- To improve business performance with the town centre;
- To provide information to local businessmen and traders on forthcoming developments, programmes and events within the town centre;
- To provide a liaison/advisory service to traders, investors, firms or persons having an interest in the town centre;
- To encourage environmental improvements within the town centre and to foster the effective provision of local services to the public and other agencies concerned with the appearance and operational management of the town centre and the doing of all such things as are incidental or conducive to the attainment of these objectives.

As an executive authority in its own right, the joint initiative has promoted Ayr Town Centre as a shopping and tourist attraction and has been committed to making Ayr Town Centre 'user and customer-friendly'. A leaflet guide to the Town centre's amenities has been produced and the installation of finger posts (tourist signposts) in the town inform the visitor where amenities are.

Source: Ayr Town Centre Management Initiative - Press Launch September 1993

They argue that by understanding these impacts (Figure 2.1), the management process can attempt to control the quality of the tourists' experience. In common with the tourism planning process discussed in Chapter 5, Graefe and Vaske (1987) identify eight sequential steps aimed at:

- dealing with problem conditions (i.e. unacceptable impacts on the tourist experience);
- identifying causal factors and;
- the selection of potential management strategies to reduce problem conditions.

The eight steps they identify are:

1 A preassessment data base review (e.g. to examine existing policy, legislation and the existing situation in relation to urban tourism).
2 A review of management objectives (e.g. to specify the visitor experience to be provided and resource management objectives to meet the specification of the visitor experience).
3 The selection of key impact indicators (e.g. to identify social and ecological variables to determine how the experience will be measured).
4 The selection of standards for key impact indicators (e.g. to restate management objectives and to identify the desired conditions for tourist experience).
5 The comparison of standards and existing conditions (e.g. the field assessment of social and ecological impact indicators to place the standards in a realistic setting – see Table 5.6 for a list of methods for measuring visitor impacts). If discrepancies occur between the standards established and the ability of the area to accommodate them, it may be necessary to go back to step 4 to redefine the standards.
6 Identify probable causes of impacts by examining patterns of tourist use and factors causing unacceptable impacts
7 The identification of management strategies (e.g. by considering the direct and indirect management strategies available to address the range of impacts).
8 Implementation.

These eight steps can be incorporated in the process of developing a visitor management strategy for tourist cities. The practical application of many of these steps to visitor management in small historic cities is described in the English Tourist Board/Employment Department (1991)

Tourism and the Environment: Maintaining the Balance – Report of the Heritage Sites Working Group which contains a number of interesting case studies, including a discussion of Stratford-upon-Avon, highlighting the need for visitor management strategies.

Visitor management strategies for urban tourism

The case study of Canterbury in Chapter 5 deals with many of the problems confronting small historic cities with large visitor markets and the principles associated with visitor management, and for this reason it is useful to identify some of the management strategies available for managing visitors before examining their use in one particular city. Many of the strategies for visitor management have been developed in outdoor recreation management, with particular reference to sensitive environments such as wilderness areas (see Hendee *et al.* 1990 for a detailed examination of their design and use). Many of these strategies can be adapted for use in urban locations which are subjected to similar pressures. These strategies can be developed to accommodate direct or indirect action and they need to be viewed in the context of each individual city so that specific action is targeted at local problems (Table 7.4). Each of the strategies selected need to be monitored in terms of their effectiveness to address specific problems, and to be evaluated to show how the tourist experience has improved/declined following their implementation. Against this background, the recent implementation of the Stratford-upon-Avon Visitor Action Management Programme is examined.

Stratford-upon-Avon Visitor Management Action Programme

Stratford-on-Avon with its association with Shakespeare, receives around 2.5 million visitors a year and it contains a host community of 23,000 people in the town (and 106,000 for the entire district). It exhibits many of the problems now affecting small historic towns and cities on the popular overseas visitor 'milk run' of organised coach tours, which commences in London and incorporates Oxford, Stratford-upon-Avon, Bath, Chester, Edinburgh, York, Cambridge and London. Canterbury is often included as a day trip destination from London (see Yale 1990 for more detail). Whilst the Stratford-on-Avon District Council developed a Visitor Management Plan in 1991–92 to deal with the mass tourism market, the Stratford-upon-Avon Visitor

Table 7.4 Visitor management strategies for urban tourism

Direct	Indirect
Enforcement of existing planning measures • to increase surveillance • to increase enforcement of rules	Physical alterations to the urban area • to improve access • to neglect access
Zoning of tourist activities • to separate incompatible uses • to separate visitors by experience level • to time	Information dispersal/communication • to advertise area and opportunities outside of pressured locations • to advertise use pattern
Ration the use of tourist resources • to limit access to area	Economic constraints • to increase prices • to decrease prices • to use differential pricing to manage visitors with premium pricing at peak times
Restrict tourist activities • by type of use • by size of group • by length of stay • by prohibiting use at particular times	

Source: Modified from Hendee et al (1990)

Management Action Programme complements the district programme. It is the first three-year pilot visitor management programme in a historic town undertaken in response to the English Tourist Board/Employment Department (1991) *Tourism and the Environment: Maintaining the Balance* report. The city was selected by the English Tourist Board:

• To research and progress the action needed to improve visitor management;
• To demonstrate and disseminate good practice in the city.

The project commenced in November 1992 as a joint public/private sector partnership with a view to input from the local community and businesses. While the general aims of the management strategy are listed in Table 7.5, the objectives of the Visitor Management Action Programme are significant because they recognise the principal issues to address. These objectives view visitor management as dealing with the issues and interrelationships associated with:

• Visitor impacts
• Visitor movement
• The visitor welcome.

Table 7.5 Stratford-upon-Avon Visitor Management Action Programme

---

The long-term strategy for tourism is to:

- Conserve the local life, beauty and character of Stratford-upon-Avon and the surrounding area.
- Ensure a satisfying and enjoyable experience for visitors to Stratford-upon-Avon.

- Support a thriving local tourism industry which can contribute significant benefits to the local economy.

The objectives of the Visitor Management Action Programme are:

- To enhance the welcome and services we provide for our visitors and develop a sustainable 'Stratford Welcome' identity.
- Improve the management of the impact of visitors on the town and its residents.
- Increase the awareness of the interdependence of the three-way relationship between the visitor, the location of Stratford-upon-Avon and the host resident community. Future action and research will consider:
- Visitor, resident and business surveys.
- Stratford Visitor Care Training Programme to ensure that visitors receive a warm and informed welcome.
- Residents Forum and Awareness week.
- Comprehensive and co-ordinated Stratford Welcome information for visitors on arrival.
- Improved signs where required.
- Key foreign language information for overseas visitors.
- Visitor welcome arrival area for coach passengers.
- Stratford Welcome Service.
- Town centre shuttle bus service.
- Out of town park-and-ride service.
- Improved rail service and facilities
- Heighten awareness of environmental and conservation aims of the programme
- To contribute positive ideas to local planning authorities.
- To involve the local community and local businesses in the future of visitor management in Stratford-upon-Avon.

Source: Stratford-upon-Avon Visitor Management Action Programme (1993)

The management of visitors in Stratford-upon-Avon seeks to 'maximise the benefits and minimise the negative impacts of visitors on the local community' (Stratford-upon-Avon Visitor Management Action Programme 1993). In addition, a range of future actions are also planned (Table 7.5). Although it is too early to comment on the success of the scheme, it does illustrate the scope of measures which some towns and cities are having to take to deal with the tourism phenomenon.

A more integrated and wide ranging approach to city management can be found in the Chester Action Programme (1993) which describes itself as a 'vision of success for all those who live and work in Chester or who visit the city'. Not only does the programme adopt an integrated approach to planning, with a private/public sector partnership, it also recognises the issues and problems facing urban managers in Chester. The Action Programme is unique in that all aspects of social and economic life in the city are incorporated in the strategy, with specific actions related to strategy objectives in a matrix format, where by the cost of achieving certain objectives in the strategy are quantified. Such an approach is both novel and forward looking, by integrating the interests of the local community, businesses and its partners in a local strategy, while recognising the need to manage tourism as an integral element of the city system. It is also likely to gain support in the 1990s as a more rational and systematic way to address activities like tourism within the wider urban environment.

Tourism needs to be viewed as a diverse and wide ranging activity within cities, in both large centres such as London, Paris, New York and Sydney and medium to small towns, as the impacts of visitors varies with each type and location. The reasons why tourists visit cities, to consume a bundle of tourism products, reflects their multi-functional nature and the way cities are sold to different target groups. As Law (1993: 168) rightly notes, 'one of the many tasks for urban tourism research is to tease out the reasons why people visit cities, the links between the various motivations and the deeper reasons why people are attracted to cities', especially the effect of place-marketing. The all-year-round tourism appeal of cities also makes it an appealing activity to market, and the short-stay nature of most urban tourist visits is offset by their relatively high spending nature. Calculating the beneficial effects for cities and local communities is notoriously difficult even where appropriate research methodologies exist. Yet selling cities for tourism does raise many issues for local communities as Bramham et al. (1989: 4) ask: 'Is a city a place to live, where people can express themselves?' Or is it a place to sell to relatively affluent visitors who are catered for by reshaping the city's image, product and environment to meet their conspicuous patterns of consumption? Haywood (1989) argues that one compromise which may address this dilemma, is to make marketing more community-based as the needs of the local community need to be considered. Urban tourism can be socially divisive and local authorities need to consider the potential effects of initiating tourism development. The trade-off for local communities is the potential employment benefit and environmental improvement which may result although leakage in the local economy may reduce the beneficial effects for the city's economy (Bath City Council 1987). Any city seeking to revitalise its ailing economy by using tourism as a tool for urban economic development will need to carefully assess the regional, national and international competition for investment, visitors, and the available resource base and the extent to which it will support a viable tourism industry. Once a local authority or city commits itself to the path of development or regeneration, the continued costs of infrastructure improvement, updating and revamping the tourism product by investing in quality, may prove an expensive future cost for urban authorities. Urban tourism can bring tangible benefits to cities and towns if developed and managed in a sensitive and balanced manner: however, it is not a quick fix to solve a locality's social, economic and environmental problems.

Questions

1 What is meant by the term service quality in the context of urban tourism?
2 How would you go about developing a strategy and action plan to promote a quality experience for tourists in a particular city? What role will research and monitoring play in this task?
3 To what extent is visitor management a vague proposition with no tangible measures to control tourist activity?
4 What are the main constraints on implementing a comprehensive visitor management strategy for a small historic town? Who is likely to support such a strategy and who is likely to oppose it? What reasons are they likely to give?

Further reading

Callan, R. (1992) 'Quality control at AVANT hotels – the debut of BS5750', *Service Industries Journal* 17(1): 17–33.

This article examines how one hotel chain has obtained certification for BS5750.

Dadgostar, B. and Isotalo, R. M. (1992) 'Factors affecting time spent by near-home tourists in city-destinations', *Journal of Travel Research*, 31(2): 34–9.

This is a useful article which examines the relationship between the destination image and tourist patronage behaviour. A range of variables are examined which consider the image score of city destinations for near-home tourists living in small communities.

Haywood, K. M. and Muller, T. E. (1988) 'The urban tourist experience: evaluating satisfaction', *Hospitality and Education Research Journal* 12(2): 453–9.

This is a good article which considers the measurement of the urban tourist experience using a range of variables.

Murphy, P. E. (1980) 'Tourism management using land use planning and landscape design: the Victoria experience', *Canadian Geographer* 24,(1): 60–73.

Although this is a dated article, it offers a number of good insights on using land use planning to ease visitor congestion.

Taylor, S. A., Sharland, A., Cronin, J. J., and Bullard, W. (1993) 'Recreational service quality in the international setting', *International Journal of Service Industry Management* 4,(4): 68–86.

This is a thorough review of service quality in relation to recreation but it is useful in terms of the discussion of service quality concepts.

Wells, I. (1991) *Town Centre Management: a Future for the High Street*, Reading: Geographical Papers, No 109, University of Reading.

Bibliography

Acernaza, M. A. (1985) 'Planificación estratégica del turismo: esquema meto-
dológico', *Estudios Turísticos* 85: 45–70.

Ambrose, P. E. (1986) 'Changing planning relations', in P. Cloke (ed.) *Policy
and Change in Thatcher's Britain*, Oxford: Pergamon, pp.97–122.

Ap, J. and Crompton, J.L. (1993) 'Residents' strategies for responding to
tourism impacts', *Journal of Travel Research* 32(1): 47–50.

Arbel, A. and Pizam, A. (1977) 'Some determinants of hotel location: the
tourists inclination', *Journal of Travel Research* 15 Winter: 18–22.

Archer, B.H. (1982) 'The value of multipliers and their policy implications',
Tourism Management 3(2): 236–41.

—— (1987) 'Demand forecasting and estimating ', in J. R. B. Ritchie and C. R.
Goeldner (eds) *Travel, Tourism and Hospitality Research: A Handbook for
Managers and Researchers*, New York: Wiley, pp.77–85.

Ashworth, G. J. (1987) 'Marketing the historic city: the selling of Norwich' in
R. C. Riley (ed.) *Urban Conversation: International Comparisons*, Occasional
Paper No. 7, Portsmouth: Department of Geography, Portsmouth
University, pp.51–67.

—— (1989) 'Urban tourism: an imbalance in attention', in C. P. Cooper (ed.),
Progress in Tourism, Recreation and Hospitality Management, Volume One,
London: Belhaven: 33–54.

—— (1992a) 'Is there an urban tourism?' *Tourism Recreation Research* 17(2):
3–8.

—— (1992b) 'Planning for sustainable tourism: slogan or reality?', *Town
Planning Review* 63(3): 325–30.

Ashworth, G. J. and de Haan T. Z. (1986) 'Uses and users of the tourist–historic
city', *Field Studies 10* Groningen: Faculty of Spatial Sciences.

Ashworth, G. J. and Tunbridge, J. (1990) *The Tourist-Historic City*, London: Belhaven.

Ashworth, G. J. and Voogd, H. (1987) 'Geografische marketing, een brunikbare invalshoek voor onderzoek en planning', *Stedebouw and Volkhuisvesting* 3: 85–90.

—— (1988) 'Marketing the city: concepts, processes and Dutch applications', *Town Planning Review* 59(1): 65–80.

—— (1990a) *Selling the City*, London: Belhaven.

—— (1990b) 'Can places be sold for tourism?', in G. J. Ashworth and B. Goodall (eds) *Marketing Tourism Places*, London: Routledge, pp.1–16.

Ashworth, G. J., White, P. E. and Winchester, H. P. (1988) 'The red-light district in the West-European City: A neglected aspect of the urban landscape', *Geoforum* 19(2): 201–12.

Ball, R. M. and Metcalf, M. (1992) 'Tourism development at the margins: pits, pots and the potential in the Potteries locality', in D. Hind (ed.) *Tourism in Europe: the 1992 Conference*, Durham, 8–10 July 1992, Newcastle: Houghton le Spring, Centre for Travel and Tourism, University of Northumbria, pp.B9–B23.

Barlow, M. (1991) *Metropolitan Government*, London: Routledge.

Barrett, J. A. (1958) The Seaside Resort Towns of England and Wales, unpublished Ph.D. thesis, London: University of London.

Bath City Council (1987) *Economics of Tourism in Bath*, London: Coopers and Lybrand.

Berkout, E. E., Abondano, C. V. N. and Deeleman, A. P. B. (1991) 'New management methodology for computer-aided tourism planning', *Industry and Environment* 14(3): 13–14.

Bjorklund, E. M. and Philbrick, A. K. (1975) 'Spatial configuration of mental processes', in M. Belanger and D. G. Janelle (eds) *Building Regions for the Future*, Notes et Documents du Recherche No. 6 Quebec: Department de Geographie, Université Laval, Quebec: 57–75.

Blank, U. and Petkovich, M. (1980) 'The metropolitan area: a multifaceted travel destination complex', in *Tourism Planning and Development Issues*, D. E. Hawkins, E. L. Shafer and J. M Ravelstad (eds) Washington DC: George Washington University, pp.393–405.

—— (1987) 'Research on urban tourism destinations', in J. R. B. Ritchie and C. R. Goeldner (eds) *Travel, Tourism and Hospitality Research: A Handbook for Managers and Researchers*, New York: Wiley, pp.165–77.

van der Borg, J. (1991) *Tourism and Urban Development*, Amsterdam: Thesis Publishers.

—— (1992) 'Tourism and urban development: the case of Venice, Italy', *Tourism Recreation Research* 17(2): 45–56.

—— (1994) 'Demand for city-tourism in Europe: tour operators' catalogues', *Tourism Management* 15(1): 66–9.

van der Borg, J. and Costa, P. (1993) 'The management of tourism in cities of art', *Tourist Review* 48(2): 2–10.

Bramham, P., Henry, I., Mommaas, H. and van der Poel, H. (eds) (1989) *Leisure and Urban Processes: Critical Studies of Leisure Policy in West European Cities*, London: Routledge.

British Tourist Authority (1993) *Guidelines for Tourism to Britain 1993–97*, London: British Tourist Authority.

Britton, S. (1980) 'A conceptual model of tourism in a peripheral economy', in D. G. Pearce (ed.) *Tourism in the South Pacific: The Contribution of Research and Development and Planning*, N.Z. MAB Report No. 6, Christchurch (New Zealand): N.Z. National Commission for UNESCO/Department of Geography, pp.1–12.

Brown, B. J. H. (1985) 'Personal perception and communtiy speculation: a British resort in the nineteenth century', *Annals of Tourism Research* 12: 353–69.

Buck, M. (1988) 'The role of the travel agent and tour operator', in B. Goodall and G. J. Ashworth (eds) *Marketing in the Tourism Industry*, London: Routledge, pp.67–74.

Buckley, P. J. and Witt, S. F. (1985) 'Tourism in difficult areas: case studies of Bradford, Bristol, Glasgow and Hamm', *Tourism Management* 6: 205–13.

Bull, A. (1991) *The Economics of Travel and Tourism*, London: Pitman.

Bull, P. and Church, A. (1994) 'The hotel and catering industry of Great Britain during the 1980s: sub-regional employment change, specialisation and dominance', in C. P. Cooper and A. Lockwood (eds) *Progress in Tourism, Recreation and Hospitality Management*, Volume 5, Chichester: Wiley, pp.248–69.

Burgess, J. A. (1982) 'Selling places:environmental images for executives', *Regional Studies* 16(1): 1–17.

Burgess, J. and Wood, P. (1988) 'Decoding Docklands: place advertising and decision-making strategies of the small firm' in J. Eyles and D. Smith (eds) *Qualitative Methods in Human Geography*, Cambridge: Polity Press, pp.94–117.

Burtenshaw, D., Bateman, M. and Ashworth, G. J. (1991) *The European City*, London: David Fulton Publishers.

Butler, R. W. (1980) 'The concept of a tourist area cycle of evolution: implications for management of resources', *Canadian Geographer* 24(1): 5–12.

Bywater, M. (1990) 'New Zealand', *International Tourism Reports* 2: 44–67.

—— (1993) 'The market for cultural tourism in Europe', *Travel and Tourism Analyst* 6: 30–46.

—— (1994) 'Religious travel in Europe', *Travel and Tourism Analyst* 2: 39–52.

Callan, R. (1992) 'Quality Control at AVANT hotels – the debut of BS5750', *Service Industries Journal* 17(1): 17–33.

Canestrelli, E. and Costa, P. (1991) 'Tourist carrying capacity: a fuzzy approach', *Annals of Tourism Research* 18(2): 295–311.

Cannon, T. (1989) *Basic Marketing Principles and Practice*, London: Holt Reinhart and Winston: third edition.

Cant, G. (1980) 'The impact of tourism on the host community – the Queenstown example', in D. G. Pearce (ed.) *Tourism in the South Pacific: The Contribution of Research to Development and Planning*, N.Z. MAB report No 6., Christchurch (New Zealand): N.Z. National Commission for UNESCO/Department of Geography, pp.87–96.

Canterbury City Council (1991a) *Canterbury District Local Plan: Background Paper No. 3 – Tourism*, Canterbury: Canterbury City Council.

—— (1991b) *Canterbury City District Plan*, Canterbury: Canterbury City Council.

—— (1993) *Canterbury City Centre Initiative*, Canterbury: Canterbury City Council.

Carroll, S. J. (1988) *Futures of Organizations: Innovating to Adapt Strategy and Human Resources to Rapid Technological Change*, Lexington, Massachusets: Lexington Books.

Cater, E. A. and Loman, G. A. (eds) (1994) *Ecotourism – A Sustainable Option*, Chichester: Wiley/Royal Geographical Society.

Chester Action Programme (1993) *Chester Action Programme: Strategies and Action*, Chester: Chester Action Programme.

Church, A. (1990) 'Transport and urban regeneration in London Docklands'. *Cities* 7(4): 289–303.

Clark, M. and Stewart, J. (1992) 'The challenge for the government of cities', *Local Government Policy Making* 18(4): 25–9.

Clark, N., Clift, S. and Page, S. J. (1993) *A Safe Place in the Sun? Health Precautions of British Tourists in Malta*, Travel, Lifestyles and Health Working Paper No. 1, Canterbury: Christ Church College of Higher Education.

Clarke, A. (1986) 'Local authority planners or frustrated tourism marketers?', *The Planner* 72(5): 23–6.

Clewer, A., Pack, A. and Sinclair, M. T. (1992) 'Price competitiveness and inclusive tour holidays', in P. Johnson and B. Thomas (eds) *Choice and Demand in Tourism*, London: Mansell, pp.123–44.

Cohen, E. (1972) 'Towards a sociology of international tourism', *Social Research* 39: 164–82.

Cooper, C. P. (1987) 'The changing administration of tourism in Britain', *Area* 19(3): 249–53.

—— (1992) 'The lifecycle concept and tourism', in P. Johnson and B. Thomas (eds) *Choice and Demand in Tourism*, London: Mansell, pp.145–60.

Cooper, C.P. and Latham, J. (1988) 'The pattern of educational visits in England', *Leisure Studies* 7: 256–66.

Cooper, C. P., Fletcher, J., Gilbert, D. G., Wanhill, S. (1993) *Tourism: Principles and Practice*, London: Pitman.

Crick, M. (1992) 'Life in the informal sector: street guides in Kandy, Sri Lanka', in D. Harrison (ed.) *Tourism and the Less Developed World*, London: Belhaven, pp.135–47.

Crompton, J. L. (1979) 'An assessment of the image of Mexico as a vacation destination', *Journal of Travel Research* 17 Fall: 18–23.

de Bres, K. (1994) 'Cow towns or cathedral precincts? Two models for contemporary urban tourism', *Area* 26 (1): 57–67.

Department of Internal Affairs (1989) *A Proposed Ministry of Arts and Culture: Discussion Paper*, Wellington: Department of Internal Affairs.

Department of the Environment (1990) *Tourism and the Inner City: An Evaluation of the Impact of Grant Assisted Projects*, London: HMSO.

Devas, N. and Rakodi, C. (eds) (1993) *Managing Fast Growing Cities: New Approaches to Urban Planning and Management in the Developing World*, London: Longman.

Dotchin, J. A. and Oakland, J. S. (1992) 'Theories and concepts in Total Quality Management'. *Total Quality Management* 3(2): 133–45.

Dowling, R. K. (1992) 'Tourism and environmental integration: the journey from idealism to realism', in C. P. Cooper and A. Lockwood (eds), *Progress in Tourism, Recreation and Hospitality Management*, Volume 4, London: Belhaven, pp.33–46.

Doxey, G.V. (1976) 'When enough's enough: the natives are restless in Old Niagara', *Heritage Canada* 2(2): 26–7.

Drake, M. (1985) 'Life in an established destination – Los Angeles', in *The Battle for Market Share*, (16th Proceedings) Salt Lake City: Travel and Research Association, pp.141–4.

DRV Research (1986) *An Economic Impact Study of the Tourist and Associated Arts Development in Merseyside*, Bournemouth: DRV Research.

Dutton, I. and Hall, C. M. (1989) 'Making tourism sustainable; the policy/ practice conundrum', paper presented at Environment Institute of Australia Second National Conference, Melbourne, 9–11 October.

Eade, J. (1992) 'Pilgrimage and tourism at Lourdes', *Annals of Tourism Research* 19(1): 18–32.

Edgett, S. and Parkinson, S. (1993) 'Marketing for service industries – a review'. *Service Industries Journal* 13(3): 19–39.

English Historic Towns Forum (1992) *Retailing in Historic Towns: Research Study*, London: Donaldsons.

English Tourist Board/Employment Department (1991) *Tourism and the Environment: Maintaining the Balance*, London: English Tourist Board/ Employment Department.

Eversley, D. (1977) 'The ganglion of tourism: an unresolvable problem for London', *London Journal* 3(2): 186–211.

—— (1984) 'Does London need strategic planning?', *London Journal* 10(1): 13–45.

Figuerola, M. (1976) 'Turismo de masa y sociologia: el caso español', *Travel Research Journal*: 25–38.

Fines, S. H. (1981) *The Marketing of Ideas and Social Issues*, New York: Praeger.

Fletcher, J. E. and Archer, B. H. (1991) 'The development and application of multiplier analysis', in C. P. Cooper (ed.) *Progress in Tourism, Recreation and Hospitality Management*, Volume 3, London: Belhaven, pp.28–47.

Forer, P. and Pearce, D. G. (1984) 'Spatial patterns of package tourism in New Zealand' *New Zealand Geographer* 40(1): 34–42.

Fox, M. (1977) 'The social impact of tourism: a challenge to researchers and planners', in B. R. Finney and A. Watson (eds) *A New Kind Sugar: Tourism in the Pacific*, Santa Cruz: Center for South Pacific Studies, University of Calfornia, pp.27–48.

Frank, T. (1985) 'Established versus emerging destinations', in The Battle for Market share (16th Proceedings) Salt Lake City: Travel and Research Association, pp.139–40.

Fujita, K. and Child, R. (eds) (1993) *Japanese Cities in the World Economy*, Philadelphia: Temple University Press.

Garland, B. R. and West. S. J. (1985) 'The social impact of tourism in New Zealand', *Massey Journal of Asian and Pacific Business* 1(1): 34–9.

Getz, D. (1986) 'Models in tourism planning; towards integration of theory and practice', *Tourism Management* 7(1): 21–32.

—— (1987) 'Tourism planning and research: traditions, models and futures', paper presented at the Australian Travel Research Workshop, Bunbury, Western Australia, 5–6 November.

—— (1991) *Festivals, Special Events and Tourism*, New York: Van Nostrand Reinhold.

—— (1993a) 'Planning for tourism business districts', *Annals of Tourism Research* 20: 583–600.

—— (1993b) Tourist Shopping Villages: Development and planning strategies', *Tourism Management* 14(1): 15–26.

Gilbert, D. and Joshi, I. (1992) 'Quality management and the tourism and hospitality industry', in C. P. Cooper and A. Lockwood (eds) *Progress in Tourism, Recreation and Hospitality Management*, Volume 4, London: Belhaven, pp.149–68.

Gilbert, E. W. (1949) 'The growth of Brighton', *Geographical Journal* 114: 30–52.

Glasson, J. (1994) 'Oxford: a heritage city under pressure', *Tourism Management* 15 (2): 137–44.

Gold, J. and Ward, S. (eds) (1993) *Place Promotion: The Use of Publicity and Public Relations to Sell Cities*, Chichester: Wiley.

Goodall, B. (ed.), (1989) 'Tourism Accommodation: Special Issue', *Built Environment* 15(2).

—— (1990) 'The dynamics of tourism place marketing', in G. J. Ashworth and B. Goodall (eds) *Marketing Tourism Places*, London: Routledge, pp.259–79.

Goodenough, R. A. and Page, S. J. (1993) 'Tourism training and education in the 1990s', *Journal of Geography in Higher Education* 17(1): 57–75.

—— (1994) 'Evaluating the environmental impact of a major transport infrastructure project: the Channel Tunnel high speed rail link', *Applied Geography* 14(1):26–50.

Graefe, A. R. and Vaske, J. J. (1987) 'A framework for managing quality in the tourist experience', *Annals of Tourism Research*, 14: 389–404.

Green, H. (1975) 'Is urban administration different?', *International Review of Administrative Sciences* 46(4): 351–60.

Green, H. and Hunter, C. (1992) 'The environmental impact assessment of tourism development', in P. Johnson and B. Thomas (eds) *Perspectives on Tourism Policy*, London: Mansell, pp.29–48.

Grenier, D., Kaae, B. C., Miller, M. L. and Mobley, R. W. (1993) 'Ecotourism, landscape architecture and urban planning', *Landscape and Urban Planning* 25(1/2): 1–16.

Grimnett, S. (1984) Planning for tourism in London, unpublished M.Sc. thesis, Guildford: University of Surrey.

Groonroos, C. (1988) '*Assessing Competitive Edge in the New Competition of the Service Economy*': Working, Paper 6, Arizona State University: First Interstate Center for Services Marketing.

Gunn, C. (1972) *Vacationscape: Designing Tourist Regions*, Austin: University of Texas.

—— (1988) *Tourism Planning*, London: Taylor and Francis, second edition.

Hall, C. M. (1991) *Tourism in Australia: Impacts, Planning and Development*, Melbourne: Longman Cheshire.

—— (1994) *Introduction to Tourism in the Pacific Rim: Development, Impacts and Markets*, Melbourne: Longman Cheshire.

Hall, D. R. (ed.) (1991) *Tourism and Economic Development in Eastern Europe and the Soviet Union*, London: Belhaven Press.

—— (1992a) 'Tourist development in Cuba', in D. Harrison (ed.) *Tourism and the Less Developed World*, London: Belhaven, pp.102–20.

—— (1992) *Urban and Regional Planning*, London: Routledge, third edition.

Hall, P. (1970) 'A horizon of hotels', *New Society* 15: 445.

Handy, C. (1993) *Understanding Organisations*, London: Penguin, fourth edition.

Harvey, D. (1989) *The Urban Experience*, Oxford: Basil Blackwell.

Haynes, R. (1980) *Geographical Images and Mental Maps*, London: Macmillan.

Haywood, K.M. (1989) 'Responsible and responsive approach to tourism planning in the community', *Tourism Management* 9(2): 105–18.

—— (1992) 'Identifying and responding to challenges posed by urban tourism', *Tourism Recreation Research* 17(2): 9–23.

Haywood, K. M. and Muller, T. E. (1988) 'The urban tourist experience: evaluating satisfaction', *Hospitality Education and Research Journal*: 453–9.

Heeley, J. (1981) 'Planning for tourism in Britain', *Town Planning Review* 52: 61–79.

Heiberg, T. and Hoivik, T. (1980) 'Centre–periphery tourism and self-reliance', *International Journal of Social Science* 32(1): 69–98.

Hendee, J. C., Stankey, G. H. and Lucas, R. C. (1990) *Wilderness Management*, Colorado, North American Press.

Henry, I. and Bramham, P. (1990) 'Leisure politics and the local state', unpublished paper, Loughborough: Department of Leisure, Recreation and Physical Education, Loughborough University.

HMSO (1985) *Streamlining the Cities, Cmmd 9063*, London: HMSO.

Holloway, J. C. and Plant, R. V. (1988) *Marketing for Tourism*, London: Pitman.

Horwath and Horwath (1986) *London's Tourism Accommodation in the 1990s*, London: Horwath and Horwath.

—— (1989) *Maltese Islands Tourism Development Plan*, London: Horwath and Horwath.

Horwath International (1990) *Worldwide Lodging Industry*, New York: Horwath International.

Hoyle, B. S. and Pinder, D. (eds) (1992) *European Port Cities in Transition*, London: Belhaven.

Hudson, R. and Townsend, A. (1992) 'Tourism employment and policy choices for local government', in P. Johnson and B. Thomas (eds) *Perspectives on Tourism Policy*, London: Mansell, pp.49–68.

Industry, Science and Technology Canada (1991) *Inventaire des Etudes Réalisees sur les Ville Canadiennes: Montreal, Toronto et Vancouver vue d'ensemble*, Ottawa: Industry, Science and Technology Canada.

Inskeep, E. (1991) *Tourism Planning: An Integrated and Sustainable Development Approach*, New York: Van Nostrand Reinhold.

Jackowski, A. and Smith, V. L. (1992) 'Polish pilgrim tourists', *Annals of Tourism Research* 19(1): 92–106.

Jansen-Verbeke, M. (1986) 'Inner-city tourism: resources, tourists and promoters', *Annals of Tourism Research* 13(1): 79–100.

—— (1988) *Leisure, Recreation and Tourism in Inner Cities. Explorative Case Studies*, Amsterdam/Nijmegen: Netherlands Geographical Studies 58.

—— (1989) Inner cities and urban tourism in the Netherlands: new challenges for local authorities', in P. Bramham, I. Henry, H. Mommaas and H. van der Poel (eds) *Leisure and Urban Processes: critical studies of Leisure Policy in Western European Cities*, London: Routledge, pp.233–53.

—— (1990) 'Leisure and shopping – tourism product mix', in G. J. Ashworth and B. Goodall (eds) *Marketing Tourism Places*, London: Routledge, pp.128–37.

—— (1991) 'Leisure shopping: a magic concept for tourism industry', *Tourism Management* 12(1): 9–14.

—— (1992) 'Urban recreation and tourism: physical planning issues', *Tourism Recreation Research* 17(2): 33–45.

Jansen-Verbeke, M. and Ashworth, G. J. (1990) 'Environmental integration of recreation and tourism', *Annals of Tourism Research* 17(4): 618–22.

Jansen-Verbeke, M. and Dietvorst, A. (1987) 'Leisure, recreation and tourism: a geographic view on integration', *Annals of Tourism Research* 14(3): 361–75.

Jefferson, A. and Lickorish, L. (1991) *Marketing Tourism: A Practical Guide*, London: Longman.

Jenkins, C. L. and Henry, B. M. (1982) 'Government involvement in tourism in developing countries', *Annals of Tourism Research* 9(4): 499–521.

Johnston, R. J. (1991) *Geography and Geographers*, London: Edward Arnold.

Johnston, R. J., Gregory, D. and Smith, D.M. (eds) (1994) *The Dictionary of Human Geography*, Blackwell Scientific Publications, third edition.

Jones Lang Wootton (1989) *Retail, Leisure and Tourism*, London: English Tourist Board.

Kent, P. (1990) 'People, places and priorities: opportunity sets and consumers' holiday choice', in G. J. Ashworth and B. Goodall (eds) *Marketing Tourism Places*, London: Routledge, pp.42–62.

Kent, W. (1983) 'Shopping: tourism's unsung hero(ine)', *Journal of Travel Research* Fall: 2–4.

Keown, C. (1989) 'A model of tourists' propensity to buy: the case of Japanese visitors to Hawaii', *Journal of Travel Research* Winter: 31–4.

Kotler, P. (1972) 'A generic concept of marketing', *Journal of Marketing* April: 46–54.

—— (1982) *Marketing for Non-Profit Organizations*, New Jersey: Prentice Hall.

Kotler, P. and Armstrong, G. (1991) *Principles of Marketing*, New Jersey: Prentice Hall, fifth edition.

Kotler, P. and Levy, S. J. (1969) 'Broadening the concept of marketing', *Journal of Marketing* January: 10–15.

Kotler, P. and Mindak, W. (1978) 'Marketing and public relations', *Journal of Marketing* October: 13–20.

Kotler, P. and Zaltman, G. (1971) 'Social marketing: an approach to planned changes', *Journal of Marketing* July: 3–12.

Kotler, P., Haider, D. H. and Rein, I. (1993) *Marketing Places: Attracting Investment, Industry and Tourism to Cities, States and Nations*, New York: Free Press.

KPMG Consultants (1993) *Survey of 34 European Tourist Bureaux*, Amsterdam: KPMG Consultants.

Lankford, S. V. and Howard, D. R. (1994) 'Developing a tourism impact scale', *Annals of Tourism Research* 21(1): 121–39.

Latham, J. (1989) 'The statistical measurement of tourism', in C. P. Cooper (ed.) *Progress in Tourism, Recreation and Hospitality Management*, Volume 1, London: Belhaven, pp.55–76.

Law, C. M. (1988) 'Conference and exhibition tourism', *Built Environment* 13(2): 85–92.

—— (1992) 'Urban tourism and its contribution to economic regeneration', *Urban Studies* 29(3/4): 599–618.

—— (1993) *Urban Tourism: Attracting Visitors to Large Cities*, London: Mansell.

Laws, E. (1991) *Tourism Marketing*, Cheltenham: Stanley Thornes.

Leiper, N. (1990) 'Tourism systems: an interdisciplinary perspective', Palmerston North, New Zealand: Department of Management Systems Occasional Paper 2, Massey University.

Leslie, D. (1989) 'The role of leisure and tourism developments in revitalising cities: lessons from Belfast, Northern Ireland', *Recreate Reeks* No. 6.

Lew, A. A. (1987) 'A framework for tourist attraction research', *Annals of Tourism Research* 14(4): 553–75.

Lewis, R. C. (1987) 'The measurement of gaps in the quality of hotel services', *International Journal of Hospitality Management* 6(2): 83–8.

Llewelyn-Davies Planning/Leisureworks (1987) *Tourism Development in Docklands: Key Themes and Facts*, London: London Docklands Development Corporation.

London Tourist Board (1987) *The Tourism Strategy for London*, London: London Tourist Board.

Lovelock, C. H. and Weinberg, C. B. (1984) *Marketing for Public and Non-Profit Managers*, New York: Wiley.

Lundgren, J. O. J. (1982) 'The tourist frontier of Nouveau Quebec: functions and regional linkages', *Tourist Review* 37(2): 10–16.

McArthur, S. and Hall, C. M. (1993) 'Evaluation of visitor management services', in C. M. Hall and S. McArthur (eds) *Heritage Management in New Zealand and Australia: Visitor Management, Interpretation, and Marketing*, Auckland: Oxford University Press, pp.251–73.

MacCannel, D. (1976) *The Tourist: A New Theory of the Leisure Class*, London: Macmillan.

McGregor, R. (1993) 'Napier, The Art Deco City', in C. M. Hall and S. McArthur (eds) *Heritage Management in New Zealand and Australia: Visitor Management, Interpretation, and Marketing*, Auckland: Oxford University Press, pp.209–17.

McVey, M. (1986) 'International hotel chains in Europe: survey of expansion plans as Europe is rediscovered', *Travel and Tourism Analyst* September: 3–23.

Madsen, H. (1992) 'Place-marketing in Liverpool: a review', *International Journal of Urban and Regional Research* 16(4): 633–40.

Marketpower (1991) *A Report on the Structure of the UK Catering Industry*, London: Marketpower Ltd.

Mansfeld, Y. (1992) 'Industrial landscapes as positive settings for tourism development in declining industrial cities – the case of Haifa, Israel' *GeoJournal* 28(4): 457–63.

Mathieson, A. and Wall, G. (1982) *Tourism: Economic, Physical and Social Impacts*, London: Longman.

Matley, I. M. (1976) *The Geography of International Tourism*, Resource Paper No. 76–1, Washington: Association of American Geographers.

Meyer-Arendt, K. (1990) 'Recreational business districts in Gulf of Mexico seaside resorts', *Journal of Cultural Geography* 11: 39–55.

Middleton, V. T. C. (1988) *Marketing in Travel and Tourism* Oxford: Heinemann.

Mill, R. C. and Morrison, A. M. (1985) *The Tourism System: An Introductory Text*, New Jersey: Prentice Hall.

—— (1992) *The Tourism System. An Introductory Text*, New Jersey: Prentice Hall, second edition.

Morris, S. (1990) *Japanese Outbound Travel Market in the 1990s*, London: Economist Intelligence Unit.

Mullins, P. (1991) 'Tourism urbanisation', *International Journal of Urban and Regional Research* 15(3): 326–42.

Murakami, K. & Go, F. (1990) 'Transnational corporations capture Japanese market', *Tourism Management* 11(4): 348–53.

Murphy, P. E. (1985) *Tourism: A Community Approach*, London: Routledge.

—— (1992) 'Urban tourism and visitor behaviour' *American Behavioral Scientist* 36(2): 200–11.

Neill, W. J. V. (1993) 'Physical planning and image enhancement', *International Journal of Urban and Regional Research* 17(4): 595–610.

Nolan, M.L. and Nolan, S. (1992) 'Religious sites as tourism attractions in Europe', *Annals of Tourism Research* 19(1): 68–78.

Normann, R. (1984) *Service Management: Strategy and Leadership in Service Businesses*, Chichester: Wiley.

Oakland, J. S. (1989) *Total Quality Management*, Oxford: Butterworth-Heinemann.

OECD (1992) *Tourism Policy and International Tourism in OECD Member Countries*, Paris: OECD.

O'Connor, A. (1993) 'World population concentrating in mega-cities', *The Independent* 13 December.

Owen, C. (1990) 'Tourism and urban regeneration', *Cities* August: 194–201.

Oxford City Council, Thames and Chiltern Tourist Board and Oxford and District Chamber of Trade (1992) *Oxford Visitor Study 1990–91: Final Report*, Oxford: Oxford Centre for Tourism and Leisure Studies, Oxford Brookes University.

Page, S. J. (1989a) 'Tourism planning in London', *Town and Country Planning* 58,(12): 334–6.

—— (1989b) 'Tourist development in London Docklands in the 1980s and 1990s', *GeoJournal* 19(3): 291–5.

—— (1992)'Perspectives on the environmental impact of the Channel Tunnel' in C. P. Cooper and A. Lockwood (eds) *Progress in Tourism, Recreation and Hospitality Management*, Volume 4, London: Belhaven, pp.82–102.

—— (1993a) 'Perspectives on urban heritage tourism in New Zealand:

Wellington in the 1990s', in C. M. Hall and S. McArthur (eds) *Heritage Management in New Zealand and Australia: Visitor Management, Interpretation and Marketing*, Auckland: Oxford University Press, pp.218–30.

Page, S. J. (1993b) 'Urban tourism in New Zealand: the National Museum of New Zealand Project' *Tourism Management* 14(3): 211–18.

—— (1994a) 'Waterfront revitalisation in London: market-led planning and tourism in London Docklands', in S. Craig-Smith and M. Fagence (eds) *Recreation and Tourism as a Catalyst for Urban Waterfront Development*, Westport: Greenwood Publishing Group.

—— (1994b) *Transport for Tourism*, London: Routledge.

—— (1994c) 'Perspectives on tourism and peripherality: a review of tourism in the Republic of Ireland' in C. P. Cooper and A. Lockwood (eds) *Progress in Tourism, Recreation and Hospitality Management*, Volume 5, Chichester: Wiley, pp.26–53.

—— (1994d) 'Developing heritage tourism in Ireland in the 1990s', *Tourism Recreation Research* 19.

Page, S. J. and Sinclair, M. T. (1989) 'Accommodation in London: alternative policies and the Docklands experience', *Built Environment* 15(2): 125–37.

—— (1992) 'The Channel Tunnel: an opportunity for London's tourism industry', *Tourism Recreation Research* 17: 57–70.

Page, S. J, Sinclair, M. T., Pickvance, C., Pickvance, K. and Piotrowski, S. (1990) *Kent and South East England's Tourism Markets in the 1990s: The Impact of the Channel Tunnel*, Consultants Report for Kent County Council and South East England Tourist Board, Canterbury: Tourism Research Centre, Canterbury Business School (2 Volumes).

Page, S. J., Nielsen, K. and Goodenough, R. (1994) 'Managing urban parks: user perspectives and local leisure needs in the 1990s', *Service Industries Journal* 14(2): 216–37.

Parasuraman, A., Zeithmal, V.A. and Berry L. L. (1985) 'A conceptual model of service quality and its implications for future research', *Journal of Marketing* 49(4): 41–50.

Parkinson, M. and Bianchini, F. (1990) *Cultural Policy and Urban Regeneration in Liverpool: a Tale of Missed Opportunities*, Liverpool Urban Studies Working Paper 19, Liverpool University.

Patmore, J. A. (1983) *Recreation and Resources*, Oxford: Blackwell.

Pearce, D. G. (1987a) *Tourism Today: A Geographical Analysis*, London: Longman.

—— (1987b) 'Motel location and choice in Christchurch', *New Zealand Geographer* April: 43(1): 10–17.

—— (1989) *Tourist Development*, London: Longman, second edition.

—— (1992) *Tourist Organisations*, London: Longman.

—— (1993) 'Introduction ' in D. G. Pearce and R. W. Butler (eds) *Tourism Research: Critiques and Challenges*, London: Routledge, pp.1–8.

Pearce, D. G. and Butler, R. W. (eds) (1993) *Tourism Research: Critiques and Challenges*, London: Routledge.

Pearce, D. G. and Elliot, J.(1983) 'The trip index', *Journal of Travel Research* 22(1): 6–9.

Pearce, P. (1982) *The Social Psychology of Tourist Behaviour*, Oxford: Pergamon.

—— (1993) 'Fundamentals of tourist motivation', in D.G. Pearce and R.W. Butler (eds) *Tourism Research: Critiques and Challenges*, London: Routledge, pp.113–34.

Peat Marwick McClintock & Land Design Research Inc (1988) *The Dover Tourism Initiative*, Dover: Dover District Council.

Potter, A. F. (1978) 'The methodology of impact analysis', *Town and Country Planning* 46(9): 400–4.

Queenan, L. (1992) *Conference Bureaux: An Investigation into their Structure, Marketing Strategies and Business*, Birmingham: British Association of Conference Towns.

Rinschede, G. (1986) 'The pilgrimage town of Lourdes', *Journal of Cultural Geography* 7(1): 21–34.

—— (1990) 'Religious Tourismus', *Geographische Rundschau* 42(1): 14–20.

Roche, M. (1992) 'Mega-events and micro-modernization: on the sociology of the new urban tourism', *British Journal of Sociology* 43(4): 563–600.

Ryan, C. (1991) *Recreational Tourism: A Social Science Perspective*, London: Routledge.

—— (1995) *Researching Tourism Satisfaction: Issues, Concepts, Problems*, London: Routledge.

Sawicki, D. (1989) 'The festival marketplace as public policy', *Journal of the American Planning Association* Summer: 347–61.

Sazanami, H. (1984) *Urban Politics: A Sociological Interpretation*, London: Hutchinson.

Schaer, U. (1978) 'Traffic problems in holiday resorts', *Tourist Review* 33(2): 9–15.

Seibert, J. C. (1973) *Concepts of Marketing Management*, New York: Harper Row.

Shaw, G. and Williams, A. (1992) 'Tourism, development and the environment: the eternal triangle', in C. P. Cooper and A. Lockwood (eds) *Progress in Tourism, Recreation and Hospitality Management*, Volume 4, London: Belhaven, pp.47–59.

—— (1994) *Critical Issues in Tourism: A Geographical Perspective*, Oxford: Blackwell.

Shirasaka, S. (1982) 'Foreign visitor flow in Japan', *Wirtschafts – und sozial Geographische Schriften*, 41: 205–18.

Sinclair, M. T. (1991) 'The economics of tourism', in C. P. Cooper (ed.) *Progress in Tourism, Recreation and Hospitality Management*, Volume 3, London: Belhaven, pp.1–27.

Sinclair, M. T. and Page, S. J. (1993) 'The Euroregion: a new framework for regional development', *Regional Studies* 27(5): 475–83.

Sinclair, M. T. and Stabler, M. (1991) 'New perspectives in the tourism industry', in M. T. Sinclair and M. J. Stabler (eds) *The Tourism Industry: An International Analysis*, Oxford: CAB International, pp.1–14.

Smith, S. L. J. (1983) 'Restaurants and dining out: geography of a tourism business', *Annals of Tourism Research* 10(4): 515–49.

—— (1989) *Tourism Analysis*, London: Longman.

Smith, V. L. (ed.) (1989) *Hosts and Guests: The Anthropology of Tourism*, Philadelphia: University of Pennsylvannia Press, second edition.

Speller, S. and Ghobadian, A. (1993) 'Change for the public sector', *Managing Service Quality* September: 29–34.

Stanback, T. (1985) 'The changing fortunes of metropolitan economies', in M. Castells (ed.) *High Technology, Space and Society*, Beverly Hills: Sage.

Stansfield, C. A. (1964) 'A note on the urban-nonurban imbalance in American recreational research', *Tourist Review* 19(4): 196–200.

Stansfield, C. A. and Rickert, J. E. (1970) 'The recreational business district', *Journal of Leisure Research* 2(4): 213–25.

Stratford-upon-Avon Visitor Management Action Programme (1993) *Stratford Welcome*, Stratford-upon-Avon: Stratford-upon-Avon Visitor Management Action Programme.

Thornley, A. (ed.) (1990) *The Crisis of London*, London: Routledge.

Thurot, J. M. (1980) *Capacite de Charge et Production Touristique*, Etudes et Memoires No. 43, Aix-en-Provence: Centre des Hantes Touristique.

Touche Ross: Greene Belfield-Smith Division (1991) *Survey of Tourist Offices in European Cities*, London: Touche Ross.

UNESCO (1976) 'The effects of tourism on socio-cultural values', *Annals of Tourism Research* 4: 74–105.

United States Travel Service (1978) *City Government, Tourism and Economic Development*, Washington DC: United States Travel Service.

Var, T. and Quayson, J. (1985) 'The multiplier impact of tourism in the Okanagan', *Annals of Tourism Research* 12(4): 497–514.

Veal, A. J. (1992) *Research Methods for Leisure and Tourism: A Practical Guide*, London: Longman.

Vetter, F. (ed.) (1985) *Big City Tourism*, Berlin: Dietrich Verlag.

Walmesley, D. J. and Jenkins, J. (1992) 'Tourism cognitive mapping of unfamiliar environments', *Annals of Tourism Research* 19(3): 268–86.

Watts, D. (1987) 'Tourism as a catalyst for the appropriate urban development of Jerash, Jordan', *Tourism Recreation Research* 12(2): 31–7.

Weaver, D. B. (1993) 'Model of urban tourism for small Caribbean islands', *Geographical Review* 83(2): 134–40.

Wellington Regional Council (1991) *Wellington Region Tourism Strategy: Summary Document*, Wellington: Wellington Regional Council.

White, P. E. (1974) *The Social Impact of Tourism on Host Communities: A*

Study of Language Change in Switzerland, Research Paper No. 9, Oxford: School of Geography, Oxford University.

Witt, S. F., Brooke, M. Z. and Buckley, P. J. (1991) *The Management of International Tourism*, London: Unwin Hyman.

Woodside, A. G., Pearce, B. and Wallo, M. (1989) 'Urban tourism: an analysis of visitors to New Orleans and competing cities', *Journal of Travel Research* 27(3): 22–30.

World Commission on the Environment and Development (1987) *Our Common Future* (Brundtland Report), Oxford: Oxford University Press.

Yale, P. (1990) *From Heritage Attractions to Heritage Tourism*, Huntingdon: Elm Publications.

Yokeno, N. (1968) 'La localisation de l'industrie touristique: application de l'analyse de Thunen-Weber', Cahiers du Tourisme, C-9, Aix-en-Provence: C.H.E.T.

Subject index

Place index